THE ACTOR AND THE CHARACTER

Transformative acting remains the aspiration of many an emerging actor, and constitutes the achievement of some of the most acclaimed performances of our age: Daniel Day-Lewis as Lincoln, Meryl Streep as Mrs Thatcher, Anthony Hopkins as Hannibal Lecter – the list is extensive, and we all have our favourites. But what are the physical and psychological processes that enable actors to create characters so different from themselves? To understand this unique phenomenon, Vladimir Mirodan provides both a historical overview of the evolution of notions of 'character' in Western theatre and a stunning contemporary analysis of the theoretical implications of transformative acting. *The Actor and the Character*:

- Surveys the main debates surrounding the concept of dramatic character and – contrary to recent trends – explains why transformative actors conceive their characters *as 'independent' of their own personalities.*
- Describes some important techniques used by actors to construct their characters by *physical means*: work on objects, neutral and character masks, Laban movement analysis, Viewpoints, etc.
- Examines the psychology behind transformative acting from the perspectives of *both psychoanalysis and scientific psychology* and, based on recent developments in psychology, asks whether transformation is not just acting folklore but may actually entail temporary changes to the brain structures of the actors.

The Actor and the Character speaks not only to academics and students studying actor training and acting theory, but contributes to current lively academic debates around character. This is a compelling and original exploration of the limits of acting theory and practice, psychology, and creative work, in which Mirodan boldly re-examines some of the fundamental assumptions of actor training and some basic tenets of theatre practice to ask: What happens when one of us 'becomes somebody else'?

Vladimir Mirodan is a theatre director, Emeritus Professor of Theatre, and was Vice-Principal and Director of Drama at the Royal Conservatoire of Scotland and Principal of Drama Centre London. He has published on topics of acting psychology, as well as the theory and practice of acting.

THE ACTOR AND THE CHARACTER

Explorations in the Psychology of Transformative Acting

Vladimir Mirodan

Routledge
Taylor & Francis Group

LONDON AND NEW YORK

First published 2019
by Routledge
2 Park Square, Milton Park, Abingdon, Oxon OX14 4RN

and by Routledge
52 Vanderbilt Avenue, New York, NY 10017

Routledge is an imprint of the Taylor & Francis Group, an informa business

© 2019 Vladimir Mirodan

The right of Vladimir Mirodan to be identified as author of this
work has been asserted by him in accordance with sections 77 and
78 of the Copyright, Designs and Patents Act 1988.

British Library Cataloguing-in-Publication Data
A catalogue record for this book is available from the British
Library

Library of Congress Cataloging-in-Publication Data
Names: Mirodan, Vladimir, 1951- editor.
Title: The actor and the character : explorations in the psychology
    of transformative acting / [edited by] Vladimir Mirodan.
Description: Abingdon, Oxon ; New York, NY : Routledge, 2019. |
    Includes bibliographical references and index.
Identifiers: LCCN 2018029136 (print) | LCCN 2018036683
    (ebook) | ISBN 9781315723433 (Master) | ISBN
    9781317527954 (Adobe Reader) | ISBN 9781317527947
    (ePub3) | ISBN 9781317527930 (Mobipocket Unencrypted) |
    ISBN 9781138852518 | ISBN 9781138852518(hardback :qalk.
    paper) | ISBN 9781138852525(paperback :alk. paper) | ISBN
    9781315723433(ebook)
Subjects: LCSH: Acting—Psychological aspects.
Classification: LCC PN2071.P78 (ebook) | LCC PN2071.P78 A38
    2019 (print) | DDC 792.02/8019—dc23
LC record available at https://lccn.loc.gov/2018029136

ISBN: 978-1-138-85251-8 (hbk)
ISBN: 978-1-138-85252-5 (pbk)
ISBN: 978-1-315-72343-3 (ebk)

Typeset in Bembo
by Swales & Willis Ltd, Exeter, Devon, UK

MIX
Paper from
responsible sources
FSC
www.fsc.org   FSC® C013056

Printed and bound in Great Britain by
TJ International Ltd, Padstow, Cornwall

For my mother, a mathematician, and my father, a playwright.

CONTENTS

ACKNOWLEDGEMENTS

My first and special thanks go to Talia Rogers, without whose insight and enthusiasm I would not have taken the first steps on this most rewarding of journeys. At various stations on the way, I was fortunate enough to receive the support and advice, most generously given, of the following: Dr Benjamin Askew, Peter Close, Simon Crawford, Professor Rick Kemp, Anita Roy and Dr Gianna Williams. To them all, my heartfelt thanks. Finally, my gratitude goes to Barbara Berkery, who accompanied me every step of the way with boundless forbearance.

Ben Piggott and Laura Soppelsa at Routledge advised on editorial matters.

Taylor and Francis Ltd (http://www.tandfonline.com) gave permission to reprint excerpts from the following material I had published previously:

'Acting the metaphor: the Laban–Malmgren system of movement psychology and character analysis', *Theatre, Dance and Performance Training*, vol. 6, issue 1, March 2015, pp. 30–45 (www.tandfonline.com/toc/rtdp20)

'Lying bodies, Lying faces: deception and the Stanislavskian tradition of character', *Stanislavski Studies*, vol. 4, issue 1, April 2016, pp. 25–45

'Lecoq's influence on UK drama schools', in Evans, M. and R. Kemp, eds., 2016, *The Routledge Companion to Jacques Lecoq*, London and New York: Routledge, Ch. 23

The excerpt from *The Long Day's Journey into Night* by Eugene O'Neill, published by Jonathan Cape, is reproduced by permission of The Random House Group Ltd. ©1956 and of Yale Representation Limited through PLSclear.

The excerpt from "An 'Aristocratic Character'" from "Childhood Phobia and Character Formation" from *Character Analysis* by Wilhelm Reich, translated by Vincent R. Carfagno, copyright 1945, 1949, 1972 by the Wilhelm Reich Infant Trust, is reprinted by permission of Farrar, Straus and Giroux.

A NOTE ON TERMINOLOGY

The pages that follow refer extensively to concepts familiar to contemporary discourses in cognitive science. While this is a field in constant development, its defining feature is an emphasis on the unity of physical and mental functions and consequent rejection of the old Cartesian mind-body dualism. When dealing with complex issues surrounding the nature of the brain, the mind, and consciousness, writers therefore use a variety of ad hoc terms designed to give graphic expression to this unity. Bodymind, body-mind, mindbrain, Brain/Mind-Mind/Brain are alternatively proposed, alongside older terms such as spirit, psyche, mind, awareness, consciousness, and others.

These terms may at times prove confusing to readers who come primarily from theatre backgrounds. To cut through the confusion, this book broadly follows the definitions offered by Susan Greenfield, seeking to make these concepts accessible to a non-specialist public. In direct quotations or references to historical perspectives, I retain, of course, the terms used by others. When referring to cognitive science debates and discoveries, I use the terms broadly thus:

Brain refers to the physical tissue and in particular to the neurons within it and the myriad connections (synapses) between them. The perspective adopted here is the 'connectivist' view of the brain, which asserts that functions (vision, taste, balance, etc.) are not located in a particular area of the brain but are the result of complex connections being established across its geography. The brain is 'plastic' in the sense that new connections are constantly being formed as a result of the organism's interactions with its environment.

Mind is taken to mean, as Greenfield proposes, the totality of the experiences that establish and maintain patterns of neural connections.

Body supplies an additional dimension to this relationship. Self-evidently, body includes brain, yet certain cognitive approaches emphasise that it is not the brain tissue alone, but rather the totality of bodily functions, including, for example, the autonomic nervous system (ANS), hormonal discharges and changes in blood pressure, that generate the experiences recorded in the mind.

Consciousness is taken to be the subjective awareness of the world, as it appears, uniquely, to each of us. There is always a degree of basic or "background consciousness", as neurologist Antonio Damasio calls it: the awareness of our own bodies. Wider consciousness – of the world around us as well as of our own mental functions – is not always present but is activated in response to stimuli that result in temporary changes in the chemistry of the brain. Consciousness is like a 'dimmer switch', a state that increases and decreases in intensity according to circumstances.

Mind and consciousness are therefore distinct but are indivisibly rooted in the physical brain. I therefore adopt wherever possible the widely used term *body–mind* to signify the integration and mutual interdependence of physical and mental processes. I use, interchangeably, *consciousness* and *awareness*, to denote the activated functions of the mind.

Finally, in common with many writers on performance practices, I found a need to distinguish between 'real' life and what happens when we act, without implying that the latter was in any way less 'real'. I therefore follow the director and scholar Eugenio Barba in using "daily" and "extra-daily" respectively.

References

Greenfield, S., 2002. 'Mind, brain and consciousness', *The British Journal of Psychiatry*, Aug 2002, 181 (2) pp. 91–93.

Damasio, A., 1999. *The Feeling of What Happens: Body and Emotion in the Making of Consciousness*. London: William Heinemann.

Barba, E., 1995. *The Paper Canoe*. London: Routledge.

1

INTRODUCTION

For over a century people have turned to psychology to understand acting. First, generations of actors, directors and teachers became fascinated by psychoanalysis. More recently, extensive work by such writers as Bruce McConachie, Rhonda Blair, Rick Kemp and John Lutterbie (to name but a few) has drawn interesting lessons regarding acting and spectating from cognitive science.

However, in both traditions, relatively little has been written about the complex psychological interplay that takes place between the actor and the fictional character. In addition, in recent books about acting by well-known directors and writers such as David Mamet or Declan Donnellan, the very concept of character is largely being dismissed, at times in peremptory terms. This attitude parallels that of many literary critics who have, since the modernist upheaval of the 1930s, been at war with the notion of character. 'The Idea of Character', Part I of this book, therefore surveys historical understandings of character and type and charts the ways in which – having flourished in the acting mainstream for most of the twentieth century – these have wilted over the past thirty years under the blast of more fashionable currents: new emphases on immediacy, authenticity, and individual difference. It seemed to me that in relation to character the 'new' had become a new orthodoxy and was thus ripe for re-examination.

Lofty directorial or lit. crit. rejections notwithstanding, in acting practice 'character' or 'transformative' acting stubbornly refuses to go away. Transformative acting remains the aspiration of many a student actor and constitutes the achievement of some of the most acclaimed performances of our age: Mark Rylance in *Jerusalem*, Meryl Streep as Mrs Thatcher, Anthony Hopkins as Hannibal Lecter – the list is extensive, and we will all have our favourites. It has even become a cliché for Oscars to be won by beautiful women or glamorous men playing monsters or characters defined by a disability.[1] However, switch on the television tonight or go to your local theatre or to the Odeon around the corner and the acting is unlikely to be transformative. For perfectly good reasons of personal inclination, commercial imperative or professional practice, much of the acting on display is rooted in an extension or refinement of the actor's personality. In the right context, this is fine; it only becomes problematic when it is assumed that this approach to acting is the only one of value. Thus, for example, Lee Strasberg: "The simplest examples of Stanislavski's ideas are actors such as Gary Cooper, John Wayne, and Spencer Tracy. They try not to act but to be themselves . . ."[2] And, six decades later, Jason Solomons, the film critic of the BBC, speaking after Christopher Lee's death: "He was always Christopher Lee, whether they put a beard on him, or a hat or anything else . . . This is the secret of film acting, to be yourself".[3] Taking another look at transformative acting therefore felt timely, if somewhat against the current. Here is one instance (among many) why I think this argument also reaches further than mere acting preferences:

Over the past few years a number of drama series based on *Fargo*, the classic Coen Brothers movie, have been made for television. The first of these series turned on two pivotal performances: the American actor Billy Bob Thornton played Lorne Malvo, a strange drifter-cum-contract-killer, whose path crosses that of Lester Nygaard, a small-town insurance clerk 'going bad'. The latter was played by Martin Freeman. Thornton's performance fell within the ambit of the 'transformative': from the sculpted hair framing his face, to the distinctive walk, to the fixed stare, he was both 'other' and 'other-worldly'. Martin Freeman, on the other hand, was . . . Martin Freeman: he attempted, with patchy results, a mid-Western accent, but his gestures, facial expressions and overall physicality not only remained stubbornly British but were recognisably within the same range as those he had used in *The Hobbit* as well as for Dr Watson in *Sherlock Holmes*. The point I would make is not that one style of performance was more successful commercially or professionally than the other, but that they were different in the way in which they affected the *meanings* of the story. From the point of view of the spectator, Thornton's transformation into an incarnation of transcendental Evil (an interpretation explicitly supported by the dialogue) lifted the story away from the personal and into the realms of the epic, from the local to the mythical, from domestic drama to tragedy. It is in this sense that this book argues that transformative acting is of particular value. At the end of Part I, Chapter 5 tests this proposition against a number of contemporary attempts at doing away with character through either dramaturgy or acting style; in the concluding chapter, I use the framework of Deception Theory to argue for the intrinsic value of such acting.

Transformation is often a matter of degree: there are 'strong' and 'weak' forms. The one that interests me, however, always goes over the 'tipping point' of perceptible physical changes. In consequence, this book foregrounds throughout body-based approaches to acting. Transformative acting entails a 'conversation' during which actors deliberately guide spectators towards a particular understanding of their characters, by means of their bodies. The language in which this conversation takes place is based, I argue in Chapter 3, on a 'language of movement' familiar to actor and spectator alike and rooted in commonly held assumptions about social and psychological categories of people or 'types'. For example, we may know that it is quite wrong to assume that all short, fat men are jolly and all tall men aloof and that this is *habitus*. But try to picture a tall, gaunt and loose-limbed Father Christmas, played by John Cleese; or Robin Hood as short and fat. Not easy . . . It seems that as soon as we dwell on the way in which we communicate through physical behaviours we revert to an atavistic certainty: that the corporeal demeanour of a person is an indication of who they are. This subliminal understanding enables actors to delineate characters by altering their bodies and in turn have their transformed shapes understood by audiences.

However, although it offers extended sections on physical and mental approaches to transformation (in Chapters 6 and 9 respectively), this book is not primarily about acting methodologies and their teaching – a vast literature on these already exists. Nor is it about the way in which acting is being received by the spectator – much excellent work, especially from a cognitive perspective, has been done in this area. This book is written from the perspective of the actor in rehearsal, in an attempt to open a few windows (and re-open some, stuck shut by layers of over-painting) onto a cross-disciplinary field of enquiry that asks what might be happening when it looks as if one of us 'becomes someone else'. I therefore start from the premise that characters can and should be considered as 'other' than the actor. As Michael Chekhov once wrote: "It is a crime to chain and imprison an actor within the limits of his so-called 'personality', thus making him an enslaved labourer rather than an artist". And, incidentally, what follows focuses exclusively on 'acting', concerned with the interpretation of extant texts; 'performance', in its numerous guises, is outside the scope of this discussion. As are complex and challenging issues to do with notions of 'self', considered within the framework of the philosophy of mind: while undoubtedly relevant, these are beyond a book principally concerned with exploring aspects of the *psychology* of acting.

From the perspective of the actor, transformation is first and foremost an act of imagination. I consider imagination in this context to be a psychophysical process, involving the body-mind of the actor in an uninterrupted flow of mutual reinforcement, a spiral of physical changes leading to psychological insights, which in turn cause further physical alterations. I am not therefore concerned with questions such as whether the use of emotional memory, say, precedes the adoption of a certain body shape or – in the opposite direction – whether choosing to wear a particular hat or stilettos rather than flat shoes triggers the emotional responses which lead to the character. I find such debates about chickens and eggs, which have defined much of the discourse on acting in the twentieth century, somewhat sterile. I am much more interested in finding appropriate frames of reference within which to place the act of transformation. These might throw some light on the elusive phenomenon of creative, focused imagination, which leads in turn to psychophysical change. And approaching transformation through the body seems to me particularly useful as a point of departure. For one thing, characterisation by physical means is readily observable. For another, turning the routine motions and gestures of daily life into expressive movement entails the activation of complex psychophysical processes – in turn, their analysis can yield useful clues regarding the mental processes involved in transformation.

As I mentioned above, much valuable research has been carried out over the past two decades on the links between acting and cognitive science, and much of what follows aligns itself with this work. I cannot help feeling, however, that attempts at developing a "science of the imagination" – interesting and innovative as these are – do not quite manage to capture the lived experience of actors contemplating and giving physical shape to personalities 'other' than their own. Part II therefore places psychophysical approaches to the creation of dramatic characters in dialogue with psychological models, which attempt to explain daily-life personality from the two (admittedly very different) perspectives of scientific psychology and psychoanalysis. The link between physical expression and personality is core to both:

From the beginning, psychoanalysis promoted the ability of the analyst to deduce personality traits from an analysand's physical demeanour. Alfred Adler was fond of quoting Luther's dictum, "do not watch a person's mouth, but his fists", and wrote: "If we want to understand a person . . . we have to close our ears. We have only to look. In this way we can see as in a pantomime".

Prompted by such observations, later generations of psychoanalysts sought to develop systematic methodologies associating certain postures with specific inner states. However, much of what psychoanalysis had to say about this topic was a reconfiguration in psychological terms of ancient tropes linking inner states and physical expression. As I outline in Chapter 3, Classical discourse on human nature and comportment had promoted the ideal of the harmonious, restrained body, expressive of a harmonious, controlled mind. Distortions of mind and body were consigned to madness or satire. Psychoanalysis, on the other hand, was greatly interested in what the deformations of the body had to say about the distortions of the psyche and their effect on shaping personality. In this view, fundamental imbalances in the psyche could also explain theatre characters: the excess of some "peculiar qualities", dominating all others, could be considered to define not only Morality Play Vices or Jonsonian humours, but characters in Chekhov, Ibsen or Miller too. This aspect of Freudian thought came to hold considerable sway over acting practices; in its Jungian adaptation, it eventually led to an elaborate system of character analysis and classification which has also had theatre applications – I examine these important influences in Chapter 8. At the same time, I note the dearth of contemporary writing on literary character from a psychoanalytic perspective. As the critic Elizabeth Fowler observes:

> It is typical of the impoverished state of thought about characterisation that even psychoanalytic theory has exiled characters. There are no characters in the writings of Jacques Lacan; figures like 'Dora' disappeared together with the genre of the case study as the discourse developed in the years after Sigmund Freud. Literary scholars interested in psychological approaches to text have followed suit, sometimes even excluding character as a potential location for the psychoanalytic process.
>
> *(2003, p. 4)*

This exclusion can in large measure be laid at the door of the scepticism contemporary writing evinces towards psychoanalytic perspectives in general. From a scientific perspective, the conceptual framework underpinning the assertions made by psychoanalysts remains that of the ancient rhetoricians and physiognomists and is just as speculative. In our case, psychoanalytical claims to 'reading' a person's traits and emotional states from their physicality (posture, gait, and gesture in particular) are wide open to the criticism that the evidence on which they were based was essentially subjective and varied from analyst to analyst. For its part, scientific psychology also seeks to ascertain, this time by experimental methods, whether personality traits can be inferred from physicality (Chapter 7). And inferences rooted in science are considered to be, as the scholar Bruce McConachie asserts, "on a firmer footing" than the "now largely discredited theory of psychoanalysis".

Trenchant differentiations such as these, while widespread, tend to ignore a growing body of research seeking to unify the intuitive outlook of psychoanalysis with the quantitative methods of scientific psychology. Such bridge-building exercises focus in particular on demonstrating that the effects of psychoanalysis are 'real' in a sense acceptable to the scientist, as measurable changes in brain structures. I find this combined, holistic approach very useful to my explorations. At its core, this book asks whether transformation is simply an actors' myth, easily dismissed by science as folk psychology, or whether a scientific basis for it might actually be found. In Part III ('The melding of actor and character') I examine the way in which transformative acting uses language and interpretation to engender deep, affective psychophysical processes. If it can be shown that these actually result, particularly when sustained over relatively lengthy periods, in the generation and modification of brain structures, then perhaps phenomena such as acting transformation are more than mere figments of our imagination.

It should also be said that, with some marginal exceptions (and recent theoretical texts notwithstanding), the application of scientific psychology to the art of performance is yet to have a widespread impact on the practices of either the conservatoire or of the professional actor. In the daily discourse of the rehearsal room, concepts loosely derived from psychoanalysis continue to be current. I do not think this is simply a matter of the acting profession being slow to adopt scientific advances. I think the enduring reliance in acting on the metaphors of psychoanalytic discourse may be due to the fact that these describe observable phenomena, while cognitive science more often than not addresses that which lies below the level of consciousness. Within the overall argument of this book, therefore, scientific psychology and psychoanalysis are placed side by side, and I draw on both traditions to explore acting processes. However, the description of traits, types, and temperaments – the key concepts of the scientific approach to personality – contained in Chapter 7 is offered as a possible opening onto a new way of looking at dramatic character, rather than the analysis of existing practices. On the other hand, the main psychoanalytic views of personality described in Chapter 8 will feel familiar to many actors and lead seamlessly to an analysis of the drives and motivation of characters (Chapter 9). Equally, when – in Part III – I turn to the complex processes by which character and actor 'merge', I begin by looking at certain psychoanalytic perspectives on intuition and creativity (Chapter 10). In Chapter 11, on the other hand, I draw on scientific models to try and understand how psychophysical processes undertaken consciously and systematically in the rehearsal room affect the body–mind at a non-conscious, automatised level.

Overall, it seems to me that, whatever their relative merits and demerits in the clinic, and despite the fact that they make awkward bedfellows, for the actor seeking to understand the elusive psychological processes involved in acting in general and transformation in particular both psychoanalysis and scientific psychology remain worth considering. Each in its own way offers interesting perspectives on the mysterious processes by which actor and fictional character interact. I am therefore considering them not in opposition, but as part of a continuum, with psychoanalysis representing one historical phase and scientific psychology another. I like Goethe's description of the marriage of the scientific method with an intuitive and creative way of thinking as a "delicate empiricism". I am also struck by the approach adopted in a recent publication by psychologist Malgorzata Fajkowska, who I do not think would mind being described as a 'hard-core' scientist. Fajkowska deals with the fraught question of whether stable and coherent personalities, based on traits that remain constant across time and life-events, can be considered to exist. She writes:

> . . . the courage to formulate the trait theory came to me from the classical (ancient) approach to exploring reality. The classical approach is founded on 'wonder' and not on the (post-) Cartesian 'doubt,' as is the modern approach. The Cartesian approach undoubtedly strives for obviousness, clearness, and transparency, whereas my use of the classical way of thinking made my solutions just possible, uncertain, or sometimes ambiguous. However, it opened a valued possibility: the application of meta-theory, not subjected to empirical validation but proposing a specialised language and tools that one can use to address specific scientific problems . . .
>
> *(2018, p. 36)*

In order to formulate her ideas, Fajkowska thus needed not only to examine the available data but to approach them with a particular *attitude*: a concept that, as I discuss in Chapter 9, has significant implications for the practice of transformative acting. Moreover, it feels as if this attitude is also well suited to explaining acting processes. In so doing, we often use a richly metaphorical language and thus embrace a form of "imaginative rationality", as George Lakoff and Mark Johnson, the proponents of Conceptual Metaphor Theory (Chapter 10), put it. This book adopts a similar approach in its examination of the interactions between the actor and the fictional character, and of the ways the two meet, break apart, then meet again in the complex, elegant, and subtle dance of mind and body we call 'transformation'.

Notes

1 See http://www.washingtonpost.com/news/morning-mix/wp/2015/02/23/since-rain-man-majority-of-best-actor-winners-played-sick-or-disabled/
2 In the *New York Times*, 2 September 1956, section 2, p. i.
3 BBC Radio 4, *PM*, 11 June 2015.

Bibliography

Personality acting: Chekhov, M., 1953. *To the Actor: On the Technique of Acting*. New York: Harper and Brothers.

"Science of the imagination": Fauconnier, G. and Turner, M., 2002. *The Way We Think: Conceptual Blending and the Mind's Hidden Complexities*. New York: Basic Books.

Adler on inferences from physicality: Adler, A., 1956. *The Individual Psychology of Alfred Adler*, edited by Ansbacher, H. L. and R. R. New York: Basic Books.

Older applications to acting of psychoanalysis: Freed D., 1964. *Freud and Stanislavsky. New directions in the performing arts*. New York: Vantage Press; Weissman, P., 1965. *Creativity in the Theatre: A Psychoanalytic Study*. New York: Basic Books.

Discredited psychoanalysis: McConachie, B., 2008. *Engaging Audiences: A Cognitive Approach to Spectating in the Theatre*. New York: Palgrave Macmillan; *absence from lit. crit. discourse*: Fowler, E., 2006. 'Shylock's Virtual Injuries' in 'Forum: Is There Character After Theory?', *Shakespeare Studies*, 34, pp. 56–69.

Bridging psychoanalysis and cognitive science: Stein, D. J., 1992. 'Psychoanalysis and Cognitive Science: Contrasting Models of the Mind', *The Journal of the American Academy of Psychoanalysis*, 20 (4), pp. 543–559; Schore, A. N., 1997. 'A century after Freud's Project: is a rapprochement between psychoanalysis and neurobiology at hand?', *Journal of the American Psychoanalytic Association*, 45, pp. 841–867; Solms, M. and Turnbull, O., 2002. *The Brain and the Inner World: An introduction to the neuroscience of subjective experience*. New York: Other Press; Ekstrom, S. R., 2004. 'Freudian, Jungian and cognitive models of the unconscious', *Journal of Analytical Psychology*, 49 (5), pp. 657–682; Rossi, E. L., 2004. 'Sacred Spaces and Places in Healing Dreams', *Psychological Perspectives*, 47 (1); Wilkinson, M., 2006. *Coming into Mind, The Mind-Brain Relationship: A Jungian Clinical Perspective*. London and New York: Routledge.

"A delicate empiricism": Pitches, J., 2006. *Science and the Stanislavsky Tradition of Acting*. Abingdon: Routledge; Fajkowska, M., 2018. 'Personality Traits: Hierarchically Organised Systems', *Journal of Personality*, 86 (1), pp. 36–54.

"Imaginative rationality": Lakoff, G. and Johnson, M., 1999. *Philosophy in the Flesh: The Embodied Mind and its Challenge to Western Thought*. New York: Basic Books.

PART I
The Idea of character

2

AN INDEPENDENT CHARACTER

Do characters have human rights?

The late Colin Dexter, creator of Inspector Morse, the famous fictional detective, is reported to have directed in his Will that no further screen adaptations of his books should be made, so that no actor other than the creator of the original screen impersonation, the late John Thaw, should ever assume the role. Two other well-known British writers, Michael Morpurgo and P. D. James, have argued that this goes against nature. Characters, they say, have an existence outside their author's wishes, and so have a "right to life".[1]

A charity dedicated to promoting the study of Shakespeare in schools organises a public trial: Hamlet, Prince of Denmark, is accused of murdering Polonius, the respected courtier. A jury is assembled, top-rank barristers argue, witnesses are cross-examined. Decked in red robes and full-bottomed wig, Lady Justice Hallett, an Appeal Court judge, presides . . . Hamlet, Prince of Denmark, is afforded his constitutional right to a fair trial.[2]

During the 2016 EU Referendum members of the public are asked for which side they think fictional characters might vote. The consensus is that Sherlock Holmes and Mary Poppins will vote Remain, while Falstaff and Basil Fawlty are definite 'Brexiteers'.[3]

We seem to take great pleasure in dealing with fictional creations as if they were real people. Harmless fun, of course, forgotten as soon as the money has been collected, the newspaper discarded, the radio switched off.

Yet something on the same spectrum also occurs in my rehearsal room: Viola, Edmund, General Gabler's daughter, Colonel Prozorov's family, are our intimates. We feel the quality of the velvet in Hedda's new, lined curtains; we cringe at Aunt Julie's dreadful new hat, we groan with Tesman under the weight of the books which had to be carted all the way from Berlin. Here the game turns serious: these are no longer words on a page, they are neighbours, relatives, schoolmates, opponents. One of my colleagues is preparing "I left no ring with her . . ." for an audition tomorrow morning. As she rehearses the speech and tries to puzzle out Viola's feelings and thoughts about that alarming ring, she moves to-and-fro on a triangular trail: between the text and herself, the text and 'Viola', herself and 'Viola'. Here is the puzzle: somewhere – outside both actor and text – a 'Viola' seems to exist. It (she?) floats somewhere in the spiritual ether, hovering, waiting to be summoned, to pour itself into the actor's body, to fill the vessel, to take over. The critic Charles Marowitz once even wrote: "as a result of being around for almost four hundred years, [characters] have now detached themselves from their original context, so they're in a sense roaming free in a kind of cultural terrain . . ."

I have also come to think of characters as having an independent, even 'ectoplasmic', existence. I know the idea of a universe populated with the ghosts of characters intent on coming to visit seems absurd. Yet here is the level-headed philosopher Denis Diderot, describing a great actress of the eighteenth century:

> Where, then, lies her talent? In imagining a mighty shape [*fantôme*], and in copying it with genius. She imitates the movement, the action, the gesture, the whole embodiment of a being far greater than herself.
>
> *(1883, p. 55)*

A notion reprised two centuries later by the actor Michael Chekhov:

> When preparing a tragic part [the actor] has to imagine that 'something' or 'somebody' is following him, driving his character to fulfil its tragic business and to speak its tragic lines. [This somebody] is much, much more powerful than his character and even himself. It should be a kind of superhuman presence.
>
> *(1953, pp. 138–139)*

Perhaps a more sensible analogy is that offered by the art philosopher Suzanne Langer. Comparing a real object with its identical yet immaterial image in a mirror, Langer labels the first "actual" and the mirror representation "virtual"[4]. Similarly, we might, in the theatre, speak of 'virtual people' – characters. Fanciful still, but no more so than having Falstaff vote in elections. And, fanciful or not, the daily practice of acting and spectating tells me that this is a legitimate way of looking at character.

Or is it? So many objections have been raised to this way of thinking, and from so many different quarters, that, after a lifetime's immersion in a tradition of theatre that treats characters as virtual human beings, I have to ask myself, *should one* and *can one*?

At one level, to the question 'should one?' there is a deceptively simple, matter-of-fact answer: if it works (in the practice of acting), do it! I say 'deceptively simple', however, because relying on the expediency of practice alone ignores the significant implications of what is after all the adoption of a strong aesthetic position. This is why:

In the year 2000, an article in *The Stage*[5], the British trade weekly, reported the following story: in Birmingham, a burglar was arrested *in flagrante*. Taken to the police station, he refused point blank to be interrogated by anyone other than Detective Inspector Burnside. DI Burnside was to be brought over from London or he would not open his mouth. It took a few hours for the puzzled Bobbies to work out who this DI Burnside might be: the tough yet fair-minded character in *The Bill*, a long-running cop-shop soap, then at the peak of its popularity.

Some four decades earlier, Kirk Douglas had just finished *Lust for Life*, his biopic about Van Gogh, and had invited a number of Hollywood luminaries, John Wayne among them, to a private screening. As the credits rolled, Wayne made his way up the aisle. "Kirk!" – he said – "How can you play a part like that? There's so goddamn few of us left. We got to play strong, tough characters." "I tried to explain" – Douglas writes – "Hey, John, I'm an actor. I like to play interesting roles. It's all make-believe, John. It isn't real. You're not really John Wayne, you know".

Jump forward to 2015 and an Australian disability campaigner blogs: "I look forward to the day when Eddie Redmayne's Oscar-winning performance as Stephen Hawking in *The Theory of Everything* is seen as having been as offensive and cringe-worthy as [a] blackface performance . . ."[6] The argument being that it is morally wrong for an able-bodied actor to play a character who suffers from motor neuron disease and that, by the same token, Dustin Hoffman should not have made *Rain Man* and Geoffrey Rush should not have undertaken his Oscar-winning portrayal of mental illness in *Shine*.

It appears that a common assumption underpins these stories: character is indistinguishable from actor. Not an attitude confined to social campaigners or deluded burglars. Leading theatre practitioners walk parallel, if more sophisticated, pathways: "There is no such thing as character", says Declan Donnellan; the question "who am I?" should be avoided at all costs, as its "paralysing anaesthetic" freezes the actor's impulses. Characteristics are "enemy words". With various nuances, similar approaches are also adopted by other avowedly Stanislavskian directors: Mike Alfreds, Katie Mitchell, and Max Stafford-Clark all turn their backs on a notion of character conceived as an entity other than the actor, and articulated in terms of traits or characteristics. Through their influence, 'action-ing' (whether as 'Physical Action' or as the more intuitive and embodied 'Active Analysis') has come to dominate those British approaches to acting and directing which consider themselves Stanislavskian. Relying on well-known sources, they consider that the actor's principal task consists first in analysing stage behaviour into its component units, then pursuing the objectives (targets, actions, tasks) that determine these. Actor and scholar Bella Merlin offers a succinct and clear definition of this influential reading: "As human beings, we are constantly and spontaneously determining objectives and setting in motion *organised patterns of behaviour* – or *lines of physical action* – to achieve those objectives". Action is all.

This approach has itself come to be challenged. "Who *actually* behaves like that?" asks Diego Arciniegas, an experienced American actor with a scholarly bent. He poses this question as an aside in the middle of a brave and lucid contribution to a book reconsidering the much-debated notion of character in Shakespeare. Describing in detail the thought processes he followed in conceiving the character of Antonio for a Chicago production of *The Merchant of Venice*, Arciniegas considers that action breakdown of the sort described above is inimical to an ideal of acting which aspires to a faithful, truthful, and natural replication of organic life on the stage. He writes:

> My approach to character is predicated on the belief that Shakespearean character emerges in the moment to moment actions, reactions and interactions of the character throughout the entire play – the character is, as some scholars say, 'processional'. This approach to character permits us, for one, to challenge the tradition of a role (e.g. romantic Romeo, bitchy Lady M., 'Dick the Shit') or discover it fresh for ourselves. More importantly, if, after the fact, I analyse what my character needs and wants in terms of goals or objectives, it is a retroactive and third-party perspective. In fact, it is often the audience member, critic, or scholar who builds a coherent, psychologised entity from the fragments of performance.
>
> *(2012, p. 112)*

As cogent an explanation as one might find of a view of character as a concatenation of actions, or – better still – reactions. Actors only need to behave naturally, intuitively, if they are to capture what Derrida famously called "the simple presence of the present act . . . [of] the living gesture that takes place only once". The character will emerge (in the minds of the spectators) as the result of *their* observation, moment-by-moment, of fragments of behaviour resulting from the responses of the actor to the circumstances of the play. Here intuition, not cerebral 'actioning', rules.

One notes, however, that Diego Arciniegas talks about the "actions, reactions and interactions" of *the character*. We are left with an inevitable question: who engages in these actions? Who reacts and interacts? The (equally unavoidable) answer here as well as in the writings of the British directors cited above is: 'the actor', or more precisely certain aspects of his or her psychophysical identity. We, the audience, are not presented with a deliberate design of character, but with the intuitive responses and actions of the actor. In this mode, spontaneity, immediacy, and sincerity are prized above all other histrionic virtues. Character is defined as actor-in-action, with an emphasis on the actor's emotional responses to the circumstances of the play, or passion-in-action. Rhonda Blair, a teacher/director seeking to address this debate using the principles of cognitive science, endorses this position: "There is no character in any objective sense, there is only the process and behaviour of a particular individual in a particular context. What the actor is doing becomes simply – and complexly – that: what the *actor* is *doing*".

So, the answer to the question "Who *actually* behaves like that?" is: no one! No normal human being behaves in real life by consciously breaking down his or her actions into tasks, activities, and units. Stanislavski and all those following him are wrong!

Unless. . . . Unless we were to alter the emphasis of the question and instead ask: "*Who* actually behaves like that?"

To try to answer, let us look at where his approach leads Diego Arciniegas (and I must stress that I am only taking advantage of his generous sharing of his process to use as a particular instance among countless similar examples). After a close analysis of Shakespeare's text, he describes his decision to play Antonio as a gay man hopelessly in love with a younger man who, in turn, falls in love with a woman. The play thus becomes the story of a fraught love triangle and everything of import that concerns Antonio's actions – his interactions with Bassanio, his willingness to enter into the absurd bargain with Shylock, the febrile impatience with which he urges the exacting of the final price, his tight-lipped retorts to Portia during the denouement at Belmont – is defined and shaped by his unhappiness in love. A perfectly legitimate approach, in fact adopted – with various nuances – in numerous productions of the play over the past few decades.

Does this matter? Only if one thinks that it might matter that this play is called *The Merchant of Venice*. Not 'Antonio's Lament', or 'Three in a Gondola', but *The Merchant of Venice*. Where, in this interpretation – and in the hundreds of others that follow similar lines – is the 'merchant'? Are we to know that this Antonio is not just a man unhappy in love, but a merchant prince whose argosies

> with portly sail
> Like signiors and rich burghers on the flood
> . . . Do overpeer the petty traffickers
> That curtsy to them, do them reverence.
>
> *(MV, 1, 8–12)*

And, then, where is 'Venice'? What does it mean for the enacting of this character that he is a *Venetian merchant prince*?

Seen in this light, the concept of character involves more than the actor-in-action. It includes the social and personal data the play offers (or at which it at least hints): not only Antonio's sexuality, but his age (what if this character is older or younger than the actor?), his social status (which *is* different from that of the actor), his upbringing, his profession, his likes and dislikes in food, drink, sports, etc., etc. This character consists of a cluster of physical and psychological characteristics and a biography different from those of the actor. Stanislavski for one had this in his bones: Russian has three different terms for character and one of these is *Deistvuiuschee litso*. The literal, etymological meaning of these terms is 'the acting faces', and they are primarily used to describe the cast list of a play, the equivalent of a *dramatis personae*. The Russian terms, however, incorporate a pregnant reading: characters have 'faces' of their own. And the Russian term for character used most frequently by actors, Stanislavski included, is *obraz* (image) – again, suggestive of 'otherness'.

It will be said that the 'processional' approach did not necessarily exclude consideration of other aspects of Antonio's biography and personality. Precisely: in making the choice he makes – in choosing to emphasise Antonio's sexuality as the prime motivator of his actions – Arciniegas selects one among a number of possible sources of motivation and so 'edits' Antonio's imagined, fictional personality in a way that suits his particular interpretation of the meaning of the play. While questioning the analytical process that leads to creating a role in the Stanislavskian tradition, both 'processional' and actor-in-action approaches are in fact blind to the fact that they inevitably engage in the selection of particular sources of motivation. A decision *is* being made, but not from the point of view of a fictional or constructed[7] character (a conflation of *imagined* biography, psychology, and physicality) but from that of the concerns and inclinations of the particular actors (with *their* biographies, psychologies, and physicality). Characters may be based on daily-life models but are not identical with them: the 'rules' they follow to arrive at motivations and behaviours are simplifications and distortions of daily life.

Theories and practices that foreground with such conviction the idea of character as actor-in-action risk not only to eliminate from acting discourse an important part of the Stanislavskian heritage and ethos but also to miss out on something visceral, something whose foundations strike deeper than either period or aesthetic tastes. Linguist Gilles Fauconnier and cognitive scientist Mark Turner, whose 2002 book, *The Way We Think*, has exercised considerable influence on recent cultural discourses, write:

> It is a central aspect of human understanding to think that people have characters that manifest themselves as circumstances change . . . to the extent that we ask 'What would Odysseus do in these circumstances?' despite the fact that those circumstances are unknown in Odysseus's world . . . Characters . . . are basic cognitive cultural instruments. We may dispute every aspect of their accuracy or legitimacy or invariance, or even their very existence, but cognitively we cannot do without them.
>
> *(pp. 249–250)*

I should therefore like to suggest a different framework for our consideration of the concept of theatre character.

I start by considering the way in which acting decisions are presented to the spectator. When I say 'presented', I mean factually, physically. What does the spectator see and hear? How is the character 'em-bodied', literally: what happens to the body, including the voice, of the actor?

In actor-in-action mode there is not much difference between the physicality of the actor in the theatre bar after the show and what has just been seen on the stage. We saw John Wayne's reaction to seeing a 'different' Kirk Douglas. As the squat, slightly gruff Lancashire-born actor Roy Kinnear was reputed to reply whenever asked "How are you going to approach this character?": "Well, he is going to be short, fat and have a Wigan accent". Which was not the case with – to take but two celebrated movie examples – Alec Guinness in *Kind Hearts and Coronets* or Geoffrey Rush in *The Life and Death of Peter Sellers*, in which both men created marked physical and vocal differences between the numerous characters they played.

Indeed, what do we perceive when we watch an actor walk on stage, before he or she has uttered a single word or performed the smallest gesture? We are struck first and foremost by their posture, by their silhouette and gait, defined by their centre of gravity. Should I so wish, I can manipulate these at will: I can slow down or speed up my breathing and my gestures; I can curve my back or 'swallow my umbrella', as the French say of a certain erect 'Englishness'; I can hold on for dear life to the ten pence piece I have inserted between my buttocks to get Hercule Poirot's distinctive walk (as David Suchet did in the long-running TV series); I can toss my dreadlocks and become Johnny Depp in pirate mode. I can, to use Michael Chekhov's phrase, adopt an "imaginary body".

The effectiveness of the imaginary body in communicating the key traits of the character is rooted in our real-life propensity to scrutinise key features of peoples' physical demeanour for clues to their personalities and status. A person's distinctive posture and way of walking strike us with the utmost immediacy. The movement analyst Warren Lamb writes:

> We do not make a posture, in the way that we make a gesture of the hand, or face, or some other part of the body . . . We have a posture which is natural to us, and except in so far as we might modify it by our own efforts, we have to live with it. These natural postures of ours decide how we perceive the world about us.
>
> *(1979, p. 22)*

A rich quote: first, it assumes that by and large we have a "natural" posture pattern – that is, one that has developed organically, as we grew up – and that deliberately altering this pattern, as in transformative acting, takes considerable effort. Second, it asserts that an intrinsic, causal link exists between our body shapes and psychological perspectives, that our posture patterns decide "how we perceive the world about us".

Several mechanisms are in play in the act of reading character through posture:

The audience establishes a rapport with the characters on stage at least in part through what psychologists call 'postural congruence' – our tendency to mirror physically those with whom we share a common viewpoint. To put it simply, we read other people by recognising aspects of ourselves in their demeanour. This in turn involves conceptualising our behaviour as psychological traits or characteristics (I was 'noble' or 'mean' when talking to Aunt Kate at Christmas). Repeated, such patterns of behaviour, although unconscious, eventually become dominant. The social psychologist Peter E. Bull conducted a range of rigorously constructed experiments that demonstrated that specific emotions and attitudes were "encoded" in different postures. Posture, he deduced, "can be regarded as a form of non-verbal communication", a conclusion supported by a classic experiment conducted by Spiegel and Machotka, who, to eliminate the effect of facial expression, used line drawings to test the decoding of postures. In this context, I also find useful neuroscientist Antonio

Damasio's concept of "background emotions". "When we sense" – Damasio writes – "that a person is 'tense' or 'edgy', 'discouraged' or 'enthusiastic', 'down' or 'cheerful', without a single word having been spoken to translate any of those possible states, we are detecting background emotions". And, Damasio also observes, the way in which we detect such emotions is precisely by means of physical signals subliminally internalised by the receivers: "We detect background emotions by subtle details of body posture, speed and contour of movements, minimal changes in the amount and speed of eye movements, and in the degree of contraction of facial muscles". In daily life, posture, like laughter, is outside our voluntary control and so is its detection. In the theatre, actors-in-action will bring their daily postures and gaits to every role (John Wayne has the same fluid walk whether playing a cowboy, a firefighter or a farmer); in contrast, actors who construct their postures do so in a conscious effort to convey a specific psychological attitude, thus offering a comment on the meanings of the play.

These two approaches, the actor-in-action and the constructed character, reflect fundamental differences in attitude toward the role of the body in expression. Two such attitudes are proposed:

One argues that the ultimate acting achievement is a state of total relaxation in which the actor's body is no longer a hindrance and in which the disappearance of barriers permits the actor's reactions to be transmitted to the audience without interference. Thought and feeling are those of the actor in the circumstances of the play and nothing must stand in their way. Grotowski would

> eliminate [the] organism's resistance to the psychic process. The result is freedom from the time-lapse between inner impulse and outer reaction in such a way that the impulse is already an outer reaction. Impulse and action are concurrent: the body vanishes, burns, and the spectator sees only a series of variable impulses.
>
> *(1968, p. 16)*

The alternative view acknowledges with interest the possibility of bodily expression related to, yet distinct from the impulse. The 'outer' is there to cover the 'inner'[8] with a protective shell. Like many shells, this one has its own beauty. Here the body is not, as for Meyerhold, a mere "instrument" to be played at will, according to the cerebral interpretations of author and director. Neither is it an obstacle to the revelation of the soul, as it was for Grotowski. Nor indeed is it an automatic follower of the psyche, as viewed by Stanislavski. In this approach, the body incarnates impulses, and the actor processes these into what the American director Anne Bogart calls "graphic shapes that turn out rather than in". As the scholar Sharon Carnicke has shown, the tradition of interpretation through the imaginary body represented by Michael Chekhov was lost in Russia because of censorship, while in America it was obscured by the dominance of the Strasberg approach. The body got lost in the struggle between emotion and action, which in many cases continues to define the two poles of the discourse on Stanislavski's legacy. By adopting a different gait and posture, the transformative actor creates, in Richard Shechner's phrase, precisely the "mask of imposture" denounced so vigorously by Grotowski and whose place in the theatrical landscape I argue should be re-considered.

If I may reiterate: this approach to acting entails the *deliberate construction of character as, first and foremost, a physical process.* Posture, gait, gestural range, vocal qualities (pitch, timbre, tone, resonance), accent/dialect, breathing rhythms, etc., are translated into a psychophysical presence which is perceptively different from that of the daily-life actor.

Seen from the perspective of the social psychologist, when such psychophysical manifestations are presented to spectators a process of encoding and decoding is initiated: posture, gait, etc., 'speak' in a language of movement. Meanings are created in the space between the signs made by actors and the interpretations afforded to these signs by spectators. Actors and directors who seek to give their texts an interpretation will also seek to 'direct' and shape the signs they transmit. Unlike 'processional' acting, in such cases encoding and decoding of posture and gesture is no longer a random process.

Once a characteristic posture has been established, we also realise that we begin to resemble others who behave or react and express themselves in similar ways – in critic Francis Fergusson's well-founded phrase, we perceive "the deeper analogies between beings". Categorisation on this basis is not without its problems. Grouping characters on the basis of personality traits or characteristics is founded on two much-contested assumptions: that one can speak of a psychological 'essence', of a stable identity 'underneath' the appearances of behaviour; and that one can therefore classify human beings (and by extension characters) into categories or types based on such immutable essences. These assumptions go back to an idea proposed by the early psychologist William James: that human personality contains a multiplicity of 'me's' which change according to circumstances, but that these are aspects of a core identity, which we as individuals recognise as our 'I'. I return to the ways in which contemporary psychology updates this proposition in Part Two. For the moment, I should record here that categorising is a basic biological function in humans; in fact, all primates are hard-wired to seek out what is predictable in an ever-changing environment. Four decades ago, scientist Eleanor Rosch demonstrated on the basis of experimentation that we categorise objects by referring to culturally determined "prototypes" and associating these with similar objects to which they bear a family resemblance. Thus, she noted, the concept 'bird' arouses the prototypical image of small, flying birds, while chickens or penguins, members of the same category, are marginal to it: "non-prototypical". Similarly, considering a particular dramatic character involves perceiving that which is non-typical by relating it to the typical. An approach that starts by describing the typical offers a useful set of reference points, which situate individual characters within a landscape. On the basis of such general observations, Bruce McConachie can confidently assert: "All spectators carry social prototypes in their mind/brains when they enter the playhouse". Does this restriction placed on the ever-changing stream of personality and/or action constitute an unwarranted simplification? Only insofar as saying 'this is Sicily' or 'we are in the Rift Valley' amounts to picking up a segment of the overall landscape in order to be able to conceive it and interact with it. And lest this position be misunderstood, I ought to stress that I am not arguing for a reliance on stereotypes, whether social, national or racial[9], to achieve effective stage communication, but for an acknowledgement that – in our anxiety to avoid such a trap – we have perhaps ignored the fact that there are not only certain aspects of social life that characterise a group, there are personality traits and behaviours too.

In the theatre, as in social interactions, one of our first reactions to encountering new presences is to seek to evaluate their social, cultural, political or familial circumstances. It is inevitable that when an actor walks on stage the audience will perceive their physicality as part of, and in relation to, a pattern. "There is a close relationship between the person and the overall pattern in which he participates", says the early ethologist E. T. Hall. That initial perception is then reinforced and amplified by subsequent stage action, both verbal and gestural. Ultimately, however, theatre, like chess, involves a large measure of pattern-recognition. A degree of complicity must therefore exist if meaning is to be transmitted between actor and spectator. For us to believe in Othello *the General*, the actor must adopt a posture and employ gestures appropriate to that social role: and not only when he surveys the Cypriot fortifications alongside Montano, but also when he receives Venetian envoys or spies on Desdemona at prayer. Even *in extremis* Antonio the patrician will deport himself in ways that are markedly different from the anxiety-ridden Lancelot Gobbo. The body reveals the 'type' of character we are watching.

Notes

1 On the *Today* programme, BBC Radio 4, 28 March 2014, 8.20 a.m. Paradoxically, while the mature Morse appears destined to be attached to Thaw forever, a 'prequel' series, entitled *Endeavour*, speculating on the life of 'young Morse' has been successfully screened. Which only goes to show that characters 'live' . . .
2 On Sunday 27 November 2016 at the Wyndham's Theatre, London. Reported in *The Times*, 29 November 2016. For those eager to know the outcome of the trial: the Prince considered pleading guilty by reason of insanity, but was rescued at the last moment by Ophelia, who produced government emails showing that the King had plotted to assassinate his nephew. The jury returned a not guilty verdict, but in her final remarks the learned judge was at pains to stress that the acquittal had been "against the weight of the evidence".
3 Poll carried out by BBC Radio 4, reported on 5 June 2016.
4 I note, however, Rick Kemp's useful distinction between "virtual" and "imagined": the first is used by some philosophers to describe theatre characters principally as mental constructs, the second implies, at least in the sense in which Kemp uses it, an embodied construct which combines psychological with physical dimensions.
5 *The Stage* 13 July 2000: 8.
6 See www.crikey.com.au/2015/03/09/why-do-we-still-think-cripface-is-ok/
7 I use "constructed" in the same sense as Bella Merlin uses the notion of "composed" or "compositional" character to describe "the transition from the actor's autobiographical self to a created role".
8 I use the traditional distinction between inner and outer only as a convenient mental construct, not to deny the integrated nature of psychophysical embodiment. The resilience of these terms in the face of recent discourses on acting rooted in neuropsychology bears witness to the fact that they are fundamental to our conceptual thinking about the body

as a "container" and should therefore be treated as a first-order metaphor in the sense described by Lakoff and Johnson.

9 In some cases, a conscious effort needs to be made to disentangle such associations from the overall concept. "Insofar as character evokes social persons (which is to say insofar as it is intelligible), – writes Elizabeth Fowler, analysing anti-Semitism in *The Merchant of Venice* – it requires the mobilisation of precisely the kind of representation of person that racist ideologies develop ... these social persons must be constantly smoked out ..."

Bibliography

Independent character: Marowitz, C., 1978. *The Act of Being*. Charlottesville, Virginia: Secker and Warburg; Diderot, D., 1883. *The Paradox of Acting*. London: Chatto and Windus; Chekhov, M., *To the Actor*. New York: Harper and Brothers; Douglas, K., 1988. *Ragman's Son: An Autobiography*. New York: Simon and Schuster; *and the notion of the "virtual"*: Langer, S., 1957. *Problems of Art: Ten Philosophical Lectures*. New York: Charles Scribner's Sons; Kemp, R., 2012. *Embodied Acting, What Neuroscience Tells Us about Performance*. London: Routledge.

Action is all: Donnellan, D., 2002. *The Actor and the Target*. London: Nick Hern Books; Mamet, D., 1999. *True and False: Heresy and Common Sense for the Actor*. London: Faber & Faber; Alfreds, M., 2007. *Different Every Night: Freeing the Actor*. London: Nick Hern Books; Mitchell, K., 2008. *The Director's Craft: A Handbook for the Theatre*; Stafford-Clark, M., 1997. *Letters to George: The Account of a Rehearsal*. London: Nick Hern Books; Stanislavski, C., 1986. *An Actor Prepares*, translated by E. Hapgood. London: Methuen; Merlin, B., 2001. *Beyond Stanislavsky: The Psycho-Physical Approach to Actor Training*. London: Nick Hern Books; Connolly, R. and Ralley, R., 2007. 'The laws of normal organic life or Stanislavski explained: towards a scientific account of the subconscious in Stanislavski's System', *Studies in Theatre and Performance*, 27 (3), pp. 237–259; Jackson, D., 2011. 'Twenty-first-century Russian actor training: active analysis in the UK', *Theatre, Dance and Performance Training*, 2 (2), pp. 166–180; *and character as actor-in-action*: Blair, R., 2006. 'Image and action: cognitive neuroscience and actor-training', in McConachie, B. and Hart, F. E., (eds.), *Performance and Cognition: Theatre Studies and the Cognitive Turn*. London: Routledge, pp. 167–186.

Challenging cerebral 'actioning': Arciniegas, D., 2012. 'Retracing Antonio: in search of the Merchant of Venice', in Yu, J. K. and Shurgot, M., (eds.), *Shakespeare's Sense of Character: On the Page and From the Stage*. Farnham: Ashgate, pp. 111–126; *and the notion of "simple presence"*: Derrida, J., 2001. *Writing and Difference*. London: Routledge.

Constructed character: Stanislavski, C., 1968. *Building a Character*, translated by E. Hapgood. London: Methuen; Merlin, B., 2015. 'The self and the fictive other in creation, rehearsal and performance', in Evans, M. (ed.), *The Actor Training Reader*. Abingdon: Routledge, pp. 119–131; *cognitive basis*: Fauconnier, G. and Turner, M., 2002. *The Way We Think: Conceptual Blending and the Mind's Hidden Complexities*. New York: Basic Books.

The body: Meyerhold, V., 1969. *Meyerhold on Theatre*, translated by E. Braun. London: Eyre Methuen; Grotowski, J., 1968. *Towards a Poor Theatre*. New York: Touchstone Books; Chekhov, *To the Actor*; Carnicke, S. M., 2009. *Stanislavsky in Focus: An Acting Master for the Twenty-First Century*, 2nd Edition. Abingdon: Routledge; Bogart, A. and Landau, T., 2005. *The Viewpoints Book: A Practical Guide to Viewpoints and Composition*. New York: Theatre Communications Group; *and its influence on psychological perspectives*: Lamb, W. and Watson, E., 1979. *Body Code: The Meaning in Movement*. London: Routledge and Kegan Paul; *and the notion of 'postural congruence'*: Scheflen, A. E., 1973. *Communicational Structure: Analysis of a Psychotherapy Transaction*. Bloomington: Indiana

University Press; LaFrance, M. and Broadbent, M., 1976. 'Group rapport: posture sharing as a non-verbal indicator', *Group and Organisation Studies*, (1), pp. 328–333; *experiments relating to*: Bull, P. E., 1987. *Posture and Gesture*. Oxford: Pergamon Press; Spiegel, J. P. and Machotka, P., 1974. *Messages of the Body*. Ann Arbor, Michigan: Free Press; *relationship to background emotions*: Damasio, A., 1999. *The Feeling of What Happens: Body and Emotion in the Making of Consciousness*. London: William Heinemann; LeDoux, J., 1996/2003. *The Emotional Brain: The Mysterious Underpinnings of Emotional Life*. New York: Touchstone Books; *and the "mask of imposture"*: Shechner, R., 1985. *Between Theatre and Anthropology*. Philadelphia: University of Pennsylvania Press.

'Inner' and 'outer' metaphor: Lakoff, G. and Johnson, M., 1999. *Philosophy in the Flesh: The Embodied Mind and its Challenge to Western Thought*. New York: Basic Books.

Character as "situational self": Kemp, 2012.

3

A BRIEF HISTORY OF . . . TYPE

Characterisation through type is an ancient and universal tradition. It spans the stock characters of the New Comedy and the *Fabulae Attelanae,* the three types of the Noh stage, Jacobean humours, the masks of the *commedia,* and, in more recent times, Delsarte's classification into "temperaments" and "social laws", Meyerhold's seventeen male and seventeen female character types and Laban's six psychological types or "Inner Attitudes". In some of these traditions, the word 'type' refers to the actor's personality. It is the actor who refines some of the attributes of his or her personality to the point where they become recognisable in themselves and for themselves. Over the centuries, these were codified into a number of categories or *emplois*, into which individual actors were said to fall. As late as the 1880s even Stanislavski, eventually the transformation actor par excellence, still thought of himself and his fellow actors in terms of these traditional role-types: 'romantic lead', 'heavy', 'comedian', etc.

But types were mostly attempts at grouping characters according to shared physical, moral or social traits. In the OED, character (in the sense I am pursuing here) is defined as a "description, delineation, or detailed report of a person's qualities". This tradition started with Plutarch and Theophrastus, who grouped their *Lives* and *Characters* according to moral dimensions. The 'military hero', the 'lover', the 'courtesan', are given (sometimes extensive) portraits designed to tease out their *mores*, their habitual behaviours and the moral dimensions which inform them. *Mores* unite those individuals who share them and separate them as a group from the rest of humanity. Theophrastus had been Aristotle's student and his writing is infused with the Aristotelian view of character: a person's deeds, repeated on numerous occasions throughout early life, solidify and take shape as moral dimensions – actions shape character. In turn, in his *Parallel Lives*, Plutarch is interested in *ethos* – in this context, human nature or personality – which he considers to be an entity apart from the actions of his heroes. For both writers, personalities are grouped first and foremost according to the moral categories they represent – human nature as a whole is measured against a code of ethics. At its most direct, the moral dimension, the *ethos*, is reflected in the *eidos*, in 'signs' which can be read on the face and the general deportment of the character.

A person's social position was also revealed through signs: typical behaviours, dress codes and other features that could be recognised socially. In certain public contexts, as well as on the stage, the language of posture, gesture and gait, created by selecting and refining certain aspects of natural movement at the expense of others, became a prime tool for communicating both function and purpose. Cicero wrote of the *sermo* and *eloquentia corporis* (the language and persuasiveness of the body) placed in the service of advocacy on the public Roman *rostra* or of political contention in the Senate. Their effectiveness was a matter of personal talent, certainly, but also of intensive and specific training. That this language could be learned implied a high degree of codification, and public orators defined themselves as a group through the skill with which they used the established signs of their trade. Similarly, in medieval societies individuals became recognisable through gestures and deportment appropriate to their particular social grouping, their *ordo*, just as much as by what they were permitted to wear by the sumptuary laws. Such ritualised uses of gesture for social purposes gave rise to what the historian Jean-Claude Schmitt calls "gestural communities". You belonged to the category called 'monk' or 'lay person', 'knight' or 'merchant', to which you declared your adherence as much by the way you expressed yourself physically as by your coat of arms, retinue, and clothes.

No sign was more significant than the speed, balance and rhythm with which a person walked: his or her gait. Aristotle recognises his *megalopsychos* (literally, the 'great-souled') – the man of poise and inner quality – by his steady, open, unhurried, graceful walk. By contrast, elaborates Theophrastus, adopting a rushed walk, ignoring those around you and rebuffing conversation, is a sign of arrogance. Such associations are not only a matter of temperament, but of social status too. Plautus writes: "it's proper for free men to go through the city at a moderate pace; I deem it like a slave to be running along in a bustle". These associations then descend through the ages and the Church Fathers extol moderation in body movement as a sign of virtue: in his book, *Formula vitae honestae*, Martin of Braga, a sixth-century Spanish bishop, recommends restraint in gesticulation, while St Ambrose considers a calm, collected bearing to be proper for a man of the cloth and crisply captures the common belief that the form of a man's mind may be read in his outer bearing: *habitus mentis enim in corporis statu cernitur*. From which it followed that if you wanted to change your state (of mind as well as socially) you needed first to change the habits of your body. In rigid medieval societies one of the few major changes possible was to be accepted into a religious order. Each order, however, had its own tradition: Cluniacs, for example, used different ritual gestures from Cistercians. As novices had to be inducted into the gestural spectrum correct for their community, their elders needed approved points of reference. This gave rise to a number of pedagogical treatises which prescribed in detail the physical aspects of a monk's daily existence: the gestures and demeanour appropriate for his daily interactions with his fellow monks and, to a lesser extent, with the laity. As one might expect, these echoed Classical requirements of decorum and restraint. They also reflected the view of human nature that lies at the heart of Christianity – an eternal soul contained in a mortal body. This in turn implied a fundamental division between *intus* (inner) and *foris* (outer). The two were separate yet interdependent: physical movements gave visible shape to the movements of the soul, but the soul could also be shaped by bodily movement. The positions and gestures to be used when the community was at prayer were designed not only to conform with ritual requirements but also to facilitate the achievement of a higher contemplative state and of religious ecstasy.

In the early modern era, Classical norms of deportment helped to shape the widely consulted manuals prescribing the rules of civilised, gentlemanly conduct. The best known among these, Baldassare Castiglione's *Il libro del cortigiano* (*The Book of the Courtier*) was quickly translated into the main European languages and, in the century following its publication in 1528, was printed in well over 100 editions. In it, Castiglione argued that the defining characteristic of being a courtier, and by extension of being a gentleman, was moral and spiritual elegance (*cortesia*, *sprezzatura* – grace), expressed in the refined understatement of those things which are visible: clothes, prowess in dance, fencing and horse riding, and physical bearing. Being born into a noble family made it easier to acquire *sprezzatura*, but nobility could also be learnt through arduous practice and by observing and imitating a suitable model. Similarly, in a lay version of the effect correct positions at prayer were said to have on the inner life of the monk, adopting a beautiful, restrained and fluid exterior could lead to inner poise and moral generosity. Secular and religious perspectives also came together in the other highly popular etiquette manual of the Renaissance, Giovanni della Casa's *Il Galateo* (1588). Della Casa was a priest and, like Castiglione's, his prescription is for elegance of bearing closely aligned to the nobility of the soul. To achieve the latter, one had to become conscious of one's gestures and carriage, and so bring them under control. By the end of the sixteenth century the notion had become established that, by altering one's behaviour until new physical habits became second nature, one could reform and improve one's inner life.

Such ideas could not help but affect the understandings brought by writers and actors to their work in the emerging professional playhouses. It was an Elizabethan conviction that outer appearance ought to reflect inner qualities: "I will believe thou hast a mind that suits/ With this, thy fair and outward character", Orsino tells Viola in *Twelfth Night*. The Shakespearean scholar R. A. Foakes writes, "Beauty of the body should indicate beauty of the soul; the fact that it frequently does not is one of the main elements of Elizabethan tragedy". In turn, awareness of the relative harmony or tension between body and soul implied a new, more complex style of acting. Iago, Richard III and Edmund dissemble, yet reveal their true natures in direct addresses. In order to play Hamlet, however, a style of (relatively) 'naturalistic' acting is introduced which, as the scholar Peter Holland writes, is "more opaque, clouding the distinction between doing and counterfeiting in acting". Gradually, actors moved from making direct statements about the personalities of the characters to slowly revealing their inner natures. By the eighteenth century, in his *Memoirs* of Charles Macklin, William Cooke could admire the great actor's portrayal of Iago for its "gradual disclosure of the character; his seeming openness and concealed revenge".

The evolution of the terminology employed by the Elizabethans to describe what we now call character is indicative of the effort needed to conceptualise the complexities of mirroring human nature through fictional entities. 'Character' in early modern English only means 'imprint', the act of writing and its outcome in characters-on-the-page. Characters in the sense of sets of fixed, emphatic traits are called 'humours' or 'elements'. But, slowly, the terms 'person' and 'personation' also begin to find their way into the vocabulary. "Person" first makes its appearance in John Marston's play *Antonio and Mellida*. "Personate", in the sense of disguising and embodying, is recorded a few years later. Florio's Italian dictionary of 1598 traces it to the Italian *personare* and gives it a playhouse-flavoured definition: "to personate, to act or play the part of any person". The historian Andrew Gurr has argued convincingly that these changes in terminology reflected the changes in acting style needed to bring to life the plays of Shakespeare and his contemporaries. To 'personate' implied observation of people so as to "qualify everything according to the nature of the person personated" and with such skill that the actor "seemed to be the very persons whom he acted", the writer Thomas Heywood noted. Gurr writes: "By 1600 characterisation was the chief requisite of the successful player", and the appearance of the noun personation "signals the growth of the concept of character-impersonation".[1] Some scholars argue that the way in which Shakespeare understood the concept of 'person' begins to move towards the modern sense of character, as a complex psychological entity distinguished by interiority and self-reflection. Even the word 'self' makes its appearance: "not merely a grammatical reflexivity but a nominal and 'personal' entity, my 'self' rather than just 'myself'". An expectation that individuality of character be expressed as individuality of deportment also eventually emerges onto the Jacobean stage.

Soon, the language of gesture became codified for the public at large too: John Bulwer's popular texts, *Chirologia* and *Chironomia* (1644), were ostensibly manuals to enable the deaf (Bulwer was a physician) to communicate by means of hand movements. In practice, concern for the deaf was no more than a starting point and the two books, published simultaneously, first catalogued common hand gestures and then attempted a "manual rhetoric", assigning specific meanings to selected gestures. Another principle of the 'language of movement' is thus established: daily gestures need to be isolated and amplified if they are to communicate clearly. The actors of the eighteenth and nineteenth centuries embraced this notion with relish: it became a universal convention of the stage for actors to stop at significant (usually emotionally charged) moments in the action and hold their poses so that the audience might appreciate the elegance and precision with which they had assumed the shapes prescribed for particular emotions or 'passions'. Such pauses came to be known as 'attitudes' or 'figures' and were familiar to actor and spectator alike: Henry Siddons's manual, *Practical Illustrations of Rhetorical Gesture and Action* (1822), for example, was popular with both. The distinction between daily gesture and a codified gestural language for the stage, which had started with Bulwer's books, became entrenched.

At the same time, a gap opened between what was acceptable on the stage and what passed in good society. We saw how for centuries restraint had been extolled, from the Classics to the medieval monastery, then to Castiglione. With the advent of the Reformation, Protestantism, alongside religious practice and ethics, also democratised gesture: the move from 'flamboyant' to 'disciplined' ways of moving, long the concern only of religious orders and the aristocracy, now extended to the daily deportment of the merchant classes and below. By the seventeenth century, restraint (in expression, clothing, display of wealth or knowledge) no longer defined gentlemanly conduct alone but was considered a social virtue for all: in Protestant circles, as a result of the emphasis on control and temperance; in Counter-Reformation circles, as a result of the need to show that the Catholic Church had reformed. (At the Restoration, the remnants of Cavalier flamboyance and excess were themselves reactions, ultimately destined to fail, against the general trend towards reserve and decorum.) By the nineteenth century, English public schools also espoused Classical ideals of restraint and self-control as the foundations of good manners.

Actors, however, called upon to express alarming 'passions', still used a much larger physical vocabulary, one all their own. It was only gradually and reluctantly that actors adopted the association between high status and gestural restraint and the trend began towards a gradual reduction in the size of expressive gestures. And yet, while for the past century and a half the language of movement in realistic acting has been moving closer and closer to daily behaviour, it is no more its facsimile than was the case in the time of Alleyn and Burbage. Over-controlled physical expression in a character still triggers in the spectator visceral associations, in-built through enculturation, which correlate deliberation with superiority and 'civilisation', while agitation or haste suggest social inferiority and dubious motives. Measured, purposeful walking is still associated with honesty, commitment and determination: while the warriors of the *Iliad* moved in this way, so too does the hero about to face his destiny in modern Westerns. Characters who define themselves in such ways signal themselves as exemplars of their type.

However, the objection continues to be made that types reduce theatre characters to only a few, traditional interpretations ("bitchy Lady M."). 'Every person is different', it is frequently asserted, therefore characters must only be seen in their individuality. At the same time, as the scholar Edward Burns points out, the idea of character as 'subject' ('I') is a modern, post eighteenth century concept. In pre-modern thinking, the only subjects of the theatre are the writer/narrator and the audience/readers who are 'subjected' (in the grammatical sense) to someone else's actions. The *dramatis personae* react to these actions, which provoke them into making choices; the latter are not there to 'reveal' the character, however, but to illustrate good or bad elections, morally or politically improving the spectator by example. The point of the play was therefore not to expose the inner nature of people, but to educate the spectator's social responses by showing how others reacted in certain situations: a view of the actors (literally, those who take actions) which was interested more in what is general and socially typical than the personal and individualistic. For the ancients, as for medieval and even some modern Far-Eastern cultures,[2] identity was determined socially, by family and state. In the wider social context, individuals did not have 'meaning' in and by themselves. Plays reflected this ancient wisdom: the classical play format involves an individual breaking the natural balance of the *polis*. By affirming their own identities, Agamemnon, Electra or Oedipus break that of the collective. The outcome of their 'passion' is the restoration of the natural balance. Only then, by returning to the collective, becoming part of a recognizable type (father, daughter, wise ruler) does their individuality regain its 'meaning'. The purpose of the character in the play is fulfilled only when the universal is perceived through the personal. Vissarion Belinsky, the Russian critic who greatly influenced Stanislavski, constantly urged the artist to "see the general in the particular".

This emphasis is inherent in the concept of type. An understanding of acting based on type inevitably takes on board the question of the various functions – moral and otherwise – of the character in the play. Actors-in-character seek to achieve (and convey to the spectator) a synthesis between what is typical and what is individual. This places each character into a wider context – as both an individual and, simultaneously, as a representative of a group.

This means asking – to take another character from *The Merchant of Venice* as an example – not only *who* Portia is but also *what* she is. If we were to imagine Portia sitting – as well she might – for her portrait, what would the painter inscribe on the canvas? The lineaments of a 'young woman in mourning', of a 'coquette', a 'vestal', an 'aristocrat' with dynastic concerns? What is the painter's moral attitude toward the sitter? Indeed, how would Portia herself wish to be seen? To address these questions is to consider the fictional character not only as an individual but also as representative of a professional, social or family category. Portia is a 'landowner' or a 'daughter' as well as having an individuality: the actor has to decide *what sort* of owner or daughter. Seen in this way, the art of the actor consists in allowing the general rule to be perceived through the exceptional details. In other words, through the process of characterisation the actor shows the norm from which the character departs at the same time as showing how it departs from it. "It is axiomatic", Elizabeth Fowler writes about yet another character in *The Merchant of Venice*

> that fictional characterisation requires the enlisting of dominant ideas or models of the person from many cultural discourses (what in my work I call *social persons*). To be intelligible, the figure of Shylock calls upon a number of familiar social persons – the Jew, the merchant, the tyrant father, and so forth . . . Social persons are abstract models of the person that act as a cognitive framework for the apprehension of character.
>
> *(2006, pp. 58–59, emphasis original)*

Fowler's notion of social persons – "sets of expectations built in the reader's mind by experience", "templates" without which fictional characters would not be intelligible – chimes with the approach to character I am outlining here. Both foreground the cognitive processes involved in recognising fictional characters. We grasp characters, whether through language on the page or a combination of visual and spoken clues on the stage, by associating them with understandings abstracted from common assumptions about group behaviours: we expect merchants, heiresses and moneylenders to behave in certain ways and we relate to individuals according to the ways in which they fulfil these expectations. This is not to imply that one can simply reduce character to a single cluster of characteristics – analysing the character of the Knight in Chaucer's *Canterbury Tales*, Fowler counts as many as 13 social persons. However, from the point of view of the actor-in-character, what matters is which one of these multiple social persons is selected to hold together the psychological portrait and translate it into a readable physicality. Of course, within this overall envelope, the physicality will alter subtly according to which of the social persons contained within the overall shell is elicited by particular circumstances. But if there is to be an independent character and not just a 'processional' actor, the consistency of certain psychophysical characteristics needs to be established in all circumstances.

A type is therefore an abstract construct, created by amalgamating and concentrating the characteristics of similar individuals, accumulated in the collective experience of both actors and spectators. It is in this sense that characters can be said to be 'independent': their 'meta-real' existence is in the form of categories which are present in the psyche of actors and spectators alike. By first identifying the category to which a particular character belongs, then recognising those characteristics in themselves, by 'tuning into' a type, actors give individuality and body to a general truth, which exists, by definition, outside their individual consciousness. Having said that, clearly the 'Idea of Viola' does not have a material existence until it is embodied by an individual actor. In becoming flesh, it acquires some of her characteristics: the colour of its eyes will be that of the actor's, as will the colour of its feelings. However, the actor makes choices and places at the service of the character only those of her attributes that she thinks appropriate. Only by having a clear-cut image of 'Viola the Idea' can the actor know which characteristics to select. And only by selecting a relatively restricted and defined posture, gait, and accent or dialect can she communicate the psychological make-up of the character physically, through the language she shares with the audience. This, at least, is what we intuit when we watch her.

Using patterns by means of which characters announce themselves to be 'shy', 'nervous' or 'blustering', actors invite the spectators to enter into a sort of contract. The contract works precisely because, in adopting certain patterns, actors declare their characters to be in certain ways limited: they include a small number of defining physical and psychological characteristics and exclude all those that do not serve their purpose. Thus, they communicate through a relatively small number of signs. The importance of the signs lies not in themselves, in their physical reality, but in what they represent. On the British stage, for example, certain accents are an efficient means of placing characters from the point of view of their social, psychological or even period provenance. And, lest this be dismissed as a relic of modern social and regional prejudices, I should point out that the tradition of identifying characters through their dialect goes all the way back to Aristophanes and then to the New Comedy. Whatever one might think of the wider context of such reductions, they work because they are read for what they are: signs, not of material reality, but of other signs – the conventions shared between stage and auditorium.

The very term character, says Burns, implies a degree of "fitness . . . a correspondence between particular 'signs' and certain categories of human being". Certain ways of walking, bending, turning, speaking are 'in', all others are 'out'. The chaos of daily behaviour is distilled into a few physical characteristics. When the realistic acting school therefore talks of 'rounded' or 'three-dimensional' characters, it does not mean by this the creation of fully-fledged 'real' human beings. On the contrary, it describes concentrations of characteristics that are nonetheless "substantive"[3] enough to give the illusion of real life. Characters are a form of *trompe l'oeil*.

This illusion, the 'Idea of character', encompasses those attributes by which we also identify personalities in daily life: intention, meaning, ethics, consciousness, agency. To exist, a character has to have a name or title, certain signature traits, and a measure of consistency of motive and behaviour, as well as of speaking, thinking and feeling. (Apparent inconsistencies can be accommodated within this overall unity.) The term 'character' also implies, in English as much as in Aristotle's *ethos*, a moral dimension – we are invited to react to the character's deeds, its actions, by applying our moral sense; to approve or disapprove.

It is therefore in this sense that I shall use the term character from now on – as an artificial construct derived from:

a.   The objective data provided by the text.
b.   The impressions made by these data in the minds of actors, where they are filtered through the actors' prior knowledge and expectations regarding the nature of the specific performances in which they are engaged. These impressions are not confined to personality traits, but – just as importantly – include the physical expression of these traits and relate to them in a mutually reinforcing, circular process.
c.   The impressions formed in the minds of the spectators by how the actors look and what they do.[4]

Notes

1 The contemporary quotes are from Thomas Heywood, *Apology for Actors* and a Puritan response to it (I.G., *A Refutation of the Apology for Actors*) cited in the same place.
2 A cross-cultural survey of norms of experiencing emotions, for example, showed that Chinese cultural attitudes regarded guilt as desirable and pride as undesirable emotions, while Anglo-Saxon attitudes were the other way around. (Eid and Diener 2001)
3 "Substantive" is the term used by Edward Burns to differentiate 'real', 'rounded', 'individual' characters from 'stereotypes' or E. M. Forster's "flat characters".
4 The literary critic Jonathan Culpeper also emphasises the process of impression formation in inference. He confines himself, however, to the dynamics between the data of the play

and the reader. When character is conceived for and perceived through performance, three elements are in play: data, actor's mind and spectator's mind.

Bibliography

Categorisation: Fergusson, F., 1949. *The Idea of a Theatre, A Study of Ten Plays, The Art of Drama in a Changing Perspective*. Garden City, New York: Doubleday & Co.; *as a basic biological function*: Rosch, E., 1977. 'Human categorization', in Warren, N. (ed..) *Advances in Cross-Cultural Psychology* (1). New York: Academic Press; Byrne, R. and Whiten, A., 1988. *Machiavellian Intelligence: Social Expertise and the Evolution of Intellect in Monkeys, Apes and Humans*. Oxford: Clarendon Press; Hall, E. T., 1959. *The Silent Language*. New York: Anchor Books; *and audiences*: McConachie, B., 2008. *Engaging Audiences: A Cognitive Approach to Spectating in the Theatre*. New York: Palgrave Macmillan; *and stereotypes*: Fowler, E., 2006. 'Shylock's virtual injuries'. *Shakespeare Studies* (34) pp. 56–69.

Character types as moral categories: Burns, E., 1990. *Character: Acting and Being on the Pre-Modern Stage*. Basingstoke: The Macmillan Press; Desmet, C., 2006. 'The persistence of character'. *Shakespeare Studies* (34) pp. 46–55.

Gestural communities: Schmitt, J.-C., 1991. 'The rationale of gestures in the West: third to thirteenth centuries', in Bremmer, J. and Roodenburg, H. (eds.) *A Cultural History of Gesture*. Cambridge: Polity Press, pp. 59–70; Dromgoole, N., 2007. *Performance Style and Gesture in Western Theatre*. London: Oberon Books.

Movement and virtue: Plautus, 1852. 'Poenulus', in *The Comedies of Plautus*. London: Henry G. Bohn, pp. 351–418; *in the Christian tradition*: Barasch, M., 1976. *Gestures of Despair in Medieval and Early Renaissance Art*. New York: New York University Press; Rijnberk, G. v., 1953. *Le langage par signes chez les moines*. Amsterdam: North-Holland Publishing Company; *and shaping the soul*: Schmitt, 1991; *in the early modern era*: Burke, P., 1995. *The Fortunes of the Courtier: The European Reception of Castiglione's Cortegiano*. Pennsylvania: Penn State University Press; *in the modern day*: Bremmer, J., 1991. 'Walking, standing and sitting in ancient Greek culture', in Bremmer, J. and Roodenburg, H. (eds.) *A Cultural History of Gesture*. Cambridge: Polity Press, pp. 1–35.

Elizabethan characterisation: Foakes, R. A., 1954. 'The player's passion: some notes on Elizabethan psychology and acting', in *Essays and Studies*. London: John Murray, pp. 62–77; Holland, P., 1984. 'Hamlet and the art of acting', in Redmond, J. (ed.) *Drama and the Actor*. Cambridge: Cambridge University Press, pp. 39–61; Cooke, W., 1806. *Memoirs of Charles Macklin*. 2nd Edition. London: James Asperne; Gurr, A., 1966. 'Elizabethan action'. *Studies in Philology*, (63), pp. 144–156; Gurr, A., 1987. *The Shakespearean Stage, 1574–1642*. 2nd Edition. Cambridge: Cambridge University Press; *and the 'self'*: Bishop, T., 2006. 'Personal fowl: The phoenix and the turtle and the question of character'. *Shakespeare Studies*, (34), pp. 65–76.

'Individual' and 'social' character: Burns, 1990; Kierkegaard, S., 1987. 'The tragic in ancient drama', in *Either/Or, Part 1*, translated by H. V. Hong and E. H. Hong. Princeton: Princeton University Press; Benedetti, J., 1988. *Stanislavski: A Biography*. London: Methuen; Gordon, M., 1987. *The Stanislavsky Technique: A Workbook for Actors*. New York: Applause Theatre Books; Fowler, E., 2003. *Literary Character: The Human Figure in Early English Writing*. London: Cornell University Press; *as understood cross-culturally*: Eid, M. and Diener, E., 2001. 'Norms of experiencing emotions in different cultures: inter- and intranational differences'. *Journal of Personality and Social Psychology*, (81), pp. 869–885.

Shared assumptions: Boegehold, A. L., 1999. *When a Gesture was Expected*. Princeton: Princeton University Press; Bogatyrev, P., 1976. 'Semiotics in the folk theatre', in Matejka, L. and Titunik, I. R. (eds.) *Semiotics of Art: Prague School Contributions*. Cambridge, Massachusetts: MIT Press, pp. 35–36.

"Substantive" characters: Burns, 1990; *in the 'realistic' school*: Connolly, R. and Ralley, R., 2007. 'The laws of normal organic life or Stanislavski explained: towards a scientific account of the subconscious in Stanislavski's system'. *Studies in Theatre and Performance*, 27 (3), pp. 237–259.

Impression formation: Culpeper, J., 2001. *Language and Characterisation: People in Plays and Other Texts*. New York: Routledge.

4

FRIENDS FOR LIFE

Character and literary criticism

The second question I posed in Chapter 2 was whether one *could* adopt an approach that ascribes psychological traits to characters and roots these in biographies. Is it legitimate to say about Lear that he is 'short-tempered', that Othello is 'dignified' and Olivia 'aloof'? And if so, to wonder how they came to be like this and speculate about their 'lives' before and sometimes after the time-span of the plays? Actors may routinely do this, but most modern literary critics certainly do not think it is right to do so.

This long-standing debate typically focuses on the touchstone for such considerations: the Shakespearian character. The writings of the Edwardian scholar A. C. Bradley, which enjoyed wide currency at the turn of the last century, probably represent the epitome of the proposition that Shakespeare's characters should be approached as representations of human subjects. "The 'story' or 'action' of a Shakespearean tragedy," Bradley writes in an oft-quoted passage,

> does not consist, of course, solely of human actions or deeds; but the deeds are the predominant factor. And these deeds are . . . thoroughly expressive of the doer – characteristic deeds. The centre of the tragedy, therefore, may be said with equal truth to lie in action issuing from character, or in character issuing in action . . . The dictum that, with Shakespeare, 'character is destiny', is no doubt an exaggeration . . . but it is the exaggeration of a vital truth.
>
> *(1904/1993, pp. 6–7)*

Action is a function of character; character is both cause and sufferer of action and the unfolding of the play's story is a result of the personalities of the protagonists and of the interactions between them. Elucidating the formative experiences of the characters (their 'back-stories'), and thus explicating their psychology, is therefore the main purpose of literary criticism. Bradley's highly influential *Shakespearean Tragedy* was published in 1904, the year of Chekhov's death and of the publication of Freud's *The Psychopathology of Everyday Life.* While Bradley mentions neither, his book shares many of their assumptions.

Bradley appends to *Shakespearean Tragedy* a number of extended 'Notes'. These were meant as editorial glosses to various texts but may also be read as a kind of actors' or directors' preparatory notes. In them, certain background-story issues are clarified: where was Hamlet at the time of his father's death?, the double timeline in *Othello,* the question of Macbeth having or not having children (Macbeth has no heirs, yet Lady Macbeth says "I have given suck . . ."), etc. Bradley articulates in the language of the emergent twentieth century a tradition of literary criticism which by then was already 200 years old: Dryden, Pope, Coleridge, all wrote as if characters had 'lives' of their own, over and above what was made explicit in the texts, and looked to character traits and motives for the keys with which to unlock the meanings of the plays. In his *Essay on the Dramatic Character of Sir John Falstaff* (1777), one of the most emphatic articulations of this position, Maurice Morgann locates the source of our fascination with Shakespeare's "round" characters in an innate "sense" we are said to possess, which enables us to intuit a character's psychological make-up beyond what may be deduced from its actions.

> [Shakespeare] . . . boldly makes a character act and speak from those parts of the composition which are inferred only, and not distinctly shown . . . it may be fit to consider [Shakespeare's characters] rather as Historic than Dramatic beings; and when occasion requires, to account for their conduct from the whole of character, from general principles, from latent motives, and from policies not avowed.
>
> *(1777/1912, p. 62)*

By the end of the nineteenth century, the editor of a popular book of extracts from the novels of Sir Walter Scott could write: "The test of a character in any novel is that it should have existed before the book that reveals it to us began and should continue after the book is closed . . . These are our friends for life . . ." This had also been the practice of generations of actors and was the tradition into which Stanislavski was born. On occasion, leaders of the profession were even moved to proselytise in print: in her *Lectures on Shakespeare,* the great Edwardian actress Ellen Terry discusses at some length whether the 'flesh but no blood' legal cavil which defeats Shylock was the product of Portia's own intelligence or of that of 'Bellario', her alter-ego; or wonders who taught the Boy Robin in *Henry V* to speak such good French.

These were some of the examples cited by the Modernist scholar L. C. Knights when, in the 1930s, he impishly asked: "How many children had Lady Macbeth?". This was the title of an article in which he argued vociferously against biographical speculation, the fascination with hidden motives and the unseemly habit of assigning personality traits to characters. Knights's main quarrel is with the underpinning assumption: that the value of Shakespeare's plays lies, over and above other merits, in their ability to bring forward complex and arresting characters. This assumption

Knights calls "the most fruitful of irrelevancies". The fact that a mere actress such as Ellen Terry, not a "critical Authority" (the capital is his), might be so emboldened as to disseminate them, and find a large audience for them to boot, vexes him profoundly. Knights's counter-argument is that the texts, the "words", are what matters and that any considerations not in the words are "preposterous".[1] His focus, as that of other prominent critics such as F. R. Leavis and T. S. Eliot, is on "Images", with a capital letter, described by Ezra Pound as "that which presents an intellectual and emotional complex in an instant of time". Knights enunciates his position thus: "A Shakespeare play is a dramatic poem . . . its end is to communicate a rich and controlled experience by means of words." He then quotes the influential scholar George Wilson Knight: "The persons, ultimately, are not human at all, but purely symbols of a poetic vision". As a result, Knights proclaims, we must treat plays "primarily as poems", from which follows that "Elizabethan drama should be non-realistic".[2] And – if we discount the disdain with which Ellen Terry's sally into print is treated – nowhere in this substantial essay are actual performances of the texts considered.

This, essentially formalist, attitude came to dominate literary criticism for the remainder of the twentieth century. Precision in text analysis aided the understanding of the plays, while resisting the siren call of common concerns with plot, character, relationships. Some critics mined the words for the interplay of rhythms, sound and imagery. Others emphasised the historical perspective: Shakespeare's plays were placed within the medieval Morality Play tradition and/or within the historical realities of the Elizabethan and Jacobean periods – literary and staging conventions (female roles played by boys, etc.), the architecture of the theatres, social hierarchies within audiences, became the main sources of illumination regarding their meanings. In Shakespeare's world, it was asserted, concepts of personality were indistinguishable from social roles – individuality and subjectivity came only later, as after-effects of the Protestant and capitalist revolutions of the seventeenth century.[3] For the 'historicist' school, characters are to be seen primarily as functions, not as individuals; it is therefore considered inappropriate to respond to fictional characters as if they were real people, even when the emphasis is on the 'as if'. For their part, Marxist critics treat the very notions of a core personality (in life) and unitary character (in fiction) with great suspicion. They quote Brecht's *Short Organum*: "the bourgeois theatre's performances always aim at smoothing over contradictions, at creating false harmony, at idealisation". The idea of a stable identity is "bourgeois" because it obscures the possibility of dialectical social and political change: "informed by contradictory social and ideological processes", the critic Jonathan Dollimore writes, ". . . [the subject] is never an indivisible unity, never an autonomous, self-determining centre of consciousness". Other critics, adopting a poststructuralist stance, cast doubt on the very ability of language to give credible and coherent depictions of reality. They therefore question whether a play, a construct made of words, can ever create entities (characters) that conduct themselves according to the norms of human psychology.

There is no doubt that the focus on the interplay of words and on historical contexts brought with it a necessary re-orientation toward the tangible materials of Elizabethan writing. At its best, as in F. R. Leavis's uncompromising essays, examinations of character rooted in textual evidence can provide startling illumination.[4] But overall concern with character came to be considered at best old-fashioned and at worst pernicious. There is no surer way of being accused of naivety and of drawing the opprobrium of scholars than to talk of characters having a 'personality' or 'identity'. And, as Knights had declared, mistrust of 'character' (always in ironic inverted commas) is inextricably linked to objections to what is perceived as the 'wrong' realistic (as opposed to 'formal') approach to acting during the 'long Stanislavskian century' that still defines most European and Anglo-Saxon theatre productions. Where on the realistic/formal spectrum the 'correct' style of performance ought to be situated is not specified;[5] nor is an analysis offered of the ways in which various understandings of character influence performance styles. But realism, by which presumably is meant simulacra of daily behaviour underpinned by psychological inferences, is judged inappropriate when making flesh the core ideas of the plays. "Macbeth is a statement of evil", L. C. Knights proclaims. In this perspective, to ask how many children Lady Macbeth had, why Desdemona's mother is never mentioned, whether Cordelia, apparently so much younger than her sisters, is the issue of a second marriage or an unexpected late arrival in a long one, is to indulge in "fruitful irrelevancies".

Such discourses have all but dominated literary and theatre criticism in the 'postmodern' era. It is not my intention to rehearse their tropes beyond what is strictly necessary to set out the background against which I formulate my own, performance-orientated, position. I cannot, however, resist the following quote, from what is arguably the most articulate exposition of the decline of the notion of character, Elinor Fuchs' highly influential *The Death of Character*. Unlike many academic sallies, this one also has the distinction of seeking to speak for "the actor":

> It is not difficult for actors to discover for themselves, without benefit of sophisticated philology, that imagining an Oedipus at the level of individual psychology does not so much enhance him with lifelike detail as dissipate his moral force. On the contrary, it is the actor's difficult task to inhabit the actions of an Oedipus with such concentration that, in effect, no 'excess' of character is left over. The actor seeks the actions, not the coherent personality that commits them.
>
> *(1996, p. 24)*

Alas, many actors remain stubbornly Bradleyan. Writing about the challenges of teaching Shakespearean character to college students, the critic Laurie Osborne notes a similar "fascinating disjunction" between student instinct and scholarly demands. One can safely say that such resistances would be detected in most of the theatre-going public, were it to be exposed to the injunctions of postmodern criticism. Fiction and the way we deal with fiction reflect a fundamental psychological investment in the recognition of coherent, stable personalities, in ourselves as much as in others. It is nonetheless a measure of the relentless scepticism of the academic critic toward performance that with increased reverence for the text also comes a tendency to read rather than to enact. This was epitomised in Knights's pronouncement: "A Shakespeare play is a dramatic poem". No room for actors in his father's mansion.

This disconnect underpins the impatience with which much academic scholarship treats mainstream acting practice. Jonathan Culpeper's otherwise excellent contemporary text on the concept of character (*Language and Characterisation: People in Plays and Other Texts*, 2001), while critical of the self-referential attitude of much lit. crit., brushes away performance-related concerns in two short pages. He also appears to subscribe to the somewhat simplistic assumption that actors "pretend". This is a loaded word, implying a distance between actor and character greater than the one I described in the previous chapters. In so doing, Culpeper appears to deny the actor the benefit of the process which he accurately allows the reader: that the character is a combined function of the data of the text, of the prior knowledge of the reader and of the context in which the reader is engaged in the act of reading. A process that I think applies equally to the relationship between actor and text.

As the critic Jin Ko Yu observes in a more recent contribution to the continuing debate on character:

> Suspicion between the theatre and academia persists, and does so because, as has been the case from the beginning, a high/low distinction operates that has many elements and cognates, including the distinction between theory and practice. On one side, the text still retains for so many the quality of neo-Platonic, metaphysical Form, to which performances remain shadowy and inadequate replicas. Additionally, superior status is granted, or self-granted, to the academic and theoretical, as opposed to theatrical and practical, knowledge. On the other side, a competing claim for priority is made based on the fact that Shakespeare's plays were first and foremost scripts for performance. Accordingly, the tables are turned to value practice and to dismiss academic knowledge as airy abstractions that are irrelevant to the living heart of drama – namely, performance.
>
> *(2012, p. 2)*

The latter statement is, sadly, true: on the whole, actors remain distant from and disdainful of critical discourse. When the director in *Looking for Richard* shouts at Al Pacino that the actor knows more about the character than any pesky academic, he articulates the prevailing view. Lately, some people on the lit. crit. side are tentatively attempting a reconciliation: those scholars who address themselves to acting processes as they find them are returning to the uses of inference. They start from the common-sense observation that, whether they consciously acknowledge them or not, people have motives for their actions. And that, just as we assess the actions of those around us by imputing motives to them, by inferring what is 'behind' them, so we (readers, actors, spectators) will inevitably assign the same relationship (motives lead to actions) to fictional characters. This perspective does not forgo the undoubted gains made by textual analysis and contextual studies to the understanding of the plays, but instead seeks to marry these with the natural human propensity towards inference. Much of this return to inference initially occurred in reaction to the historicist strictures of the Original Practices school: as a result, this approach is generally subsumed under the general title of 'presentism'. Michael Bristol, one of its most nuanced exponents, confesses:

> I have a guilty secret: I want to know how many children Lady Macbeth had. When I read Shakespeare I compare the dramatic characters with real people . . . It is reasonable to think about the literary characters in the way we think about real people because that is how we actually make sense of stories.
> *(2000, pp. 18–19)*

Whether Lady Macbeth had children, whether they were fathered by Macbeth and in particular what then happened to render Macbeth childless in the timeframe of the play are, he argues, questions relevant to understanding the play as well as to – the main concern of the actor playing her – the way in which the character will be portrayed. On this basis, Bristol chooses to believe that Lady Macbeth had one child and that it either dies during the play (unlikely) or had died before the action begins. This changes the way one reads the character: "On this view Lady Macbeth is not an abstract symbol of evil, or of the unnatural", – Bristol replies to L. C. Knights – "but rather a person who commits an evil deed".

A distinction ought to be drawn here, however: for directors, an emphasis on the analysis of imagery is helpful when constructing the world of the production. Indeed, this approach can be said to have defined English directing: since the Second World War, the major English theatre companies have been mostly led by directors initially educated in the Leavis/Knights/Wilson Knight tradition of textual analysis. They took note of scholarly concerns regarding the relationship between imagery and theme and embodied their responses, not only in visuals (set, costumes, etc.), but also – with the cooperation of the actors who became their regular collaborators – in characters. Distilling the plays into tight metaphysical abstractions remains intellectually very attractive – a pithy, meaningful answer to the question: "What might this play be about?" This is not to argue for a single interpretation of complex texts backed by "Authority" in the way Knights does ("Macbeth is a statement of evil"). But it is to recognise that, while the great plays will yield multiple meanings, from the actor's point of view a fundamental choice needs to be made: one approach – widespread in Anglo-Saxon productions, though less so on the Continent – is to 'let the play speak for itself', to give voice to the words but not to guide the spectator towards a particular interpretation. This approach, I would suggest, inevitably leads to 'processional' and personality acting. The alternative is to examine the various possible interpretations and select an explicit thematic line. Its embodiment through acting cannot be achieved without constructing defined characters. To 'let the play speak for itself' is an abrogation of the right (one might say the duty) to interpret. And interpretation can nourish itself on the fruits of literary criticism.

I therefore fully subscribe to the need to define a governing idea that informs a play's interpretation. At the same time, if one adopts this perspective in production, a line needs to be drawn from ideology to enactment. Every kind of decision, from casting to the emphases one gives to certain lines, from physical and internal aspects of characterisation to sets, costumes, lighting and music, must follow from that initial, 'ideological' decision. In turn, interpretative choices, the selection of an 'Idea of the play', become intrinsically linked to what is credible in the stage realisation. The governing idea must be consistent not only with the words, but also with the characters and actions that are inferred from them. The point being that the interpretation one adopts should be dictated not by the random reactions of the actors, but by the governing idea through which the play is transformed into a production. For their part, however, the actors are duty bound to test this governing idea against *their* primary responsibility – the creation of characters.

And so, we return to the practices of the rehearsal room. Regardless of lit. crit. objections, actors routinely perform improvisations beyond the action covered by the text: Hamlet at Wittenberg drinking with Rosencrantz and Guildenstern, Laertes in Paris. For some actors, characters also *exist*. Ruth Draper, the great American actor famous for being able to create a vast range of characters, alone on stage and with the bare minimum of props or costume changes, was once found by a childhood friend "with her hair tied up, on her knees on the kitchen floor, scrubbing away for all she was worth". When her friend expressed surprise, "Draper paused for a moment in her labours as she told a long tale of being a 'widow with all these children' and how hard she had to work to feed them". And here is Sir Ian McKellen, talking about Estragon in *Waiting for Godot*: "It's probably the way he walks, you know. All human beings walk differently. And his walk is probably due to bad feet".[6] For such actors, the point of this approach, its ultimate achievement, is transformation.

Notes

1 In "The Question of Character in Shakespeare", published in 1959, Knights softens his stance: he revisits Bradley with more understanding, yet maintains his view that the latter's consideration of the "words" was too constrained.
2 When a few years later S. L. Bethell comes to consider Elizabethan acting, he adopts the same attitude: "Poetry and its decent delivery" are "the only real essentials of Elizabethan drama."
3 Alan Sinfield makes the very good point that in this case one would at the very least expect to find "embryonic" traces of concern with individuality in the early seventeenth century, which operated in social conditions strongly anticipating later developments.
4 At their worst, applications of postmodernist 'theory' to character analysis are of little use to the realisation of the plays on the stage. In his trenchant critique of the poststructuralist approach, Bruce McConachie adopts a science-led perspective, with which this book is also aligned. And, as Alan Sinfield says, the upshot of poststructuralist analyses of theatre appears to be that the plays, all plays, are ultimately unrealisable.
5 This complaint was noted by John Russell Brown as early as 1953.
6 *Front Row*, BBC Radio 4, 25 March 2014, 7.15 p.m.

Bibliography

Literary approaches to character: Sinfield, A., 2006. 'From Bradley to cultural materialism', *Shakespeare Studies*, (34), pp. 25–34.

Characters as subjects: Bradley, A. C., 1993. *Shakespearean Tragedy: Lectures on Hamlet, Othello, King Lear and Macbeth*. Harmondsworth: Penguin; Babcock, R. W., 1931. *The Genesis of Shakespeare Idolatry, 1766–1799: A Study in English Criticism of the Late Eighteenth Century*. Chapel Hill: University of North Carolina Press; Morgann, M., 1777/1912. *Essay on the Dramatic Character of Sir John Falstaff*. London: Henry Frowde; Terry, E., 1932. *Four Lectures on Shakespeare*. London: Martin Hopkinson; Warren, N. (ed.), 1979. *The Letters of Ruth Draper, A Self-Portrait of a Great Actress*. London: Hamish Hamilton.

Twentieth-century criticism: Knights, L. C., 1946. *Explorations: Essays in Criticism, Mainly on the Literature of the Seventeenth Century*. London: Chatto & Windus; Knights, L. C., 1959. 'The question of character in Shakespeare', in Garrett, J. (ed.) *More Talking of Shakespeare*. London: Longmans, pp. 55–69; Norman, C., 1962. *Ezra Pound*. New York: Funk & Wagnalls; Eliot, T. S., 1934. *Elizabethan Essays*. London: Faber; Wilson Knight, G., 1930. *The Wheel of Fire*. Oxford: Oxford University Press; Bethell, S. L., 1950. 'Shakespeare's actors', *The Review of English Studies*, 1 (3), pp. 193–205; *and historicist approaches*: Stoll, E. E., 1927. *Shakespeare Studies: Historical and Comparative in Method*. New York: Macmillan; Bradbrook, M. C., 1935. *Themes and Conventions of Elizabethan Tragedy*. Cambridge: Cambridge University Press; *and Marxist perspectives*: Brecht, B., 1964. *Brecht on Theatre*, translated by J. Willett. London: Methuen; Dollimore, J., 1993. *Radical Tragedy: Religion, Ideology and Power in the Drama of Shakespeare and his Contemporaries*. Durham: Duke University Press; *and postmodernism*: Fuchs, E., 1996. *The Death of Character: Perspectives on Theatre after Modernism*. Bloomington and Indianapolis: Indiana University Press.

Critiques of poststructuralist approaches: McConachie, B., 2008. *Engaging Audiences: A Cognitive Approach to Spectating in the Theatre*. New York: Palgrave Macmillan; Sinfield, 2006.

Tension between theory and practice: Brown, J. R., 1953. 'On the acting of Shakespeare's plays', *Quarterly Journal of Speech*, (34); Meyrick, J., 2003. 'The limits of theory: academic versus professional understanding of theatre problems', *New Theatre Quarterly*, 19 (3), pp. 230–242; Osborne, L., 2001. 'Shakespeare and the construction of character', in Bleeher, S. A. and Klein, H. (eds.) *Shakespeare and Higher Education: A Global Perspective*. Lewiston: Edwin Mellen Press, pp. 312–331; Culpeper, J., 2001. *Language and Characterisation: People in Plays and Other Texts*. New York: Routledge; Yu, J. K., 2012. 'Introduction', in Yu, J. K. and Shurgot, M. (eds.) *Shakespeare's Sense of Character, On the Page and From the Stage*. Farnham: Ashgate, pp. 1–18; *attempts at reconciliation*: Falco, R. et al, 2006. 'Forum: is there character after theory?', *Shakespeare Studies*, (34).

Presentism: Bristol, M., 2000. 'How many children did she have?', in Joughin, J. J. (ed.) *Philosophical Shakespeare*. London and New York: Routledge, pp. 18–33.

5

THE DRAMA OF NO CHARACTER

The process of transformation remains elusive, mysterious even. Empirically, one senses that a complex psychophysical process is taking place, but what precisely this involves remains uncharted. At the same time, both the concept and the process of transformation raise some interesting, sometimes puzzling, theoretical questions. The chapters that follow seek to open a few windows onto questions relating to the techniques and the psychology of transformation. Here are a few, preliminary thoughts:

If transformation suits certain actors better than others, can one also say that it suits certain characters better than others? Is it equally appropriate, for example, to pre-modern theatre and to contemporary film work? Can one apply it with equal success to Sophocles and to Beckett?

There is a current of opinion which considers that the idea of transformation, and its twin notion of character, are essentially modern, that is post-1870, concepts. The Original Practices school, for example, points out that the plays of Shakespeare's time were written in 'parts', that is as pieces of dialogue handed out separately to individual members of a company and only assembled into a whole in rehearsal. Moreover, writers were commissioned to write to suit individual performing strengths within the companies: the parts were written for the clowns Kempe or Tarlton, for leading men such as Burbage and Alleyn, and so on. These men were, says this view, 'types' of actors, and their parts were written to reflect aspects of their personalities. This could not be any other way, seeing that rehearsals and play runs were notoriously short and many players were asked to undertake a multiplicity of parts in the same performance, thus coming in and out of role at frequent intervals. Such actors (as well as their counterparts after the Restoration, who played an astonishing number of roles in one short season, often with little rehearsal) were said to "produce a multiplicity of 'characters' of his or her self".

Edward Burns adduces a telling case in support. One and the same actor in *King Lear*, he points out, is called upon radically to change identity, to play two distinct parts, as it were: Edgar and Poor Tom. He writes: "Modern actors, searching for Stanislavskian wholeness or 'character', blur and make unnecessarily puzzling such moments in Shakespearean texts – they are, quite rightly, seen as an embarrassment to 'correct' modern acting . . ."

Burns submits that the players of the Elizabethan stage were "rhetoricians" who assumed "parts" distinct from each other, without looking for psychological connections between them. As a refinement of this thesis, he proposes the idea of the specialist actor whose *persona* was a fixed character essence in itself, a "type" from which he played variations throughout his career. Seductive as this conclusion is, I cannot help feeling that it does not quite square the circle between Edgar and Poor Tom. Was he played by a Poor Tom specialist, a clown wishing to try his skill at light juveniles, or by a melancholy juvenile out to experiment with eccentric comedy? In any case, there is evidence that a degree of assimilation between character and actor was appreciated by the spectators and was, at least on occasion, practised by the players. In 1664 Richard Flecknoe remembered seeing Burbage in *Two Gentlemen of Verona*, as "a delightful Proteus, so wholly transforming himself into his part, and putting off himself with his clothes, as he never (not so much as in the tiring-house) assumed himself again until the play was done". And some evidence also suggests that Elizabethan actors were quite capable of shorthand identifications of character types by means of quick alterations of their facial expressions and bodily shapes.

Seen in the light of an independent character, however, the question for the modern actor is not how to jump back and forth between two distinct identities, but how to find in Edgar's psychological make-up the source of his transformation into Poor Tom, and back into Edgar. Edgar might be conceived as a bookish dreamer who, in his loneliness, is given to 'playing roles' in his often overwrought imagination. He thus has the psychological background to play-act Poor Tom. We are presented with three layers: an imaginative actor, playing a character (Edgar), who in turn plays another character (Poor Tom). Far from being an "embarrassment", the idea of a character-playing-a-character offers a wealth of possibilities for internal comment. The delight comes precisely from watching, live on stage, how one characterisation transforms into another.

This process is particularly exciting in plays that require the characters to assume a series of masks (literally as well as metaphorically). This is the thrill of watching unyielding Pentheus transformed before our eyes into a compliant woman in *The Bacchae*. In the Greek theatre in general one actor usually played several characters – each time he entered wearing a new mask and robe, the difference from his previous character would have been reinforced by a change of gait, perhaps of posture, and appreciating that artistry would have been part and parcel of the spectator experience. Brecht's *Lehrstück*, *The Measures Taken*, tells the story of a group of international activists who are sent to China to organise the revolutionary underground. The actors are presented with a complex chain of characterisation: actor → main character (European Communist International agitator) → disguised (masked) as local Chinese so as to 'hide in plain sight' → then assuming the various identities (different masks) of the people they encounter (coolie, merchant, policeman, etc.). Each actor also has to assume, without the help of a mask, the character of the Young Comrade, the idealistic guide whom they ultimately have to kill in order to avoid detection. The 'learning' is precisely in experiencing – and, having experienced, mastering – the feelings of the man they have killed. I therefore disagree with Elinor Fuchs's analysis, which sees the play as "one of the more extreme experiments of the modernist turn against character" in which the Four Agitators are meant to play the Young Comrade "impassively". How can 'learning' about mastering emotion take place through the act of acting if one does not experience the emotion in the first place? How can one 'agree' to the obliteration of individuality if one does not first yield fully to the sense of a unique 'I'? As Peter Brook shows, the essence of Brechtian characterisation is the speed with which actors change roles within the epic play: the episodic structure of the epic plays implies that characters appear to the spectators as flickering glimpses, firing their imaginations to fill in the gaps. This does not mean that there are no characters – only that the playwright gives the actors minimal means to present them. Character there must be – someone with whom the actor can identify. I feel strongly that the photographic and filmed evidence of Brecht's own productions for the Berliner Ensemble points towards a high degree of realistic identification between actor and character, despite his theoretical pronouncements to the contrary. Anyone watching recordings of Helene Weigel acting can see that such theoretical assumptions melt under hot stage lights.

What then of the writer who sets out to make the playing of individual characters impossible by asking his actors to portray two characters *at once*? In his *Hamletmachine*, Heiner Muller asks one and the same actor to play both Hamlet and Ophelia, or rather a Hamlet who declares "I want to be a woman" and "dresses himself in Ophelia's clothes". He now moves between identities, finally 'revealing the trickery' by taking off make up and costume and speaking in 'his own voice'. Or rather with the voice and words of a character the author identifies as "The Actor Playing Hamlet". What are actors to do? Do they create two characters, one called 'Ophelia', the other 'Hamlet', and endeavour to portray each fully, while at the same time switching at the speed of light from one to another? Or do they abandon any such thought, reducing the performance to the enunciation of the lines? If the latter, an awkward question returns to prick us: Who is it that speaks the lines? The 'actor'? If so, which part of him? Does s/he change intonation, pitch, posture? Does s/he turn this way for Hamlet and t'other for Ophelia? Does s/he enhance these thumbnail sketches of the characters with the aid of costumes and props? (This is the way Robert Lepage treated the same problem in *Elsinore*, his solo performance based on *Hamlet*.) Or does s/he just stand upright, face front and spew the lines? If so, 'with feeling'? With 'understanding'? Whose? I am afraid that, however militant the attempt at denying character, the theatre idiom will not allow it. In the final analysis, we are left with the same conundrum: the performance radiates either from the actor's or from the character's personality. There is no way around this. The only thing one can say is that certain modes of performance demand very sketchy characterisation. For such demands, a complex structure designed for transformation is not useful. Not because its principles are wrong – it is simply inefficient to work in such detail on characters that may last for only a few seconds.

A variant of the same theme is the insistence of some post-war dramatists on 'ambiguity'. Stephen Rea played Clov in the 1976 Royal Court production of *Endgame*, directed by Donald MacWhinnie, with Beckett present throughout rehearsals. At one of these rehearsals, Rea asked Beckett about the meaning of a particular line and was told: "It is always ambiguous". "For me", Rea says, "acting begins at that moment".[1] The implication is that the truly Beckettian, and by extension 'modern', actor, has no need to 'interpret', that is to define the meaning of the text, then make it concrete and thus communicate it. Rea's sole task is to remain 'open', his performance a challenge to the audience to 'guess' a multiplicity of meanings in his actions and demeanour on stage or screen. Readers familiar with Stephen Rea's most interesting roles, as Manus in *Translations* by Brian Friel, for example, or as the doomed hero in one of Neil Jordan's Ulster movies, may recognise this overall approach: a slouching, brooding, enigmatic *persona* hiding much more than it reveals and implying, above all, a thoroughly 'modern', tortured confusion about itself and everything around it. 'Being here' is all there is, says Rea's deportment – an act of physical presence, as ambiguous and chaotic as life itself. There is nothing else, nothing 'behind' or 'beyond'. In consequence, 'character' is irrelevant. There is no unitary personality revealing itself gradually by exfoliating the skins of action. If there at all, the personality is split, fragmented. The actor is 'no one'.

In *Attempts on her Life*, Martin Crimp, one of the most interesting of the Royal Court writers to emerge from under Beckett's mantle, even creates a character who is literally not there. Anne ('Annie, Anny, any'?) is a woman, but also a car; a young bohemian, but also a middle-aged do-gooder; a revolutionary idealist but also a sentimental *petite bourgeoise*. She never appears, yet the entire play consists of descriptions of her different 'faces', narrated by an undifferentiated company of actors. Ambiguity in the portrait calls for the abrogation of characterisation in acting.

At the root of this approach to drama is the post-war aesthetic of the 'open work'. In a television interview about Antonioni's *oeuvre*,[2] Alain Robbe-Grillet gave what I think is one of the clearest examples of the difference between 'closed' and 'open' meaning in a work of art: in a film by Hitchcock, the French novelist explained, while the meaning of the pictures is constantly delayed, it is eventually fully revealed. At the end, we understand everything – who the murderer was, why he did it, how opportunity aided his intention. The meaning is closed. In Antonioni's films, on the other hand, the images themselves are crystal clear – we know exactly what we see, nothing is hidden from view. But at the end, the meaning of the accumulation of images remains obscure, given to different interpretations by different spectators – ambiguous. The meaning is open – the film is *écriture*, independent of what its author may or may not have intended.

At first sight, transformative acting appears inevitably to lead to closed meaning. By knowing so much about the character, by dissecting it psychologically, the actor 'solves' it. By the end, we know what the character did as well as why. In a very fine production of *Uncle Vanya*[3] directed by Peter Stein, the Italian actress Maddalena Crippa 'solved', in this sense, the character of Yelena. Yelena is often a problem: is she genuinely attracted to Astrov but too bound by convention to follow her desires? Is she a bored coquette, ("so drunk with idleness that she cannot walk straight") out to find entertainment during the long summer months? Is she the confused victim of an oppressive marriage? Crippa's interpretative line was crystal clear: Yelena's attraction to Astrov was genuine, her desire imperative and her renunciation harrowing. Her refusal to have an affair, however, was not based on social prejudice or on fear of physical commitment – two of the traditional, unsatisfactory explanations – but on her sense of self-worth. Here was a woman whose main motivation was 'to keep my self-respect'. But was this 'faithful' to Chekhov's intentions? Who knows? Stanislavski thought he was being truthful to Chekhov when he played Astrov like a martyr, lacerated by the pettiness of provincial life, clinging to Yelena in the climactic scene in Act III "like a drowning man clutching at a straw" – yet in a letter to Olga Knipper, who played Yelena in that first production, Chekhov was adamant that "Astrov has no respect for Yelena. In fact, when he leaves the house afterwards, he's whistling". Where is the truth? The acting process through which Maddalena Crippa found her own solution for Yelena is a kind of conversation: a nocturnal tête-à-tête between assumptions about the writer's intentions (based on intimate acquaintance with his writing as well as the historical context) and the personal outlook of the actor. Chekhov's text is 'open', in the sense that it offers several possible choices and an infinity of nuances within each option. But the actor 'interprets' – chooses one of these options; the choice informed not by a concern with historical accuracy, but by the actor's own, contemporary, attitudes (I shall return to 'attitude', a multi-layered concept with important ramification for the psychology of transformation).

The objection to such interpretations is that by solving the character, the actor also closes it. Our conversation on the way to the bar, the complaint goes, is not about possibilities, but a confirmation that we understood, that we 'got it'. No unnerving ambiguity here, only the satiety that comes with a job well done, with a story well rounded. Can actors respond, within the terms of their own craft, to this insistent literary call for ambiguity and openness?

Typically, in the Royal Court production of *Attempts on her Life*[4] the company never sought to forego the idea of personality. Although the lines of the script are unattributed and the author's only indication is for "a company of actors whose composition should reflect the composition of the world beyond the theatre", in performance the actors assumed quite distinct personalities: the story was told now by a 'small man with glasses, clumsy and shy', now by a 'forceful woman', now by 'an elderly gent' – character sketches derived from extensions of the personal identities of the actors. In the same way, we speak about the 'Winnie' of Madeleine Renaud and compare it with that of Billie Whitelaw. Ambiguity or not, in the absence of a distinct character, the actor falls upon personality. At his most extreme – often his best – Beckett actually encourages the emergence of the actor-clown, the supreme personality actor: a character/persona. There is a famous photograph of Jack McGowran as Clov in *Endgame*, which might have been taken at a latter-day version of the *Grand Guignol*. This is not 'no one' – Jack McGowran has definitely created a 'character' out of an extravagant extension of a personality trait. For him, as for Stephen Rea and all actors, there is no escape from the call of the character – the writer may turn his face against character and succeed brilliantly on the page, but the actor is bound to turn back and embrace it. This is a condition of acting itself, as inescapable as the need to be present, physically, on the stage. The only real choice available to the actor is between transformation and personality. This argument is as old as Meyerhold's sorties against Stanislavski. For Meyerhold, the virtue of characterisation lay in the firework display, in the constant changes through which actors enthral with their "chameleonic" power. Characterisation was an accumulation of "masks", provided by the actors. Stanislavski, on the other hand, was fond of quoting Shchepkin's statement: the actor "must begin by wiping out his self . . . and must become the character the author intended him to be".

I think there is a meaningful difference between transformative acting and watching the firework display of another individual's personality, however exciting. In the former, the satisfaction lies in discovering the heart of the chameleon beating underneath the skin, however many colours this adopts. It consists in penetrating through to the essence of another human being, and by this means intuiting something of the meaning of a human existence. The implications of transformative acting for *interpretation* go far beyond the mere technicalities of 'building a character' – they go to the heart of what theatre is about. When Meyerhold declares: "For Molière, Don Juan is no more than a wearer of masks" he does not tell us *who* Don Juan is. Is this a pointless question? A frivolous one? I do not think so. Acting from personality is a selfish act. Transformation means a rapprochement between actor and character on the one hand; between the embodied character and spectator on the other. The Idea of character leads to a concern with *knowing*, in the sense of grasping a metaphysical entity in its totality. 'Being Don Juan' means 'knowing Don Juan'. This implies penetrating, through empathy, into another human being. It is, as Grotowski put it, an answer to our solitude.

In the chapters which follow I will therefore look at transformation from three perspectives: the actor's tools and processes; approaches to personality in psychology and psychoanalysis which may also be applied to characters; and the mechanisms by which actors and fictional characters 'merge'. Ultimately, I argue for a qualitative difference between transformative and personality acting.

Notes

1 Interview in the *Observer*, 15 September 1996.
2 "Dear Antonioni", *Arena*, BBC2, 18.01.1997.
3 Teatro di Roma with the Teatro Stabile di Parma (1995–6).
4 First performance at the Royal Court Theatre Upstairs, March 7 1997.

Bibliography

Shakespearean 'parts': Burns, E., 1990. *Character: Acting and Being on the Pre-Modern Stage*. Basingstoke: The Macmillan Press; Yu, J. K. and Shurgot, M. (eds.), 2012. *Shakespeare's Sense of Character, On the Page and From the Stage*. Farnham: Ashgate; Gurr, A., 1987. *The Shakespearean Stage, 1574–1642*, 2nd Edition. Cambridge: Cambridge University Press; *contemporary perspectives*: Flecknoe, R., 1957. 'A short discourse on the English stage', in Spingarn, J. E. (ed.) *Critical Essays of the Seventeenth Century*. Bloomington: Indiana University Press, pp. 91–96; McNeir, W. F., 1941. 'Gayton on Elizabethan acting', *PMLA*, 56 (2), pp. 579–583; Heywood, T. and I. G., 1612/1941. *An Apology for Actors & A Refutation of the Apology for Actors*. New York: Scholars' Facsimiles & Reprints.

Brechtian characterisation: Fuchs, E., 1996. *The Death of Character: Perspectives on Theatre after Modernism*. Bloomington and Indianapolis: Indiana University Press; Brook, P., 1968. *The Empty Space*. New York: Avon Books.

Denying character: Muller, H., 1984. *Hamletmachine and Other Texts for the Stage*, edited and translated by C. Weber. New York: Performing Arts Journal Publications; Muller, H., 1995. *Theatremachine*, translated and edited by M. v. Henning. London: Faber and Faber; Kalb J., 1989. *Beckett in Performance*. Cambridge: Cambridge University Press; Crimp, M., 1997. *Attempts on her Life*. London: Faber and Faber.

Character and interpretation: Frayn, M., 1988. 'Introduction to *Uncle Vanya*', in Chekhov, A. *Plays*, translated by M. Frayn. London: Methuen; *and Jack McGowran as Clov*: Worth, K., 1972. *Revolutions in Modern English Drama*. London: G. Bell & Sons.

Meyerhold on character: Meyerhold, V., 1969. *Meyerhold on Theatre*, translated by E. Braun. London: Eyre Methuen; *and Stanislavski quoting Shchepkin*: letter to Alexandra Schubert 27 March 1848, in Cole, T. and Chinoy, H. K. (eds.), 1970. *Actors on Acting*. New York: Crown.

PART II

Transformations in body and mind

6

CONSTRUCTING THE CHARACTER

Contemplation

What is a role? At the most rudimentary level, it is composed of 'facts' about the character: its biography, deeds and decisions – words on a page. To go back to an earlier example, from the narrow standpoint of her biography, Viola is young, orphaned, unmarried and one of a pair of twins – the well-educated, well-travelled daughter of a rich merchant. So far, so obvious. At this point, the actor begins to draw inferences from the raw data: she asks herself what it means to have a twin brother, to have been brought up in the household of a Renaissance merchant, to be shipwrecked. From here, an imaginary biography and back story will begin to emerge. The actor probes the character's decisions further: that Viola chooses to remain in Illyria, disguises herself as a boy and joins Orsino's Court helps her make fundamental choices regarding Viola's characteristics. Viola's decisions may lead the actor to think that she is 'adventurous, brave, inquisitive, nonchalant, refined . . .' Or, on the contrary, her need to disguise herself may point to a Viola who is 'timorous, unsure of herself, who wants to get lost in a crowd: a shy, delicate, sensitive' Viola.

Stanislavski and Boleslavski used to call this technique "searching". By this they meant the process by which actors systematically relate inferences drawn from text data to personal experiences. In this respect, the acting process is a specialised application of the cognitive process whereby we constantly theorise about what others think and feel by registering their behaviours and comparing these with our own experiences. Through inference, the cognitive foundation of the creation as well as the reception of artefacts, we also relate fictional realities to our own.

One might call this process 'reading for character'.[1] Cognitive linguists have shown that when we listen to someone telling a story, we make assumptions about the speaker's intentions. We also take into account the social contexts from which the story emerges. In the case of literary fiction, our reading will, in addition, be informed by our familiarity with the literary genre within which the story inscribes itself: we look at characters in a Jacobean drama differently from those in a French farce. Crucially, and this is especially important when turning a literary text into live performance, actors and directors interpret the text to suit *their own* motivations and goals. The interpretative angle shapes the way in which characteristics are selected, extended and 'customised'. Jonathan Culpeper makes a useful distinction between what he calls "faithful" and "unfaithful" characteristics, so classified in accordance with their proximity to the historical context and the assumed intentions of the author. The range of possible "unfaithful" characteristics is much greater than "faithful" ones, and startling interpretations may emerge from them. In any case, my friend working on Viola will have to take some deliberate decisions about who she *does* want to play, while remaining conscious of those alternatives she has discarded – in Brecht's famous phrase, she will have to "fix the 'not . . . but'".

Below the threshold of full consciousness, as she reads her script, a character begins to take shape – literally: an as yet amorphous, fluid shape, only dimly distinguished through the fog of first impressions. But her "histrionic sensibility", that "basic, primary, or primitive virtue of the human mind", is fired up. Associations from her own life begin to rise to the surface: the way an acquaintance strides purposefully, how another flexes her wrists while speaking . . . Outlines of paintings and sculptures, half-remembered from visits to museums, an illustration in a childhood book, a pen portrait in a Dickens novel, coalesce to bring the diffuse shape into ever greater focus. My friend could think of her Viola as a humanised animal, or even as a marionette or a cartoon character. Whatever the sources, a 'model' begins to emerge before her inner eye. Once established, this can be projected, as it were, on an imaginary blank screen and contemplated at leisure. It can be put to work, taken shopping or for walks. Crucially, it can be tested outside the immediate time/space parameters of the play: "How do you walk in the park on a lazy Sunday afternoon?" my friend will ask her imaginary model. "How do you get angry or hug a baby or dance?"

Conceptual models of this type are relatively simple cognitive structures, essential for our understanding of the world. Our ability to reflect on our own mental processes allows us to build an explanatory model for the intentions and motivations of other people. Models inform and shape our reasoning processes and therefore our decisions. Scientists also construct such 'theoretical models' or 'theoretical objects' prior to testing them experimentally. In our case, the experimental laboratory will be the rehearsal room. But for the moment, we are still in solitary contemplation.

Exploration

As her next step, my friend will begin translating the characteristics suggested by the model into specific ways of standing, walking, speaking – a physical life. As I emphasised earlier, acting-in-character soon turns to the body. Not, however, the 'daily' body of the actor, shaped by the accretions of a lifetime. Instead, a body deliberately and systematically made ready for entering a state of psychophysical 'neutrality', from which to start changing toward characterisation. While this principle also features strongly in Stanislavskian acting methodologies, I find other offers, drawing directly from body-based traditions of acting, even more useful. Two main approaches, both widespread on the Continent, have traditionally been used in the training of Western actors: Expressionist dance, and the tradition of playful theatricality regenerated in France by the revolutionary director Jacques Copeau.

Copeau's innovative work led to the creation of an influential school of acting, not least through the work of his nephew and principal disciple, Michel Saint-Denis. Before and after the Second World War, Saint-Denis established no fewer than five highly influential acting schools, on both sides of the Atlantic. When designing their curricula, he married the traditional English focus on classical text and voice work with the best of the Copeau practices: mask work, animal observation, circus skills, and an emphasis on improvisation and play. Others, such as the director Jean Dasté, the teacher and movement director Jacques Lecoq, or the great French mimes Etienne Decroux and Marcel Marceau, also drank deeply from the well opened by Copeau.

Copeau had called for actors to be

> . . . brought back to a naïve state that is not an artificial or literary attitude, but is their natural position before a world of possibilities where nothing is corrupted by habit or imitation, nor perverted by an acquired virtuosity . . .
>
> *(1990, p. 169)*

Following on from this injunction, twentieth-century movement and voice directors consider that a form of receptive neutrality is a necessary precondition for attaining the openness and malleability needed to engage creatively with the character and with one's partners. They therefore tend to promote the concept of 'centring'. This is typically described as "the collection of energy into its central source", from which specifics of breath, bodily movement, vocal qualities and positions in space emerge. Opinions vary as to the precise position of this "central source" and Western schools of movement – some also drawing on yoga, tai chi, Suzuki and other Eastern traditions – devise complex systems of exercises according to whether the origin of expressive movement lies in the solar plexus, the five vertebrae at the bottom of the spine, the pit of the stomach, strongly grounded feet or other areas of the body. There are any number of texts describing exercises designed to achieve this state; what interests me here is the principle which underlies them all: that an 'extra-daily' state of muscular relaxation, what Copeau called a "*décontraction préalable*", combined with mental alertness and a readiness to react, place both the mind and the body of the actor in the right state for effective acting.

This applies, of course, just as much to the actor-in-action as to the actor-in-character. However, those teachers who combine Copeau-inspired techniques with Stanislavskian approaches offer additional tools, encouraging psychophysical transformation. Among these, the Israeli-American movement teacher Moni Yakim[2] is typical. His offer to the actor highlights three principal approaches to transformative characterisation: work on natural elements (rain, storms, clouds), on man-made objects and, at a more advanced stage, on animals.

In a process that, though frequently parodied, remains highly effective, the student actor is told early in training:

> . . . simply lie on the floor and put yourself wholly into the subject of study – whether it be thunder, a caterpillar, or a toothbrush . . . assume the subject's traits, to the point where you integrate with it. By becoming one with your subject, you take its qualities into yourself.
>
> *(1990, p. 84)*

Acting teachers use injunctions such as these frequently and with confidence. Nonetheless, an important qualification imposes itself: such exercises are primarily designed for the training studio, while students learn the technique and develop their imaginations. In professional practice, other considerations come to the fore. As we have seen, for the experienced actor (our Viola) 'working on rain' – that is, imagining and physicalising the qualities of rain – is primarily concerned with making specific, character-driven choices: *her* rain falls 'gently', is 'steady and heavy' or 'drums furiously on the roof'. Nouns describing elements or objects ('cloud, storm, oak, car, arrow') are accompanied by a qualifying adjective ('fluffy, brooding, solitary, polished, deadly'). The choice of object narrows the field and offers a hook on which to hang the character exploration: while specific attributes will be consistent with the object (cars are not 'fluffy' nor oaks 'fast'), they will be those assigned by the actor to the character. The actor's prior decisions about the key features of the character define the exploration. Natural elements and man-made objects are useful when they act as triggers for personal readings of character traits. It is what they *trigger*, not what they *are* that matters.

While work on elements and objects can provide useful associations, in the process of physicalising character models two more complex approaches, also derived from the Copeau tradition, are likely to prove most rewarding: animal and mask work.

'Working on animals', that is – within the limitations of the human anatomy – imitating their stalking, leaping, stretching, etc., is an effective way of changing body shape.[3] Yakim explains:

> Through the exploration of an animal's character and essence – the *animalisation* of your own person – you'll . . . act and react instinctively as someone other than yourself . . . the goal is to capture and experience the inner life of the particular animal you choose to become . . . Once you absorb this inner life, the substance of its structure, shape, and behaviour develop naturally.
>
> *(1990, pp. 85–86, emphasis original)*

While common in this type of acting discourse, terms such as "essence", "inner life", and "motivation" are nonetheless challenging. Whether animals actually possess a psychological essence or whether it is only our anthropomorphic projections that confer one upon them is disputed territory, and I have no intention of blundering in where angels fear to tread. But picture a hawk in your mind's eye. You are likely to think of it as 'majestic', or perhaps 'free' or 'fierce'. Yet those who breed and train hawks will tell you that they are actually excellent parents, dedicated to their offspring, and very playful. As with elements and objects, in acting the useful starting point is not the animal, but the actor's decisions about the character. The question is not 'can I create a convincing shark or giraffe?' but whether – while searching for a psychophysical identity for Macheath or Andrew Aguecheek – a shark or a giraffe might provide useful triggers. We draw on the animal's behaviours to give physical shape to psychological characteristics: the animal acts as a fairground mirror, magnifying and distorting those things we seek yet struggle to define. Laurence Olivier's seminal Richard III, for example, echoed powerfully in its silhouette the ravens of the Tower of London, with their mythical associations. In another celebrated performance of the same role, Ramaz Chkhikvadze, the lead actor of the Georgian *Rustaveli* company, is remembered by Antony Sher as "a species of giant poisonous toad". And here is Sher himself, "on the prowl for bits of Richard" by way of animal parallels: contemplating the nature of Richard's physical deformity, Sher sketches in his rehearsal diary "An image of massive shoulders like a bull or ape. The head literally trapped inside his deformity, peering out". This image is then blended with a memory of lions in South Africa:

> . . . *find myself thinking* of . . . lions . . . . *Remembering images* from a trip long ago to the Etosha Pan Game Reserve – lions lying in the sun breathing heavily, short heavy pants, mouths slightly open. Great strength resting . . . You also see severely deformed people do this – breathing with heavy little gasps . . .
>
> *(2014, loc. 976, my emphases)*

Finally, Sher turns to the text for the animal image that will eventually prevail:

> Margaret calls him a 'bottled spider' – a striking image, whatever it means (I'm not bothering to look up the editor's notes yet) . . . crutches could help to create the spider image.
>
> *(loc. 1183)*

I emphasised "thinking" and "remembering" in the first quote: Sher's point of departure is an act of imagination, not of direct observation. Actors scan their texts purposefully, the ultimate goal of physical representation ever-present. Moreover, actors read for character with trained eyes: theirs is not the haphazard emotional arousal of the reader for pleasure, but a systematic search. As I argued earlier, 'reading for character' is shaped by the craft of the actor: while looking for inferences, actors develop specialised forms of attention and concentration. Sher's physical search eventually leads him to a psychological insight: "I had set out to look for a physical shape, but maybe what I found is something about being disabled".

When it comes to constructing models for well-known characters, another element comes into play: great historical performances throw a long and threatening shadow over the contemporary actor's endeavour. I have already mentioned Charles Marowitz's notion of characters "roaming the land". "And worst of all, the lips I have drawn are not my own, but Olivier's" Sher agonises. Part of character creation in these cases must involve a dialogue with the past, and it would be foolish to pretend otherwise. The imagination is informed by the models created by others and a permanent tension exists between these and the search for originality. It is the way in which one resolves this tension that distinguishes transformative acting from the actor-in-action approach. We saw how Diego Arciniegas responded by looking to find originality through spontaneity. This was also Lee Strasberg's call. Their approach relies primarily on emotion and reactions, with no objective correlatives in a model. Sher's purposeful search for a model, on the other hand, involves him manipulating his own body. His face becomes an object of contemplation: long stares in the mirror capturing, as he describes it, those moments when a peculiar angle of the light reveals features expressive of some key character trait. It is the same with his animal work: imitating an animal with intent (that is while focusing on the character trait) leads to certain animal movements transferring into the posture and gestures of the character. Finally, when Sher arrives at a silhouette that is radically different from those of his predecessors, this still arises as a matter of intuition – the crutches that eventually became the hallmark of his interpretation are discovered by chance as he convalesces from a ruptured Achilles tendon. But intuition is unlikely to have arisen without the painstaking, methodical search for a model during the long rehearsal weeks.

Realist and Expressionist traditions differ in their approaches to animal work. Copeau-inspired exercises usually require that animals should be observed directly: it used to be standard practice for drama schools to buy season tickets to their local zoos and send students to observe the animals at close quarters; this custom has recently been supplanted by giving them access to collections of filmed nature programmes. The Expressionist school of movement, on the other hand, deliberately eschews direct observation. Instead, actors and dancers are encouraged to recreate the physical life of the animal from memory and imagination. In this approach, once an overall physicality has been established, the actor is asked to select a small number of animal-inspired moves, usually three, and link each of these to corresponding psychological characteristics. The upward swing of an elephant's trunk becomes an *irritable* shrug of the shoulders; a pointer sniffing the air leads to an *alert, questioning* turn of the head. And, in the Expressionist approach, the effectiveness of these gestures is instantly tested: the actor presents the animal-derived work to the rest of the company, whose members are invited to deduce the psychological characteristic from the physical gesture. Only when sufficient agreement emerges does the actor proceed to incorporate the selected, animal-derived gestures into the physical life of the character.[4] The process thus involves a level of objective selection, based on assumptions shared across the company of players, assumptions themselves based on what is effective in communicating through the language of movement. This approach moves away from the generalised exploration implied by direct observation, imitation and 'immersion' and towards a deliberate, conscious construction of character, in which gestures are purposefully designed to be expressive of key characteristics. As Anne Bogart, whose company adopts similar practices, observes: "it's not a guessing game, but an opportunity to note what was legible, expressive, moving". 'Reading for character' is on everyone's minds throughout.

If gestures derived from animal work make a useful contribution to characterisation, donning a mask, an ancient craft in performance traditions the world over, arguably constitutes the most complex way of exploring character by means of external stimuli. Covering one's face unequivocally proclaims: "I want to look different, to be other than I am". At the same time, masks can be used just as much to 'liberate' certain aspects of the actor's personality as to enable transformation. This distinction is given physical form in the two types of masks used in the tradition that concerns me here: 'noble' (sometimes also called 'larval' or 'neutral') masks on the one hand and 'character' masks on the other.

Copeau called the former 'noble' because they recreated the expressionless face coverings used by Renaissance aristocrats to hide their identities when descending into the pleasure quarters of the town. Noble masks obliterated their wearers' features and liberated them from social restrictions. Likewise, Copeau asked his trainee actors to make clay models of their own faces but neutralise any distinctive features, so as to create an image which I would describe as 'engaged relaxation', the inner state of *décontraction préalable* turned into an artefact. When you wear a mask with indeterminate features you are no one and everyone – everything is permitted to the mask. The point of wearing a noble mask as preparation for acting is to achieve a state of openness to impressions and thus of 'authentic', intuitive reactions devoid of preconceptions or stage conventions. Jacques Lecoq's 'neutral' mask exercises, arguably the most widely used contemporary version of Copeau's noble mask work, are meant to enable the actor's body-mind to become a soft wax on which the world can leave its impressions. A young actor describes the experience thus:

> As the mask stands in the water, the mask becomes the water, as the mask stands on the plateau and views the horizon, it becomes the horizon, as the mask holds a bird in its hands, the breath and heartbeat of the bird become the breath and heartbeat of the mask. The mask is a conduit through which its environment or encounters are made physical.[5]

As used here, the word 'mask' carries two meanings: the physical object, made of leather, papier-mâché or wood and canvas; and the character which emerges from the interaction of object and actor. Above all, 'the Mask' is curious – the actor putting it on is seized by an unstoppable urge to explore and experiment. It is as if the mask unshackles that most basic of animal instincts, the urge to seek in one's surroundings for the tools of survival. The body responds with an immediacy outside awareness; there is a sense in which we surrender conscious control and allow ourselves to exist in a permanent sense of wonder, in which everything is genuinely surprising. The actor forsakes being impressive, so as to become impressionable.

Many of its champions elevate neutral mask work to a creed of purity and authenticity, a way towards self-knowledge and insight. Through neutral mask-work, writes one, "The self that thinks and acts needs firstly to retire from the constructions put upon it by the language of others. . . and then to create itself". However, work with neutral masks is ultimately not that different in its outcomes from a plethora of exercises used in contemporary actor teaching to discard encul-turated habits, 'centre' the actor and so enable organic, intuitive reactions to arise. Ultimately, such exercises tend to lead to actor-in-action approaches. From my perspective, the interest of neutral mask-work lies primarily in the way in which it serves as preparation for working with the character mask, or – to use Copeau's distinction – with *"le masque expressif"*. David Gaines, founder of the celebrated physical theatre company *The Moving Picture Mime Show*, uses an inspired simile: "If larval mask is a three-stroke sketch, then character mask is the detailed Dürer engraving of character".

Character masks – whether Greek-style, full-face masks with openings for the eyes and mouth, or *commedia*-style half-masks which leave mouth and chin visible and do not distort speech – wear distinct expressions. Skilful mask-makers build faces which are recognisably human, yet with certain features exaggerated, so that when the masks are static, they convey an overarching attitude to life: lust, naivety, authority, arrogance, stupidity, enthusiasm, greed. When the actor moves and shows the mask to the spectator at different angles and in different lights, subtler charac-teristics are added, but always within a range demarcated by the core expression.

Individual character mask-work starts with looking in the mirror and respond-ing intuitively to the face/mask staring back: a peculiar inclination of the head, lips pursed or smiling. . . then a tentative walk. The angle of the head might turn into an overall posture; the walk could suggest a way of breathing, then an overall rhythm. If the mask is being used to explore a text, the characteristics embodied in the model intervene: the mask looks back from the mirror and words such as 'snide' or 'light-footed' arise in consciousness. Clichés (universals) often suggest themselves: a Uriah Heep-like rubbing of the hands, a crooked smile. To move beyond these, the actor combines characteristics and mask with an animal – let's say a lizard. This produces interesting alternatives: the lizard's tongue extended to catch a fly turns into the character nervously licking its lips; the way the claws jerk when the lizard is startled turns into an over-precise adjustment of the trouser seams when the character sits; the swish of the lizard's tail turns into the precious, over-emphatic flick of a tail coat, and so on. "Ultimately", writes John Harrop, a skilled exponent of this type of work, "each actor will discover a basic physical composite, comprised of two or three simple characteristics which form a strong physical outline, but in no sense limit the character in terms of detail".

Once these are on their way, the mask-character engages – in silence – with sim-ple, mundane tasks: making coffee, mending a bicycle. Simple, yet still requiring imaginative exploration: "Where was the coffee bought?", "Who broke the bike?" As a character identity begins to emerge, more important questions have to be asked: "Who is this person?", "How old?", "What profession?", "Where does she live?"

Deprived of the most immediate means of communication – the face and the voice – the actor has to convey the answers through the body alone: posture, gait, gesture. Communicating without the aid of facial expressions imposes precision of gesture: a robust and pointed "articulation of actions". Only when the actors become proficient in this technique is the voice added, first through unformed grunts and sounds, eventually through Copeau's famous *Grammelotage*, an onomatopoeic, made-up language with words fresh-minted from body shapes and rhythms.

The mask imposes a further discipline: it cannot be seen unless it constantly faces the audience. Actors cannot become lost in introspection. Indeed, working with masks, both neutral and character, gives actors permission 'to be big', to measure the size of their gestures by what is expressive, not by what is 'natural'. The mask is there to give shape to compulsive urges and compelling intentions. In his essay, *A Note on the Mask*, Edward Gordon Craig extolled the "conviction" he detected in the mask. The body language of the mask-wearer, characterised by assurance and definition, becomes, again in Craig's words, "the visible expression of the mind". The Italian playwright and actor Dario Fo expands:

> What is the purpose of the mask? To magnify and simultaneously give the essence of the character. It obliges you to widen and develop your gestures, which must not be arbitrary if you want the audience, your immediate mirror, to follow you and to grasp the flow of the piece. . .
>
> *(1991, p. 35)*

Movements and gestures are thus said to become those of the mask-character, not of the actor. The actor and teacher Keith Johnstone, whose approach to improvisation is widely followed, even goes so far as to maintain that masks have "shamanistic" powers, that they place actors in heightened states of receptivity akin to "possession".

Any notion of "possession" in the sense of loss of control must, however, be challenged. In fact, one of the essential features of character construction by means of mask-work is the dynamic it engenders between impulse and control. Michel Saint-Denis inserted mask-work into the curricula of all the acting schools he established precisely because, as he explained, "it enables the student to warm his feelings and cool his head". The masked actor can acknowledge powerful, often dangerous, emotions; yet these are safely presented as the emotions 'of the mask' rather than of the actor. At the same time, the need to express these emotions by means of bodily movements that feel 'unnatural' implies a high degree of conscious control, of "detachment and lucidity".

The transformative exercises described above eventually lead to wider improvisation sessions, first in pairs, then in larger groups. In these so-called 'choral improvisations'[6] increasingly complex, idiosyncratic characters are brought together in order to create a world through and of bodies. A recognisable world, yet one hovering between the real and the mythical: *Saul on the Road to Damascus, An Irish Fishing Village After a Violent Storm, Waiting for Immigrants on Ellis Island*, etc. "The mask", writes Saint-Denis's biographer, "becomes a liberating experience, leading to a world of myth, dream, and poetry". Used in this context, masks become powerful exploratory devices for storytelling as well as character creation.

Here, however, a significant bifurcation takes place: Jacques Lecoq's many followers generally saw the creation of original dramatic material – plays or *commedia*-like 'scenarios' generated by actors – as the natural extension of improvisation-based theatre, both masked and not masked. In the English-speaking theatre, however, mask-work has often been deployed in the investigation of extant, not least classical, texts. In the 1950s and 1960s, early exponents of this approach gathered around Michel Saint-Denis's disciple George Devine, at that time Artistic Director of the Royal Court Theatre. A good measure of English guts was grafted onto the masks, and directors such as John Blatchley and William Gaskill created work that was smutty, sun-baked and earthy. And, in 1960, the radical playwright John Arden even wrote *The Happy Haven*, a full play for masks, which was produced by the Royal Court with Susan Engel and Frank Finlay in the leading roles.

Perhaps the clearest illustration of the way in which mask-work continues to be used to develop characters in text-based performances comes from the work of the British director John Wright. Wright had first read Copeau as a young trainee actor and only later attended workshops with Jacques Lecoq and the latter's disciple, Philippe Gaulier. Copeau fundamentals thus shaped the vision behind his two influential theatre companies: Trestle and Told by an Idiot. Early Trestle work was almost wordless, but very soon the company moved from improvised work to text-based productions. Moreover, at a workshop in the early 1980s, Wright had watched Lecoq playing *The Jesuit*, a mask many 'Lecoqians' disliked because they considered it to be 'psychological'. For Wright, psychology did not have negative connotations and he developed a new set of teaching masks, this time based on six archetypes: The Fool, The Trickster, The Innocent, The Mother, The Hero and The King.[7] These became tools with which to investigate the personality traits of characters in extant texts. Wright was subsequently invited to work at the National Theatre Studio, the Royal Shakespeare Company and the Royal Court, using his archetypal masks to explore classical characters: The Mother, for instance, morphed into Medea. Working with, among others, leading British directors Rupert Goold and Michael Boyd, Wright also introduced counter-masks – those ostensibly going against the grain of the character. Using counter- or contra-masks compels actors to contemplate those things that are other than what is expected, whether as a result of theatrical convention or of intuitive responses. An actor playing Puck, for example, might be intuitively drawn to the mask of an impish, ruddy-cheeked, snub-nosed *putto* (perhaps, in the *commedia dell'arte* tradition, Brighella's mask). Invited to select a counter-mask, he might explore Puck by means of the high forehead, heavy eyebrows and long nose of the *Dottore* or *Capitano* masks. In the end, he might stay with the impish Puck, but with added layers of arrogance or cruelty. Mask and counter-mask explorations enable the actor to manipulate the context from which the character emerges and thus illuminate it from unexpected angles.

Throughout, Wright's relationship to text was founded on the conviction that in the British context this was the correct approach. He writes:

> [Lecoq's] process. . . is a unique grounding for a theatre maker but as a pathway for an actor it is incomplete. A highly creative individual with an articulate and responsive body is only part of what is required in an actor. To produce a performer without an equally responsive voice and an imaginative response to language is like training a pianist to only use one hand.
>
> *(2002, p. 82)*

In this, Wright and his school were actually building on Saint-Denis's legacy: the latter had also stayed close to Copeau, their common inspiration in seeking to inject new energy into the classical repertoire. The influential movement teacher Litz Pisk once declared: "Lecoq people are drunk on movement" and, in the tradition of character creation with which I am concerned, extant text remains the keystone of the theatre edifice. This approach, echoed by a number of drama schools in Britain, also expects body-based work to be aligned with a realistic, 'psychological' methodology: intentions, motives, objectives are just as important as physical expressivity and 'play'. The result is a style of playing John Wright describes as "physiological realism".

Ultimately, as Jacques Lecoq himself emphasises, exploratory mask-work is there for transformation:

> There is a huge difference between actors who express their own lives, and those who can truly be described as players. In achieving this, the mask will have had an important function: the students will have learned to perform something other than themselves, while nevertheless investing themselves deeply in the performance. They have learned not to play *themselves* but to play *using* themselves.
>
> *(2001, p. 61, emphases original)*

Altered bodies, altered selves

Michael Chekhov's notion of the "psychological gesture" is arguably the most complex and sophisticated application of this principle. Chekhov starts by distinguishing between mundane and revelatory gestures. He recognises that human beings turn impulses instinctively into "natural and usual" movements, but then calls on the actor consciously to refine some of these intuitive reactions into expressive and evocative gestures. These are essentially symbolic gestures, products of the actor's imagination: extending the Expressionist principle of imaginative recreation, Chekhov calls on the actor to approach physical characterisation in the first instance without actually moving, but by 'rolling the film' of movements in the imagination. As the scholar Jonathan Pitches comments: "Necessarily, the choices of movement are coloured by the artistic imagination when they are performed 'in the mind' and this leads to unexpected creative aberrations which can then be fed back into the work". At the top of the hierarchy of meaningful gestures lies the psychological gesture, a concentrated movement or action that reveals the character's "secret, innermost motivation and personality trait". Michael Chekhov's own psychological gesture for Hamlet was an imaginary arm endlessly stretching through prison bars. The psychological gesture was intended primarily as a rehearsal device, a way of capturing and recalling instantaneously the essential shape and drive of the character. At times, however, these supremely expressive gestures also find their way into performances: Chekhov's celebrated portrayal in Gorki's *Lower Depths* of a hopeless tramp with nothing left in life but to wait for death was captured by endlessly, pointlessly stirring a spoon in a cup of tea. When Alec Guinness played George Smiley in the TV adaptation of John le Carré's tetralogy *Smiley's People*, he encapsulated the spymaster's drive – to 'see' the source of personal and national betrayal through the fog of conflicting emotions and information – by, as le Carré had described, repeatedly, absent-mindedly wiping his spectacles with the end of his tie.

Ultimately, the overall physical life that grows from such shoots gives the character a unique tempo or "kinetic melody". The Russian neuropsychologist Alexander Luria used the term "kinetic melody" to describe the way in which acquired complex motor skills, such as writing or driving, are automated and integrated to the point at which, like the various instruments of an orchestra, they act as one. In character work, I am arguing, this is not only a physical but a psychophysical melody.

Tempo and melody, musical terms, acquire specialist meanings in the work of the actor. Tempo, of course, means first of all speed: how quick or how slow are a character's movements. In *Building A Character*, Stanislavski describes an exercise in which actors speak and move at speeds set by metronomes. As the speeds change, so does the meaning of their actions. Tempo as a psychophysical tool was adopted early by Stanislavskian disciples: Robert Lewis called it the "inner beat" and Michael Chekhov refined it into "inner and outer" tempi reflecting, respectively, the psychological processes ("the change of thought, images, feelings, will impulses, etc.") and their outcomes in the (physical) "actions and speech" of the character. At points in his career, Stanislavski even had assistants stand in the prompt box and, visible only to the actors on stage, 'conduct' with their hands the pace of live performances. Bizarrely, even a few years ago I recall seeing the well-known Russian director Yuri Lyubimov 'conducting' from the back of the auditorium, with the help of a small torch, the pace of actors performing in his productions.

Stanislavski also combined tempo with the more elusive idea of rhythm and wrote about the "tempo-rhythm" of a sequence of movements. For him, "tempo-rhythm" was the magic pathway to emotion. In the last months of his life, though bed-ridden, Stanislavski even had an assistant turn at various speeds a wheel of coloured electric bulbs and noted the effects on his emotions of changes in colour and tempo. But, while Stanislavski was exercised by the ways in which movement affected the actor's own feelings, I am interested in how tempo can shape characterisation. In this, I find of greatest help the method of movement analysis devised by the movement director and thinker Rudolf Laban.[8]

In order to determine the dimensions of movement, Laban undertook a sort of 'chemical analysis'. He studied the various 'molecules' and 'atoms' which make up movement with the aid of four 'instruments', four fundamental questions:

a. which part of the body moves and what relationship exists between it and those parts of the body which remain still?
b. what is the duration of the movement and in what relationship does it stand to other movement durations around it?
c. how much muscular power is exerted in effecting the movement?
d. which direction in space is the movement leading towards or away from?

Laban also makes the common-sense observation that people move in response to a need. We react before we act. The reaction may be hard to detect at first sight, but we have to absorb the impact of the outside world before we respond with an exertion of our own. Our movements can therefore be said to fall into two broad categories: movements that absorb the impact of the environment (Laban says "yield" to it) and movements that exert themselves on the world ("contend" against it). In consequence, movements should be analysed not only in accordance with the four questions, but also according to where they are on a 'scale', from their most yielding aspect to their most contending. Answering his four questions:

Laban observed that in order to lift a heavy weight the muscles strain to over-come the force of gravity. Equally, lifting a light object necessitates only the lightest of muscle exertions. Thus, Laban declared, one of the four components of movement is its Weight. According to the intensity of the energy deployed, Weight can be either Light (yielding) or Strong (contending).

Movements also have a direction in Space. Someone hammering will go as cleanly as possible between the raised arm and the nail – the movement is Direct. But a coachman whipping his horses will raise the whip, move it first to the left of his head, then to the right and only then crack it forward. The movement is convoluted, roundabout, Flexible.

Movements take place in Time. Here Laban pointed out that the important factor was not whether the movement was slow or quick, but how slow or quick in comparison with other movements around it, either of parts of the same body or of external objects. A movement is therefore said to be Quick or Sustained (slow) not in an absolute way, but in comparison with its surroundings.

Finally, effective movements involve a degree of co-ordination: they are either free and easy or halting and tight. This Laban defined as the Flow of movement, which could be either Free or Bound.

Actors can deliberately play with movements along these four dimensions, increasing and decreasing speed, choosing to move on more or less convoluted path-ways, opposing gravity or yielding to it in different degrees. These components, or "Motion Factors", of movement rearrange themselves constantly: now one, now the other occupies the foreground, while the remainder take a supporting role. When combined, they create 'cocktails' of movement which amount to a *tempo*. A strong, direct and quick movement, like that of a man chopping wood with an axe, has the tempo of a 'punch'. At the other end of the scale, a feather will float down in a light, flexible and sustained movement. In between these two extremes are several other physical tempi. Laban calls these combinations the eight "Working" or "Effort Actions", into which all human movement can be broken down and analysed. They are given names suggestive of everyday, familiar actions: Punching, Pressing, Gliding, Dabbing, Wringing, Slashing, Flicking, Floating.

By the same token, entire characters can be constructed using one of these categories as a starting point. A character whose movements are predominantly Dabbing can be more precisely described as 'dotting' or 'nibbling'. These adjectives define its overall tempo and can amplify the sensation through animal comparisons ('sparrow-like', 'squirrel-like') because animals often display a clear-cut tempo. Restoration playwrights often conceived their characters in terms of a tempo and expressed it in a revealing name: Mincing, Mrs. Millamant's woman in *The Way of the World*, for example, 'minces': her speech and movements are Quick/Direct/Light and full of pretentious affectation.

The actor Michael Mears offers an example of the way in which this analysis translated into professional practice when he was creating Mr. Brisk, a character in *The Double Dealer* by Wycherley. As his name suggests, Mr. Brisk is always in a hurry and uses short, sharp gestures. Responding intuitively to the writing, Mears took as his point of departure the image of a young boy trying to keep a balloon in the air by Dabbing at it with his index finger – a Light/Direct/Quick movement. From this simple gesture a tempo arose, which was eventually stitched into the character's patterns of speech. Sooner or later, says Mears, the physical tempo affects the psychological traits of the character. In turn, charac-teristics – 'dynamic', 'relaxed', 'powerful', 'indecisive' – can be defined in terms of Light or Strong, Sustained or Quick and so on.

Warren Lamb, an early Laban follower, combined the latter's principles of movement with the findings of kinesics, the study of communicative body move-ments in anthropology, linguistics and social psychology. Kinesics stresses that our movements must be considered as integrated *sequences* of posture and gesture. Lamb therefore proposed the concept of "Posture–Gesture–Merger" or PGM. His emphasis is on 'merger': the key definer of PGM is the integration of its components and the way these flow organically into one another. PGM, Lamb says, offers the means by which to understand "the secret language" in which movement conveys personality. Lamb shares with other Laban followers the assumption that, whether they want it or not, peoples' deep-seated personality traits are revealed in their movements. People are said to have a constant "signa-ture tune" of movement, regardless of the activities in which they are engaged. Once formed, a person's PGM remains constant throughout adult life: analyses of movement sequences in the same people carried out at 15-year intervals demon-strated little change. We are, says Lamb, "hallmarked" with our patterns. Which does not mean, of course, that these cannot be changed temporarily and accord-ing to circumstances. Which schoolboy has not straightened up and changed the rhythm of his walk before entering the head teacher's office; which teacher has not changed both posture and voice before addressing a packed classroom?

The possibility of temporarily altering the PGM and through it one's tempo offers a useful entry point into the phenomenon of transformation. Through tempo, imagined characteristics are made objective, concrete, corporal. If our imaginary Viola is 'forceful' and 'outgoing', she will naturally express herself through strong Effort Actions: 'Punches', 'Slashes' and the like. The sequence can be reversed: my friend can prepare for her speech by using a 'Punching' gesture: she will 'butt', 'pummel', 'stamp', and so on. We speak of the psychosomatic effect of gesture.[9]

Manipulations of this type apply just as much to the movements of the speech organs as to those of the rest of the body. Kate Fleming, the first Head of Voice at the National Theatre, used to speak of the "breath of life", by which she and other traditional voice teachers meant the frequency and intensity with which an actor took in and exhaled air. The rhythm generated by the breath would then permeate the entire body and dictate the way it was shaped and moved, as well as its distinctive pattern of speech.[10]

Characteristics can also be inferred from, and expressed through, the rhythms and prosodic structures of play texts, in particular those written in verse. Verse has been described as "sounds moving in time". The veteran voice coach Cicely Berry highlights the "huge variety of movement" to be found in Shakespeare's verse. Well-drawn characters have individuated 'voices', discernible in their patterns of speech. Such tempi ask to be interpreted: why is Hotspur speaking in one rhythm and Hal in another? By means of Laban's analysis, the tempi of speech as well as of gesture can be broken down to common denominators and distilled to their 'spirit' – Motion Factors and Effort Actions.[11]

If I may illustrate the point from another angle:

Many British actors adopt credible American accents (and *vice versa*). But how many British actors are aware that American males tend to cross their legs in distinctive ways or that most Americans will raise their heads slightly at the end of statements to which they expect an answer? Do such national characteristics matter in performance? Does one attempt to replicate Dublin working-class physicality when playing O'Casey? Most actors in the English-speaking world would probably answer 'yes'. What then of Sicilian demeanour when playing Pirandello? Not so clear-cut. An interesting debate on this issue arose around a production in the early 2000s at the Southwark Playhouse in London of *Through the Leaves,* a two-hander by the German writer Franz Xaver Kroetz. The play was originally written in Bavarian dialect, so the English translation sought to find dialectal equivalents. In this particular production, the two roles (a butcher and his wife) were played by two distinguished British actors: Simon Callow and Ann Mitchell. Callow adopted a Lancashire accent, a dialect he considered would give his characterisation certain affinities with the Bavarian original. Ann Mitchell chose to stay in her native London accent. During a post-show discussion, these interpretative choices were laid bare: Mitchell considered spontaneity and immediacy to be the most important aspects of her rendering of the role and chose to ignore the Bavarian context, remaining close to her own vocal and physical expressive range. For his part, Callow thought it important to approximate in English certain traits which he associated with the original Bavarian: a certain ponderous weight, a clumsy gruffness, a sense of brutality – all contributing to the creation of a social identity for this character, who was not only Bavarian, but a Bavarian *butcher*. Changing from his habitual Received Pronunciation to Lancashire made an important contribution to the growth of his character from imaginary chrysalis into a fully-fledged psychophysical identity. Adopting the accent changed not only the shape of his mouth but of his entire physique: dialect, gesture, demeanour and gait fused into a single entity.

Windows on movement

The principles underlying body-based approaches to transformation are beginning to emerge. First, the stimulus always starts outside the private world of the actor, in the observation or imagining of natural elements, man-made objects, animals or human models. Character traits and motivations are then communicated, economically, by means of consciously selected gestures or actions. These concentrations of daily movements distinguish them from the surrounding 'noise'. It has been noted that human beings can only mentally integrate around seven pieces of information at one time, and only four if the sources of information are in motion. Lecoq instinctively knew this when he asked his actors to select only three characteristics or "lines of force" in order to establish a character. Most actors working towards psychophysical transformation similarly tend to restrict changes to their voices and bodies to a limited number of easily recognisable alterations. The leading dialect coach Barbara Berkery points out that she only suggests changing a small number of key sounds even when enabling such radical transformations as those of Gwyneth Paltrow into Emma or of Renée Zellweger into Bridget Jones.

Concentration and amplification of gestures are thus the means by which the actor-in-character turns daily motion into expressive movement. Both are achieved through the manipulation of the elements of natural movement: Weight, Time, Space and Flow. Overall, re-shaping the body follows key principles articulated long ago by Etienne Decroux:[12]

- Design – the geometry inherent in the shape of a silhouette, underpinned by an *inner tension* or *opposition*. Great political cartoonists, from Gillray or Daumier to Searle, knew this and drew characters whose bodies were extended and distorted by forces pulling in opposite directions. When our bodies are in motion, in order to stay upright we constantly adjust our balance through myriad small movements. In transformational acting, these adjustments are larger. As I mentioned earlier, the key change consists in shifting the centre of gravity of the body, an important technique in the materialisation of a model into an imaginary body. Michael Chekhov suggests finding the character's "imaginary centre", that is, moving the daily centre of gravity of the actor to other parts of the body. One can easily see what he means: compare Brando as Terry Malloy in *On the Waterfront*, leading with the head, body tilted forwards by a centre of gravity placed in the shoulders, with Brando's rolling gait as Stanley Kowalski, centred on the hips. In his own work, Chekhov created characters who 'led with' or 'moved from' the belly (for Falstaff or Sir Toby Belch) or from one eye (for Tartuffe or Quasimodo). Laban, Grotowski and Lecoq describe similar approaches. Once a new centre of gravity has been established, the body re-organises its functions accordingly. Importantly, in approaches such as these, by moving the centre of gravity of the body to that of an imaginary model, actors are compelled to focus on the differences between their own physicality and that of the character.

- Intensity – Gesture is at one and the same time *larger than life* (in order to be read) and *concentrated* (in order to condense the psychological traits). The vocabulary of movement is, as Bella Merlin writes about Dario Fo's work, "simultaneously *expanded* to a dramatic size and condensed to a psychological essence". Strong urgencies turn into movements; "emotions become gestures".
- Rhythm – as discussed earlier, the body in action manifests itself as an overall tempo–rhythm, what Beckett called the "physical theme" of a character. This is punctuated by 'accents' (psychological gestures, nervous tics, stares, etc.) that help to fix its expressive meanings. Transformation is perceived in the interplay between movement and stillness: the transformed body is easiest to grasp when motionless, yet the actor remains fully engaged; when movement finally occurs, it does so with the full force of the kinetic energy contained in the stillness. "In immobility is emphasis, and in movement is rhythm and flow", writes David Gaines.

Viewpoints – an increasingly influential acting and directing approach – integrates many of the principles of movement and expression outlined above. Originally developed in the 1970s by the American dancer and choreographer Marie Overlie, it was initially concerned with structuring dance improvisation according to the perspectives or 'viewpoints' of Space, Shape, Time, Emotion, Movement and Story. These combined the use of abstract physical dimensions, in the Central European modern dance tradition, with psychological concepts such as emotion and with aesthetic concerns such as narrative structures. Extending these to theatre work, director Anne Bogart added a number of other elements, in her case derived from architecture and fine art. Coming out of the experimental New York theatre scene of the 1960s and 1970s, her approach offered a strong challenge to dominant, Strasberg-influenced acting orthodoxies.

At the heart of Bogart's approach lies the separation of core elements involved in creating theatre by means of the body. By asking the participants to focus on each of its elements at a time, Viewpoints invites constant changes of perspective on character, story, meaning, and so on. In an illuminating passage from a recent essay, Bogart recalls the way in which Mary Overlie introduced its principles to her:

Mary told me that early on she had considered calling the Viewpoints 'Windows'. I understood immediately. Look at a specific theatrical moment through the *window* of space. Look at the same moment through the *window* of shape. Look at the moment through the *window* of story or the *window* of time. The specific window through which we look determines how we look and what we are looking for; it defines our particular experience of the moment.

(2014, p. 110, emphases original)

Bogart charts the path of creativity on lines that are close to the description I gave earlier: "from associative ruminations to critical thinking to intuitive action to objective judgement". In her more recent writing, Bogart also alludes to certain findings of cognitive science, in particular to cognitive blend theory and to the hypothesis that the so-called mirror neuron system forms the foundation of our ability to imitate and empathise. Her approach remains essentially intuitive, however, and inscribes itself within the wider family of body-based techniques, from Laban to Grotowski to Lecoq, which rely on physical changes to generate ideas and sensations.

Viewpoints can prove exciting and enriching, both as a methodology for sensitising actors in training and as a way to generate images and test ideas in rehearsals. Bogart describes Viewpoints as a practice for generating fiction collaboratively by means of improvisation. As such, work on character forms only a part, and a relatively small part at that, of the overall approach. In fact, the movement teacher Stephen Wangh, who is familiar with Bogart's work, once wrote (only slightly tongue-in-cheek) that she actually "denies that character exists". Viewpoints does, however, draw on the overall tradition of body-based approaches to include techniques such as working with objects, music and changes of tempo to explore the emotions, memories and desires of the character. Bogart also writes eloquently about the creation of physical shapes as well as about relying on recognised national characteristics to communicate in the language of movement. Like Laban analysis, Viewpoints traces its artistic roots to the modernist tradition. Bogart readily acknowledges influences as varied as those of Virginia Woolf, Martha Graham and Vasyli Kandinsky. Body shapes and gestures are distilled into lines and curves, then re-combined to create recognisable, though strongly delineated postures and stage arrangements. Expressive gestures are "abstract and symbolic rather than representational".

Descriptions of body-based techniques such as these and the others I have described earlier might give the impression that I am talking of a rigid shell for the character, of a stiff pose, held for the appreciation of the connoisseurs in the audience. Nothing could be further from the truth: when I speak of conscious manipulation of physicality, I do not mean in any way to imply exaggerated artificiality or rigidity. To explain the way in which, in the practice of the realistic stage, the outer shape of a character remains recognisable while retaining organic fluidity, the Russian school of movement borrows from Pavlovian psychology the concept of "dynamic stereotype". The physical shell created by the actor is conceived as a set of conditioned reflexes, acquired through repetition in rehearsal; these are "dynamic" in the sense that they adapt constantly to changing circumstances. The movement teacher Galina Morozova writes:

> In physiology, a dynamic stereotype is the specific result of conditioned reflexes: influenced by a [multiplicity] of factors, certain conventionalised signs appear, which follow a set pattern. A dynamic stereotype is [responsive] to change, having an ability to adapt to external conditions. . . in his creation of human behaviour patterns, the actor's memory preserves the represented structure and sequence of actions (the stereotype). However, paying careful attention to his stage situation, he allows the stereotype to change according to the changing stage circumstances – making it 'dynamic'.
>
> *(1999, p. 97)*

What Morozova calls "plastic agility" ("plastic" is a word Stanislavski uses often) provides the catalyst through which the silhouette is transformed into an organic, believable and attractive simulacrum of a human being. Expert physical ability – flexibility, coordination, balance, control – correlates with mental openness, bestowing the ability to react at speed to one's partner's movements while adjusting one's own. Think kung fu or capoeira: agility of both mind and body. Copeau extolled the "distinctiveness and reverence" brought to acting executed with "taste and lightness". Not a word which Russian teachers formed in Soviet times would use, but this is what we might call 'grace'. Morozova writes:

> Every agile movement looks beautiful – and every awkward one ugly. An actor who possesses a high level of agility is capable of consciously creating the plastic features of his character. . . while an actor with a low level of agility will look the same in all his roles – even if he is able to transform internally for the role.
>
> *(1999, p. 86)*

Agility is needed for grace and grace for transformation: transformation possesses its own, particular beauty.

*   *   *

We have now reached the question that will occupy most of the rest of this book: How is it that, by changing my body, I end up playing 'something other than myself'?

First, a relatively straightforward answer, directly linked to the body-based techniques described in this chapter:

Bella Merlin relates how during rehearsals the simple act of smiling deliberately (constant alterations to her facial muscles) led to psychological changes. Her observation is supported by scientific studies showing, for example, that when we smile in response to someone else's smile, feedback from our facial muscles to the brain affects our social judgement. Underpinning such observations is the phenomenon of proprioception.

The term 'proprioception' comes from two Latin words, *proprius* (one's own, personal) and *capere* (to grasp). Combined, they mean self-perception. Proprioception describes the feedback mechanism going from the skeletal muscles, tendons and joints of the body to the brain. This enables the brain to sense how the body moves in relation to its surrounding environment; the brain in turn responds by triggering the autonomic nervous system (ANS). This activates the muscles, so we can run away from danger or turn to fight it. In turn, new movement patterns affect our internal organs, hormonal discharges, blood pressure, etc., and eventually register in consciousness. This is particularly relevant to emotion: mood has been shown to be affected by changes in posture and it is well documented that the autonomic functions of the body respond to and generate emotions in direct and specific ways.[13] It has frequently been observed that actors can become angry by banging their fists on a table or distressed by imitating the outer actions of crying. Research has shown that emotion can be triggered in this way, since physical movement is accompanied by somatic sensory-feedback to the brain, with consequent changes in the neo-cortical circuits as well as the hormonal and autonomic nervous systems. By deliberately adopting a certain physical position or repeatedly executing a gesture, actors trigger physiological responses that translate into psychological correlatives, through an organic progression Bella Merlin tellingly describes as a "re-assembly of the actor's instrument". As Rick Kemp explains: "Given that proprioception is linked to conceptual thought and emotional attitudes, it follows that *using postures and gestures that are different from those we employ in everyday life is likely to create and alter the sense of self*".

The various views on the complex psychological mechanisms that underpin this "altered sense of self" are the subject of the forthcoming chapters.

Notes

1 I consciously echo Jonathan Culpeper's similar "reading for character".
2 Yakim first studied in Paris with Etienne Decroux, then came to New York to study acting with Stella Adler. When in 1967 Michel Saint-Denis set up the drama department of the Juilliard School, Yakim became a founder-member and its long-serving and influential Head of Movement.
3 In Britain, teachers such as Catherine Clouzot (at the Drama Centre London and the Arts Educational Schools), Helena Kaut-Howson (at LAMDA)) or Ian Ricketts (at the Guildford School of Acting), among many others, taught exercises based on the direct observation of animals.
4 This way of working was described to me by the Laban-inspired dancer and teacher Yat Malmgren, who had observed it in, among other places, the practices of the Kurt Jooss dance company. Copeau's company also practised a form of "collective testing" of the effectiveness of character gestures.
5 Mathew Wernham, contribution to "Mask and Masking" symposium, Central Saint Martins, 25 March 2015.
6 In Saint-Denis's schools, choral improvisations were done with or without masks. I stress the use of masks here as it best illustrates the methodology of character creation through responses to external, physical inputs.

7 But, Wright says, "I am not a Jungian and I have since regretted calling them archetypes".
8 Affinities have often been noted between Laban's analysis and the work methods of some of his contemporaries, notably Suzanne Bing, Copeau's movement teacher, and Michael Chekhov.
9 Stanislavski uses the word "reflexive" to describe the effect of gesture on emotions.
10 This approach, outlined by Antonin Artaud, also influenced the thinking of major experimental directors such as Peter Brook and Joseph Chaikin.
11 The actor and scholar Benjamin Askew discusses from a Laban perspective the analysis of verse as movement.
12 In his comparisons of Eastern and Western acting approaches, Eugenio Barba discerns a similar set of principles: opposition, changes in balance and "consistent inconsistency" – the need for the performer to maintain a constant distance between daily and performative or "extra-daily" behaviours.
13 Theories of emotion, in particular of the interaction between emotion and cognition, are a hotly debated area of scientific enquiry. I am using here the principles outlined by so-called 'read-out' theories which, as things stand, remain the dominant models in the field.

Bibliography

Imaginary biographies: Bradley, A. C., 1993. *Shakespearean Tragedy: Lectures on Hamlet, Othello, King Lear and Macbeth*. Harmondsworth: Penguin; Hagen, U. with Frankel, H., 1973. *Respect for Acting*. New York and London: Collier Macmillan; Wangh, S., 2000. *An Acrobat of the Heart, A Physical Approach to Acting Inspired by the Work of Jerzy Grotowski*. New York: Vintage Books; *and "searching"*: Boleslavski, R., 1933. *Acting: The First Six Lessons*. New York: Theatre Arts Inc.; Benedetti, J., 1988. *Stanislavski: A Biography*. London: Methuen; *cognitive processes*: Byrne, R. and Whiten, A., 1988. *Machiavellian Intelligence: Social Expertise and the Evolution of Intellect in Monkeys, Apes and Humans*. Oxford: Clarendon Press; Tomasello, M., 1999. *The Cultural Origins of Human Cognition*. Cambridge, Massachusetts: Harvard University Press.

Reading for character: Culpeper J., 2001. *Language and Characterisation: People in Plays and Other Texts*. New York: Routledge; *cognitive basis*: Dijk, T. A. and Kintsch, W., 1983. *Strategies of Discourse Comprehension*. London: Academic Press; Gernsbacher, M. A. et al., 1992. 'Do readers represent characters' emotional states?', *Cognition and Emotion*, (6) pp. 89–111; *and deliberate decisions*: Brecht, B., 1964. *Brecht On Theatre,* edited by J. Willett. London: Eyre Methuen; *and the "histrionic sensibility"*: Fergusson, F., 1949. *The Idea of a Theatre: A Study of Ten Plays, The Art of Drama in a Changing Perspective*. Garden City, New York: Doubleday & Co; *and "purposeful reading"*: Zwaan, R. A., 1993. *Aspects of Literary Comprehension*. Amsterdam and Philadelphia: John Benjamins.

Character models: Boleslavski, R., 1933; Stanislavski, C., 1994. *Creating A Role,* translated by E. Hapgood. London: Methuen; Hagen, U., 1973; Chekhov, M., 1953. *To the Actor: On the Technique of Acting*. New York: Harper and Brothers; Wangh, S., 2000; *as cognitive structures*: Zbikowski, L. M., 2006. 'The cognitive tango', in Turner, M. (ed.) *The Artful Mind: Cognitive Science and the Riddle of Human Creativity*. Oxford: Oxford University Press, pp. 115–132.

Naïve states: Copeau, J., 1990. *Copeau on the Theatre,* edited by J. Rudlin and N. Paul. London: Routledge; *and 'centring'*: Yakim, M. with Broadman, M., 1990. *Creating a Character, A Physical Approach to Acting*. New York: Back Stage Books; Bogart, A. and Landau, T., 2005. *The Viewpoints Book: A Practical Guide to Viewpoints and Composition*. New York: Theatre Communications Group; Mitchell, T., 1998. *Movement: From Person to Actor to Character*. London: The Scarecrow Press; Wangh, S., 2000.

Animal work: Yakim, 1990; Mitchell, 1998; Mekler, E., 1989. *The New Generation of Acting Teachers*. New York: Penguin; Sher, A., 2014. *The Year of the King: An Actor's Diary and*

Sketchbook. Kindle Edition. London: Nick Hern Books; *collective testing*: Rudlin, J., 2010. 'Jacques Copeau: the quest for sincerity', in Hodge, A. (ed.) *Actor Training*. 2nd Edition. London and New York: Routledge; Bogart and Landau, 2005.

Mask work: Copeau, 1990; Rudlin, 2010; Chamberlain, F. and Yarrow, R., (eds.), 2002. *Jacques Lecoq and the British Theatre*. London: Routledge; Gaines, D., 2016. 'Full-face masks, pantomime blanche and cartoon mask', in Evans, M. and Kemp, R., (eds.) *The Routledge Companion to Jacques Lecoq*. London and New York: Routledge, pp. 135–141; Harrop, J. and Epstein, S. R., 1982. *Acting with Style*. Upper Saddle River, New Jersey: Prentice-Hall; Fo, D. and Rame, F., 1991. *The Tricks of the Trade*. London: Methuen; Johnstone, K., 1981. *Impro: Improvisation and the Theatre*. London: Eyre Methuen; Saint-Denis, M., 1982. *Training for the Theatre*. New York: Theatre Arts Books; Baldwin, J., 2003. *Michel Saint-Denis and the Shaping of the Modern Actor*. Westport, Connecticut and London: Praeger; Mirodan, V., 2016. 'Lecoq's influence on UK drama schools', in Evans, M. and Kemp, R. (eds.), *The Routledge Companion to Jacques Lecoq*. London and New York: Routledge, pp. 208–217; Wright, J., 2002. 'The masks of Jacques Lecoq', in Chamberlain, F. and Yarrow, R. (eds.), 2002. *Jacques Lecoq and the British Theatre*. London: Routledge, pp. 71–84; Lecoq, J., 2001. *The Moving Body: Teaching Creative Theatre*, translated by D. Bradby. London and New York: Routledge.

Psychological gesture: Chekhov, 1953; Pitches, J., 2006. *Science and the Stanislavsky Tradition of Acting*. Abingdon: Routledge; Yakim, 1990; Gordon, M., 1987. *The Stanislavsky Technique: A Workbook for Actors*. New York: Applause Theatre Books.

Character tempi: Luria, A. R., 1973. *The Working Brain: An Introduction to Neurophysiology*. London: Penguin Books; Stanislavski, C., 1968. *Building a Character,* translated by E. Hapgood. London: Methuen; Bogart and Landau, 2005; Boleslavski, 1933; Lewis, R., 1958. *Method or Madness*. London: Heinemann; Chekhov, 1953.

Movement analysis: Laban, R., 1971. *The Mastery of Movement,* edited by L. Ullman. 2nd Edition. London: Macdonald and Evans; Rudlin, 2010; Mirodan, V., 2015. 'Acting the metaphor: the Laban–Malmgren system of movement psychology and character analysis'. *Theatre, Dance and Performance Training*. 6 (1), pp. 30–45; *and PGM*: Lamb, W. and Watson, E., 1979. *Body Code: The Meaning in Movement*. London: Routledge and Kegan Paul.

Callow and Mears examples: Mirodan, V., 1997. 'The way of transformation (the Laban-Malmgren system of dramatic character analysis)', Ph.D. Thesis. Royal Holloway, University of London.

Rhythm and breath: Artaud, A., 1958. *The Theatre and its Double*. New York: Grove Press; Hulton, D., 2010. 'Joseph Chaikin and aspects of actor training', in Hodge, A. (ed.) *Actor Training*. 2nd Edition. London and New York: Routledge, pp. 151–173.

Poetry and expressive movement: Beum, R. and Shapiro, K., 2009. *The Prosody Handbook: A Guide to Poetic Form*. New York: Dover Publications; Berry, C., 2000. *The Actor and the Text*. London: Virgin Books; Askew, B., 2017. 'The action to the verse: Shakespeare, Stanislavski and the motion in poetry metaphor'. *Stanislavski Studies*, 5 (2), pp. 141–157.

Information processing: Edelman, G. M. and Tononi, G., 2000. *A Universe of Consciousness: How Matter Becomes Imagination*. New York: Basic Books.

Reshaping the body: Barba, E., 1994. *The Paper Canoe: A Guide to Theatre Anthropology,* translated by R. Fowler. London: Routledge; Murray, S. and Keefe, J., 2007. *Physical Theatres, A Critical Introduction*. London and New York: Routledge; *and design*: Chekhov, 1953; Chekhov, M., 1991. *On the Technique of Acting*. New York: Harper Collins; *and intensity*: Merlin, B., 2015. 'The self and the fictive other in creation, rehearsal and performance', in Evans, M. (ed.), *The Actor Training Reader*. Abingdon: Routledge, pp. 119–131; Fusetti, G., 2016. 'Commedia dell'arte and Comédie Humaine', in Evans, M. and Kemp, R. (eds.), *The Routledge Companion to Jacques Lecoq*. London and New York: Routledge, pp. 142–149; *and rhythm*: Gaines, 2016.

Viewpoints: Bogart and Landau, 2005; Bogart, A., 2014. *What's the Story: Essays about Art, Theatre and Storytelling*. Abingdon: Routledge.

Dynamic stereotypes: Morozova, G. V., 1999. *An Actor's Plastic Culture, A Short Encyclopedia of Stage Movement Terms*. Moscow: GITIS Publishing House.

Altered bodies, altered selves: Merlin, B., 2001. *Beyond Stanislavsky: The Psycho-Physical Approach to Actor Training*. London: Nick Hern Books; *smiling*: Hatfield, E. and Cacioppo, J. T., et al, 1994. *Emotional Contagion*. New York: CUP; Niedenthal, P. M. et al, 2005. 'Embodiment in the acquisition and use of emotion knowledge', in Feldman Barrett, L., Niedenthal, P. M. and Winkielman, P. (eds.), *Emotion and Consciousness*. New York: Guilford Press; *banging fists*: Hagen, 1973; Carnicke, S. M., 2009. *Stanislavsky in Focus: An Acting Master for the Twenty-First Century*. 2nd Edition. Abingdon: Routledge; Stanislavski, 1994.

Proprioception: Stepper, S. and Strack, F., 1993. 'Proprioceptive determinants of emotional and nonemotional feelings'. *Journal of Personality and Social Psychology*, 64 (2), pp. 211–220; Damasio, A., 1999. *The Feeling of What Happens: Body and Emotion in the Making of Consciousness*. London: William Heinemann; *and physical movement triggers emotion*: Gellhorn, E., 1964. 'Motion and emotion: the role of proprioception in the physiology and pathology of the emotions'. *Psychological Review*, 71(6), pp. 457–472; Panksepp, J. and Biven, L., 2012. *The Archaeology of Mind: Neuroevolutionary Origins of Human Emotions*. New York: Norton; *generates ideas*: Kemp, R., 2012. *Embodied Acting, What Neuroscience Tells Us about Performance*. London: Routledge.

Theories of emotion hotly debated: Mirodan, V., 2019. 'Emotion', in Kemp, R. and McConachie, B. (eds.), *The Routledge Companion to Theatre, Performance and Cognitive Science*. London: Routledge.

7

PSYCHOLOGIES

I – Trait, type and temperament

The taste of onions

By now it should have become abundantly clear that the kind of acting approach with which I am concerned is founded on the assumption that such a thing as a character exists, that it can be described in terms of adjectives, that its motivations and goals may be guessed at, and that when an actor is 'on', a palpable sense of a different 'I' is felt by both actor and audience. It would have become equally evident that any discussion of the nature of the 'independent' character must involve an examination of concepts of daily life personality. However, most actors will readily acknowledge that theirs is no more than a vague, folk understanding of such concepts. If a discussion on the possibility or otherwise of transformation is to be meaningful, it now needs to examine how our rough-spun psychology maps against recognised ways of scientific thinking on personality.

Gordon Allport, the father of trait psychology, offered this definition: "Personality is a dynamic organisation, inside the person, of psychophysical systems that create the person's characteristic patterns of behaviour, thoughts and feelings". In terms of my examination of dramatic character, two aspects of this classic formula are particularly useful: its emphasis on the "dynamic" nature of personality on the one hand and, on the other, the recognition of "characteristic patterns".

Psychologists also sometimes define personality as a 'mode' or 'style' of dealing with the world, and in particular with other people. Do you flounce off in high dudgeon if the queue for coffee is too long and the barista too slow? (I do.) Do you live for the next time you can samba down the waterfront at the Carnival in Rio or finally solve the *Times* crossword? (I don't.) These, and a multitude of similar preferences, contribute to what scientists call the psychology of individual difference. In each one of us certain features can be considered to be stable over time and across situations. These are our defining personality *traits* – the accepted term for characteristics in the psychology of personality. It is these core traits that cause us to desire certain things above others and to fall regularly into certain patterns of behaviour. A key question then arises: if such patterns take root, are they mine and mine alone, or are they recognisable across groups and *types* of people? Answers to this question define two extremes in psychological constructions of personality.

The 'nomothetic' perspective argues that traits exist in the same way in every person. Commonalities can be identified and comparisons between individuals are, therefore, possible. Thus, support is offered to the actor-in-character approach. The so-called 'idiographic' perspective, on the other hand, takes the view that no two individuals, not even identical twins, are alike. Traits are said to be particular to each individual and, therefore, people cannot be compared or grouped, because everyone is on a different scale. A further refinement of this position, the 'learning' perspective, foregrounds continuous change as the governing driver in personality formation. Claims for consistency are, therefore, regarded with scepticism: we learn from new experiences and learning constantly changes who we are. The actor-in-action can draw a great deal of comfort from this view.

A middle view argues that traits – sociability or aggression, for example – can, in fact, be detected across individuals, but that each of us is unique in respect of the *levels* at which we display these inclinations. A desire to explore, for example, can be said to exist in us all, but I may be much less inclined to take risks than my brother; by extension, in Ibsen's *Hedda Gabler*, Tesman is much more stuck in his ways than Judge Brack, who, in turn, is more cautious than Ejlert Lovborg. Such a view, still essentially nomothetic, considers individual personalities as variations on a theme. The overall dimensions on which we measure personality are the same for all; each of us, however, contains each of these elements in different measures. Personality, therefore, is mapped on two competing vectors: on the one hand, the stability and rigidity of form offered by adherence to a pattern; on the other, the inner dynamism conferred by the interactions between competing sets of characteristics.

Scientifically, our personality traits are recognised by whether they

- can be measured through appropriate tests and predict real-life behaviours and are therefore *valid*;
- are constant regardless of circumstances and thus *reliable*.

Let me start with the simplest questions arising from the description of 'contemplation' of the character model outlined in the previous chapter: can we *actually* infer a person's traits from the way he or she behaves, or is that a folk fallacy? Second, are 'proper' investigations, by means of rigorous scientific psychological profiling, etc., needed if we are to arrive at reliable views of personality? If so, is an analysis of dramatic characters in terms of characteristics/traits based on shaky foundations?

To the first question, most psychologists would answer wryly, "Well, it's not that simple . . ." To the second, unsurprisingly, "Of course!" For them, personality traits are constituent elements of complex psychic structures, affected by genetic, physiological, and environmental factors. Observable behaviours may be influenced by deep-seated traits, but this does not mean that we can directly infer from them what these traits are. Folk psychology, they would say, is to be treated with scepticism.

This "dogma of complexity" has come to be questioned of late. Psychologist Juri Allik starts his illuminating challenge by declaring, "There seems to be no privileged source of information because information is everywhere, and its retrieval requires unsophisticated skills". Almost everything we do and say in interactions with others leaves a trace. These 'impressions' are easily interpreted by our fellow human beings, without the need for specialist training. True, we cannot observe personality traits directly, as if through a microscope. We can, however, infer them with relative ease from information about our personal inclinations, made freely and universally available by us all. There even exists, some psychologists have argued, a "personality judgement instinct", developed through evolution as part of our survival armoury. This is unproven, yet it is tempting to speculate that our histrionic sensibility is a specialised application of this development.

In support of their assertions, Allik and his colleagues adduce some solid empirical evidence. A typical scientific method of assessing personality, for example, is to compare judgements made by people about themselves with judgements made about them by other people (so-called self–other agreement studies). Agreement ratings between self and observer typically come in at between 40 and 50 per cent, so statistically less than what might arise simply through random probability. This has led psychologists to distrust the ability of lay people to make accurate judgements about the personality traits of others. However, such conclusions are generally based on studies involving small groups of subjects *who do not know one other*.

To test these assumptions, Allik and his colleagues undertook a self–other agreement study on a sample of over 11,000 subjects, in two different countries, Estonia and Holland. Participants were asked to rate themselves and others on the basis of two different, though widely recognised, personality questionnaires. These typically rate people on a graded scale in terms of being, for example, 'outgoing' or 'reserved', 'expressive' or 'impassive', 'dynamic' or 'laid-back', and so on. Unusually, however, Allik and his colleagues recruited people who knew one another well. This time, self–other agreement on key aspects of behaviour expressed as personality traits was recorded in about 95 per cent of cases.[1] Allik and his colleagues concluded that in everyday situations, and if one is reasonably familiar with the other person, estimating someone's personality is not actually very difficult. They liken this natural process to riding a bike: one gets a few bruises at the beginning, but once acquired, this becomes a mundane, automatic skill we can all exercise with ease.

How well do we need to know someone before our assessment of their personality matches their own? A number of studies have established a consensus on this question: it takes only between 5 and 10 minutes of observing a person before we can make a relatively accurate assessment of their personality. Moreover, they don't need to do very much in that short time span. Watching them perform up to around twenty simple activities is sufficient; after that, a plateau is reached and any improvements in accuracy are very small. In life, as on stage, we seem to be able to make up our minds about others quickly and accurately. Calling for a rethink of the belief that knowing someone else is a slow and gradual process, psychologist David Kenny uses a telling comparison:

> A persistent metaphor is that of 'peeling an onion' . . . which implies that it takes considerable time to know what a person is really like. A better metaphor might be to 'scratch the surface of the onion'. After all, the distinctive taste of an onion is as marked in its outer layer as it is in the innermost layer.
>
> *(2004, p. 277)*

Contemporary psychology appears to be moving towards an acceptance of the fact that the common practice of drawing general inferences about people's identities from observing their everyday behaviours is a natural, and fairly accurate, part of our social interactions. To bring our intuitive inferences to consciousness, in daily life we use the language of traits and in acting, of characteristics. Spectators watching characters in plays exercise this natural skill; presented with a constructed character, they will draw the conclusions regarding its characteristics towards which the actor has led them.

Grid coordinates

Personality traits are a sort of shorthand with which to summarise our impressions of other people as well as understand ourselves. These adjectives describe ways in which we and others are likely to act. Not the acts themselves, which vary according to circumstances, but what is, as it were, 'behind' them: the psychological inclinations or tendencies that cause us habitually to approach the world in this fashion and not in that.

Please close your eyes for a moment and consider the following statement: "The doctor examined little Emily's growth". What came to mind? Did you think her dad took little Emily to the doctor because she was a bit on the short side for her age; or did you think Emily had discovered a sinister lump? Were you, in other words, intuitively drawn towards a down-to-earth, simple, and benign explanation or, on the contrary, inclined to assume the worst? The way in which we react to such ambiguous phrases is a measure of our 'interpretative bias' – the concept that says that we are guided in how we interpret external inputs by fundamental personality inclinations. Classical psychology described these as our defining traits – those things that affect our key cognitive functions, our decisions and judgements and, thus, 'make us who we are'.

Psychologists also drew a distinction between personality *traits* and psychological *states*. Hans Eysenck's classical model of personality defined traits as *permanent dispositions* and states as *transient conditions*. Such models assumed a causal relationship between the two: states are always seen as reflections of a trait – a person who is high on the trait of neuroticism, for example, is likely to experience frequent bouts of sadness. On the other hand, states – sadness, elation, or interest, for example – though they may last for weeks, months, or even years at a time, are given to change. Even casual changes in context, such as finishing work and meeting friends for a drink, may cause us to shift from one state to another.

Psychology theorists also adopted fairly strong positions on the role played by genetics and often linked personality traits with early life experiences. Traits were considered to be biologically determined, permanently embedded in our personalities and very difficult, if not impossible, to change through life experiences. We are who we are and any changes we might undergo are likely to be superficial and short-lived. Early psychologists Wilhelm Wundt and William James postulated the existence of such fundamental, stable traits, and Gordon Allport, Hans Eysenck, and others sought to confirm it through both observation and experiment. In the 1970s and 1980s, however, the theory of stable traits came under sustained attack. Walter Mischel's book, *Personality and Assessment*, described a study that found only a modest correlation between self-reported traits and actual conduct. If traits could not account for behaviours in a consistent way, they could not be considered stable. Only states existed.

These two extremes represent the so-called 'essentialist' and 'situationist' models of personality. The first holds dear the idea that personality traits are mainly genetic and set. The second argues that we only react moment-by-moment, according to the situations in which we find ourselves and that therefore our personalities are fluid, indeterminate, and unpredictable. As a result, situationists assert that only what is observable in our behaviours can be described; anything else – by implication traits, which may only be *inferred* from behaviour – is at best irrelevant and at worst sits outside the domain of strict scientific study. For this extreme view, the mind is flat and thin, like a computer disk standing ready for experience to burn impressions on to it, day-by-day and moment-by-moment. Our sense of ourselves as coherent, unitary beings is an illusion. Mischel wrote: "the conceptual split between person and situation is absurd": the implication being that there is no such thing as a consistent set of characteristics adding up to a coherent personality, but only a series of variable reactions to different circumstances. The 'processional' actor would readily identify with such a sentiment.

A series of now widely accepted studies has, however, demonstrated that this assumption is, in fact, wrong. Here is one example why: mothers were asked to describe where they thought their pre-teen children stood in relation to shyness and temper. The children, as well as their partners and their own children, were then interviewed at age 30 and again at 40. The study concluded that boys who had been prone to temper tantrums in childhood had become, by their own admission, irascible adults. Girls who got angry in their childhood did not see themselves as crotchety in adulthood, but their families *did*. Equally, shy boys were slow to progress in their careers as adults and married later than the average in their age group. Shy girls married at the same age as the average but were statistically more inclined toward conventional home-building rather than professional careers. This and similar studies demonstrated that personalities were stable over long periods of time. This is now generally agreed: the so-called 'dispositional' perspective in psychology, arguing that we possess relatively stable inclinations (or 'dispositions') and that these cause us to act consistently and fairly predictably in different situations, is now dominant. This is no longer taken to mean, however, that a particular trait would necessarily lead to the same type of behaviour in every situation – our actions are both trait- and context-dependent. In the end, Mischel himself accepted the validity of traits, while arguing for the interaction between personality and situations to be afforded a greater role in our models of the personality.

If all this sounds strangely like the 'core character' versus 'action-is-all' argument, it is because the latter is a specialised instance of the same fundamental perceptions of the human experience: the sense of a constant and unitary 'I', pitted against the equally powerful sense of an 'I' who is forever changing in reaction to changing circumstances. One way of squaring this circle is to acknowledge that moment-to-moment fluctuations do take place, but that – seen across long time spans – we habitually default to 'set-points' which constitute the norm of our personalities and anchor transient states. Like all organisms, we are genetically pre-programmed to respond with the speed of light to changes in the environment that we perceive as threats: to retreat or attack. To do otherwise could place us in mortal danger – the time is simply too short for traits to intervene. It is these lightning changes we describe as 'instinctive' or 'intuitive' and they are invariably accompanied by physiological alterations: hormonal releases, skeleto-muscular dispositions, and so on. Once the danger has been dealt with, we revert to a "steady state", in which "fixed" traits play the defining part.

I am particularly attracted by the way recent thinking builds on such observations in order to revisit the question: "What do traits actually do?" Psychologist Malgorzata Fajkowska claims that the main function of personality traits is to control the way in which we process external stimuli. As living organisms, we are constantly exposed to sensory, emotional, and cognitive prompts and have to react – we are aroused by them, experience cognitive, motor, and motivational changes as a result of this arousal and are moved to act on these changes. Certain, mainly innate, personality traits which psychologists label 'temperaments' (I shall come back to these) are particularly suited to regulate our reactions. They define what Fajkowska calls the "style" of our behaviours, their "intensity, energy, strength, speed, tempo, fluctuation, mobility". In acting terms, they give each character a fundamental, recognisable 'tempo'. Individuals as well as characters should, therefore, be described not by whether they have one or the other of these traits but by their relative intensity.

Going all the way back to Aristotle, we have also devised systems by which to group and classify personality traits. Charles Macklin, for instance, using the language of the Natural Sciences to describe acting processes, talks about the need for the actor to know "the genus, and species, and characteristic that he is about to imitate . . ." Classifications not only group characters, but also attempt to explain similarities and differences between the groups by cross-referring them with the wisdom of the age. This may be the four elements of earth, air, water, and fire, or the Renaissance humours, whose relative balance in the body was said to determine four temperaments, "peculiar qualities" or personality types: sanguine, phlegmatic, choleric, melancholic. They may even be explained in terms of astrology, or by equating character types with animals – social types seen as different breeds of dog was a well-known conceit of Victorian cartoonists. However idiosyncratic (and I am *not* suggesting that they can all be relied on equally), these provide an indispensable map: without agreed reference points for the classification of variables in personality, we would be forever meandering, trying to describe one another.

Words, words . . .

Ultimately, traits and types provide a language with which to describe human characteristics and a method by which we can give this language a structure: a 'vocabulary' and a 'grammar', if you wish. Historically, two approaches have been adopted in this endeavour: the *empirical* approach sought to list as many traits as possible and then group them according to certain criteria; the *theoretical* approach postulated that certain traits existed and then evaluated them "for goodness of fit" with experimental findings. Prevalent empirical approaches rely in the main on the so-called 'lexical hypothesis' to identify and list personality traits. As this leads directly to the system of traits classifications currently dominant in psychology, I shall dwell on it longer than on theoretically based approaches.

Simply put, the lexical hypothesis asserts that some aspects of human behaviour are so prominent, so easily observable and so meaningful to human interactions that most languages will have developed terms for them.

In the 1930s, Gordon Allport identified 17,953 terms in the English language describing personality. His colleague, Warren Norman, then scanned the entire *Webster's Dictionary* and found 27,000 terms in all. After eliminating obscure, inappropriate, and archaic terms, they still retained 3,600 of these, which Allport labelled "stable biophysical traits". These were considered to denote genuine personality traits, as distinct from words describing social roles, physical characteristics, etc. That generation of psychologists then endeavoured to establish reliable criteria by which to group this gargantuan lexicon into manageable categories or 'inventories' of traits. Raymond Cattell, one of the first to introduce mathematical tools into psychological investigations, used factor analysis to spot recurring features or patterns of association in large sets of data. Factor analysis thus provided a basis for arguing that some traits mattered more than others – if a factor accounted for a lot of the variables in the data, it reflected an important trait; if it accounted for less variability, the trait was less important.

In this way, the huge variety of behaviours in which personality manifests itself was reduced to a smaller set of 'underlying' traits. Cattell came to the conclusion that personality traits could be classified according to a set of 16 overriding dimensions or "primary factors". As a result, he devised a 16 Personality Factor Inventory, or 16PF, arranged across 16 pairs of contrasting labels such as

Reserved versus Warm

Reactive versus Emotionally Stable

Deferential versus Dominant

A large number of such inventories have been devised since, addressing differ-ent aspects of personality and at times reflecting the particular research interests of the investigators. More often than not, these are in the format espoused by Cattell and place individual behaviours on a spectrum ranging from a trait to its opposite. Inventories are then translated into questionnaires which ask the respondents to place themselves on a scale of agreement or disagreement with statements related to one of the factors being studied: 'I rarely feel lonely or blue', 'I handle myself pretty well in a crisis',[2] and so on. By answering such questions, respondents describe perceptions of their own conduct (self-reporting) and may also classify others' behaviours.

Traits are therefore recognised:

a. Because they reflect a reality of perception, as self-reported
b. Because they reflect certain cognitive processes in the observers themselves.

The mechanism which governs self-reporting appears to be this: from the earliest age, we come into contact with others – first parents and siblings, then society at large – and observe their reactions to us. These reactions are stored in our memo-ries; it is from them that we construct images of who we are. When we describe ourselves in response to self-reporting questionnaires, in fact we rely on the per-ceptions of others, which we have internalised. Yet, memory is not exact: it is a construct affected by the emotional and physical circumstances in which it arises as well as by the context in which it is summoned in the present. "Memories are our theories of how we were", writes psychologist Robert Hogan and self-descriptions "are self-presentations, not self-reports".

It should be said that the lexical approach to trait identification is not without its critics. Objections are often raised on the grounds that it relies on terms and descriptions that are also used by "novices", that is, lay people not qualified to opine on scientific matters. The obvious response to this criticism goes back to the very assumption on which the lexical hypothesis rests: if certain words are used frequently and have a broad range of synonyms and related word families, it is reasonable to assume that what they describe is important. Common speech reflects the significance for both individuals and societies of the psychological pro-cesses these words describe. Moreover, studies of trait descriptors across dozens of languages have demonstrated that, regardless of geography or culture, the more a particular attribute was important to the relationships between human beings, the more languages had terms to describe it.

Objections to reliance on common words are the obverse of the oft-encountered reluctance of artists to engage with scientific concepts. In both instances, an unwarranted limitation to the rewards of cross-domain fertilisation is rooted in mistrust of those who think differently. It would, therefore, be a mistake to ignore these as a foundation, "necessary but not sufficient", for a science of personality. The "necessary but not sufficient" qualification is key, however, and works both ways: scientific classifications are indeed necessary (isolating ourselves from them is an act of solipsism just as absurd as that of the scientist ignoring common parlance), but – while being necessary – are not sufficient to describe fully the creative process.

A more substantial objection is that traits rely on circular reasoning when they seek not only to describe what can be seen, but also explain its causes. If a colleague tends to act all the time in a heavy-handed manner, in meetings, with visitors, and even her family, we might describe her as 'aggressive'. But if I ask "how do you know she is aggressive?" and the answer is "because she always behaves aggressively", I have come full circle. In the absence of other explanations of her behaviour, empirically based trait theories are indeed open to this criticism. Inferring the causes of motivations and drives appears to demand a different approach.

The best known theoretically based approach to traits remains that proposed by Hans Eysenck over half a century ago. Eysenck started by trying to bring a contemporary scientific outlook to historical classifications going back to Galen and Hippocrates. He revisited, among other perspectives, the findings of Wundt, Pavlov, and, in particular, C. G. Jung's 1921 treatise, *Psychological Types*. Eysenck put forward the hypothesis that personality types should be considered as a combination of high and low levels of two vectors or 'super-traits'. One vector was 'introversion–extraversion' and the other 'neuroticism', defined in terms of emotionality–stability. The first describes our relative inclinations to seek more (or less) excitement, to be active, to interact with others socially, and to be dominant. Neuroticism establishes a scale on which we can place the ease and frequency with which we become distressed and fearful. In order to assess where a person is situated on these two overriding dimensions, Eysenck devised the *Eysenck Personality Questionnaire*, or *EPQ*. When this was mapped on Cattell's 16PF lexically based system, the two measures showed significant similarities and overlaps, thus reinforcing each other's validity. Moreover, both systems established a hierarchy in which each super-trait incorporated a number of component traits. As a tool for predicting future conduct, however, Eysenck held to the view that the higher levels, that is, the types, were most reliable, as they were linked to aspects of the physiological mechanisms of the nervous system. Eysenck's approach, though now less used in contemporary psychology, remains of considerable interest for the classification and understanding of theatre character. I shall return to the concepts of introversion–extraversion, in relation to some of the concepts used in Laban's analysis of movement, which I outlined in the previous chapter.

Ocean

Eysenck eventually came to add to his model a third scale – aggressive/empathetic. This resulted in eight combinations of traits or types, compared with Cattell's 16.

More recent researchers have considered that two or three scales were too few but 16 too many. However, they retained the methodological principle behind Cattell's and Eysenck's models, looking for commonalities across large numbers of trait descriptors. Over the past quarter of a century, a consensus has emerged around a system of trait classification called the Five-Factor Model or FFM, sometimes also described as 'the Big Five'. While, strictly speaking, the two are not identical, for our purposes they are sufficiently similar to be treated as one.

An easy-to-remember acronym for the five factors in OCEAN. This stands for scales of:

Open/closed to experience

Conscientious/non-conscientious

Extravert/introvert

Agreeable/non-agreeable

Neurotic/stable

These five Factors are then further refined through bipolar and unipolar adjective scales which reflect each of the overarching factors. Thus, Extraversion is further qualified as:

Bipolar	*Unipolar*
Bold–timid	Gregarious
Forceful–submissive	Outspoken
Self-confident–unassured	Energetic
Talkative–silent	Happy[3]
Spontaneous–inhibited	

As with any system of classification, a trade-off is inevitable between ease of use and complexity. There is no doubt that when using the five Factors alone to look at personality, something is lost. Better descriptions as well as more accurate predictions (of clinical outcomes, for example) can be arrived at if one uses the sub-traits. On the other hand, the broad brush of the OCEAN super-traits can evoke a quick, intuitive picture that is easier to access.

The FFM model has been tested for reliability and stability in large populations and is considered to provide a credible tool for assessing personality in a variety of contexts, from the clinic to the workplace.[4] The vocabulary of the FFM has also been tested across diverse cultures, and rating scales translated into German, Japanese, or Chinese found similar Factor structures. The five super-traits also predict real-world behaviours: the Factors have been shown to weigh heavily on cognitive abilities, the likelihood of success or failure in marriage, performance at work, and even the likely outcomes of heart conditions; all supporting the validity of the model.

To the best of my knowledge, the FFM has not yet been applied to the analysis of theatre characters and it would be interesting to see what results its application in this area might yield. It will be said that some of the terms used by the FFM are more suited to the clinic or the HR department than the stage. But its proponents are keen to emphasise the strong kinship that exists between the scientific terms and everyday concepts. 'Neuroticism' need not mean psychiatric disorder, only nervousness, 'Extravert' is simply another word for energetic and enthusiastic, 'O' might just as well represent originality and 'A' affection. The model appeals because it dovetails with everyday experiences. The easy to grasp associations of its core terminology have given it considerable communicative power and have contributed to its popularity.

A brief description of the Five Factors thus seems to be in order, even in a book about theatre character. On one level, this could serve as a rough crib-sheet for initial approaches to character: the Factors provide easy to access points of entry ('this fits my character; this does not . . .') as well as a foundation on which to build. On another, they illustrate the striking extent to which these scientific, rigorously tested descriptors match older classifications, rooted in the earlier psychologies of Freud and Jung, on which so much acting theory relies.

Openness to Experience is related in certain respects to intelligence and creativity: people who score high on this dimension tend to be described as imaginative, perceptive, and sensitive to aesthetic beauty. They are often inclined towards daydreaming and also tend to be unconventional and to need constant stimulation. On this dimension, people (and characters – Blanche du Bois, Romeo) can be described by whether they are more or less responsive to, and excited by, fantasies, emotions, and ambiances.

Conscientiousness is readily grasped: some people are neat, well organised, meticulous, and industrious. Others are prepared to cut corners, bend the rules, have no interest in details, 'delegate' with gusto (characters in French farces and in Oscar Wilde plays spring to mind, as do quite a few contemporary politicians). Conscientiousness has also been linked to restraint and to strong focus on professional achievements. Poor Bob Cratchit, Scrooge's put-upon clerk, would definitely score high on C, as would Tesman or Woyzeck.

Extraverts are positive, enthusiastic, cheerful, and lively. They tend to talk a lot and dominate the conversation, yet feel warm and friendly – they form relationships easily and tend to stick to them. Extraverts are often ambitious and take risks in the pursuit of their goals. Cyrano's fellow Gascons are typical of this extreme, as are any number of action heroes, from Achilles to Rambo. Those low on E are described both in self-reports and in reports by others as reserved, quiet, and withdrawn. They tend to keep their impulses and emotions in check (Laura in *The Glass Menagerie* belongs here as – on a different level altogether – does the Buddhist monk who sets himself on fire in *U.S.*, Peter Weiss's anti-Vietnam play).

Agreeableness is essentially a social trait, but does not simply measure how pleasant or otherwise a person might be. High A scores denote well-developed caring qualities, the ability to nurture and give emotional support to others (Aunt Julie in *Hedda Gabler*; the Nurse in *Romeo and Juliet*). Low A scores, on the other hand, describe a self-centred, spiteful, jealous, and hostile personality – an 'Iago' *par excellence*.

Finally, *Neuroticism* – probably the trait studied in most depth because of its clinical implications – measures the way in which we react to distress. Those with high N scores tend to describe themselves as frustrated, guilty, and fearful. They often suffer from low self-esteem, are self-conscious, and find it difficult to control their impulses and cravings. They are prone to depression and other psychiatric disorders (dramatic literature is full of such characters – Richard II, Orsino, our old friend Antonio, are but a few). Those with low N scores are not immune to mental illness but are generally relaxed, even-tempered, self-possessed, and cool under pressure: not quite as well represented as the high Neurotics, but Fortinbras might be a good example, as might Horatio.

The sharp-eyed reader will no doubt have spotted an obvious flaw: some of these examples are interchangeable. Romeo could be given as an example of high A and the Nurse of high E. Quite: these basic descriptions are not to be taken to imply that the FFM can be applied, simplistically, to describe a person solely by means of one of these super-traits. The traits cannot and should not be taken in isolation: research has shown that visible aspects of personality are, in fact, blends of two or more super-traits. Thus, someone described as 'shy' reflects a combination of relatively high Neuroticism with low Extraversion. Equally, the same behaviour may be assigned to more than one super-trait: adjectives such as 'temperamental' or 'aggressive' can reflect either low Agreeableness or high Neuroticism. Someone scoring average to low on Extraversion could be either energetic yet reserved, or languid yet approachable. The five Factors merely represent a bird's eye view of personality; to arrive at detailed descriptions one has to drill down into the sub-traits and assess their relative strengths. In particular, from our point of view, one has to distinguish between those traits which are intrinsic to the personality (the character at home, in bed, with the blankets drawn over its head) and those that reflect the character's interactions with others. In their overview of the Five Factor Model, psychologists McCrae and John summarise:

> Although individuals differ on their standing on the five factors, the factors themselves point to universal issues. All people must be responsive to danger, loss, and threat; interact with others to some degree; choose between the risks of exploration and the limitations of familiarity; weigh self against social interest; balance work and play. Personality processes, by definition, involve some change in the thoughts, feelings, and actions of an individual; all these intra-individual changes seem to be mirrored by inter-individual differences in characteristic ways of thinking, feeling, and acting – differences that are summarised, at the broadest level, by the five factors.
>
> *(1992, p. 199)*

Elsewhere, the five Factors have been compared to Jungian archetypes: first, because they are innate structures; second, because their function is to assess whether other people or events are likely to make a positive or a detrimental contribution to the well-being of the person, the family or the group. One must append an important caveat to these claims of universality: like all such endeavours, the FFM is very much a product of our times. Had a similar system been devised for ancient Athenians, psychologist Jerome Kagan points out, dimensions such as loyalty to one's community are likely to have featured highly; if for seventeenth century Puritans, piety would have weighed heavily. The vectors of the FFM reflect those values on which contemporary Western societies set most store: sociability, work ethic, and tolerance. By contrast, a study of Chinese words for the most important aspects of interpersonal relations found that the majority referred to aspects of selfishness and dependence on others. I am sensible to this overall cultural critique; I am even more interested in pointing out that any analysis of theatre character using FFM criteria would need to correct for either historicist or contemporary perspectives.

None the less, the psychological method of starting with high-level super-traits, combining their relative strengths, and then drilling down to individual characteristics seems to me to hold valuable lessons for the analysis of theatre characters.

Of babies and biases

As we have seen, the so-called 'dispositional' perspective in psychology argues that we possess relatively stable traits and that these cause us to act consistently and fairly predictably. If the current state of personality psychology is to be believed, it appears that we can, in fact, speak of stable 'inner natures'. How are these formed?

Jerome Kagan, the long-serving professor of psychology at Harvard, spent much of his professional life studying the ways in which babies and infants react to unexpected change. He brought into his laboratory more than 450 four-month-old babies, placed them in high chairs and, in the presence of their mothers, exposed them to something benign but which they did not expect: a mobile started to turn above their heads, a tissue giving out a slight smell of alcohol was waved under their noses, or a stranger's voice was heard coming from a speaker. Around 40 per cent of the infants sat contented, babbling away. Twenty per cent of infants, however, became agitated, and always in the same pattern: their upper-body muscles tensed, their legs and arms flailed, and they eventually started to cry. Most importantly, they arched their backs so as to lift themselves out of the chair. This is significant because adults also arch their backs when they fear danger. In infants and adults alike, the amygdala – a small, almond-shaped structure in the middle of the brain that is heavily involved in how the brain reacts to unexpected stimuli – sends powerful signals to another part of the brain that, in turn, triggers this distinctive response.[5]

These infants were then followed through their education experiences and professional choices for over two decades. The findings were startling: those who had become agitated – the "high-reactives", Kagan calls them – continued throughout their development to respond strongly to new and unexpected encounters. As a result, they developed defence mechanisms to avoid stress: they became vigilant, shy, and cautious. One, otherwise not particularly neurotic, high-reactive even went so far as to declare: "I do not like spring because the weather is so unpredictable". They also tended to avoid too much contact with other people and overall chose professions that could be exercised in relative isolation: writers, programmers, scientists. On the other hand, those infants who had reacted placidly – the "low-reactives" – turned out to be extraverts: chatty, laid-back, friendly. They were more inclined to take risks and chose professions such as airline pilot, firefighter, or entrepreneur. These temperamental biases could even be observed in the physiological reactions of the two groups. Temperaments, writes Kagan

> . . . produce variation in the reactivity of, or sensitivity to, a change in heart rate, breathing, gastric motility, skin temperature, or bitter taste. Children who like very sour tastes also prefer bright colours and foods with unfamiliar flavours.[6]
>
> *(2007, p. 176)*

Interesting support for this division into high- and low-reacting individuals comes from animal studies. One study found that birds that looked for food quickly and further afield (so-called 'fast explorers') had better immune functions and lower testosterone levels than slower explorers. Another study, looking at how animals coped with stress, found that "proactive" individuals attacked more quickly and were more defensive and that "reactive" individuals had lower hormonal activity on the key hypothalamic–pituitary–adrenal (HPA) axis than "proactive" ones.

As he was able to demonstrate that these traits were consistent across large numbers of subjects, Kagan feels confident enough to describe the two groups as "types" and to draw parallels between these and ancient classifications. The resilience dimension he detects in "low-reactives" is linked, for example, to Galen's sanguine temperament. Neither is he reluctant, as scientific psychologists often are, to acknowledge the continuity of thought between his classification and the attempts at grouping personalities of earlier psychologists such as Pavlov or Jung. Common sense observations, Classical literature, early psychology, and modern scientific investigation all point toward the notion that, seen across a population, individual differences can and should be grouped into temperaments or types.

Temperament, therefore, describes the biases with which we all begin our lives. It is a form of "biological preparedness", made of those things a child brings into the world at birth and which manifest themselves in differences in the neurochemical functions of our brains. Evidence emerging from parallel research has shown that there are good physiological reasons for this to occur. While we are in the womb, during birth and then in the first hours and days after our entry into the world, fundamental interactions take place between our DNA and the environment. Our genes, which are very active until birth, normally shut down soon after as a result of a process called methylation, in which a chemical compound attaches itself to the DNA. The rate at which the genes shut down can vary considerably across individuals, however. Experiments on rats have shown, for example, that licking and grooming in the first seven days of life has a powerful effect on the degree to which the DNA structure of the oestrogen receptor alpha gene (the so-called 'attachment' gene, which plays an important role in the development of maternal behaviour) is modified. Biologists think that what happens is this: licking is a tactile stimulation similar to massage – they both increase the levels of the growth hormone. High levels of growth hormone bind to DNA and, in so doing, prevent methyl groups from binding to it. The more licking occurs, the less methylation is found in the cells. As a consequence, the 'attachment' gene is kept active for longer during this crucial period of development. Enhanced attachment dispositions are then sustained into adulthood. Conversely, if an organism does not get that type of stimulation, the gene is methylated quickly and shuts down; this also affects the organism throughout its lifespan.[7] The genetic effects are, in turn, passed down the generations: high licking–grooming mothers have high licking–grooming daughters, and so on. Sociability – defined as our ability to connect with, or attach ourselves to, other people, from parents and siblings to lovers and co-workers – is a key personality trait. Genetically informed dispositions toward or against forming attachments thus play an important role in determining this aspect of our personalities.

Thus, temperaments *predispose* us toward certain feelings, moods, and behaviours. They make it easier or harder to be joyful, easier or harder to become tense, easier or harder to feel guilty. They are the strings of the harp on which the environment plays. "Experiences", Kagan says, "act on these biases to create personality types, such as agreeable with peers or impulsively aggressive following frustration".

One must not fall into the common trap of equating temperament with personality, however. An innate propensity exists, but only as a general direction. The environment will always play a crucial role in determining how temperament actually expresses itself in personality. Even identical twins, who share the same genes at the moment of conception, will not be identical in every respect nine months later, as chance events during gestation will have affected them in different ways. Once born, if all 'goes well' for the child, that is, if the temperament is reinforced by a sympathetic environment, then strong biases (a very active baby, for example) will be compensated and the person end up balanced and integrated. However, no matter how positive the environment, a person with one type of temperament will never reach the other extreme. The shy will not become bold or the lively, docile. And what happens if things do not 'go well' for the child? The answer can only be that temperamental inclinations, unchecked, develop into overemphatic personalities. This is the psychological basis of lopsided theatre characters, captured culturally by the tradition of humours, types, and masks with which I am concerned.

Temperaments are, says Kagan, like the block of marble before the sculptor has started work: its shape, texture, and colour restrict the sculptor's choices, but still leave a vast array of creative possibilities. Few 'sculptors' are as effective at shaping our personalities as our parents: mothers and fathers sense very early on that a child is inclined to be energetic or passive, focused or dreamy, and so on. Their image of what their child *ought to be like* then intervenes: parents reinforce temperamental tendencies when these correspond to this image and suppress them when they do not. According to their own expectations, for example, mothers presented with a "high-reactive" and therefore shy, hypersensitive child, will become either very protective or, on the contrary, get tough so as to make their child resilient.

The concept of temperament is far from being settled in psychological theory. None the less, there is relatively little challenge to the observation that certain fundamental behaviours appear so early in an infant's life that the only explanation is that their origins are either genetic or pre-natal/immediately postnatal. Such objections as there are to this view of innate and early-life propensities come from psychological and psychiatric concerns with therapeutic methodologies and their effectiveness; these are counterbalanced by solid research on animals, primates in particular, which reinforce with biological and chemical analyses behavioural observations made about humans. The old saying that psychoanalysts do not believe in temperament until they have had their second child is also worth remembering. For our purposes, the following summary might be useful: from the earliest stages of development, temperament acts in the way a filter operates on a camera – it emphasises certain colours on the spectrum while excluding others.

*   *   *

The language of traits describes what can be *seen* in our behaviours. Does it also point to what *causes* them? From the earliest days of trait psychology Gordon Allport had noted that "a trait is known not by its cause, but by what it causes; not by its roots but by its fruits". Because it describes a person's behaviours, but not the dynamic which takes place within, trait psychology has sometimes been labelled the "psychology of the stranger". It devises a taxonomy of traits and groups them into categories but does not account for the all-important sense of 'I'. Applied to theatre characters, it could tell me that Proctor is upright and Tamburlaine foolhardy, but not *what motivates them*.

To answer that question, we may need to look at personality not simply as a cluster of traits, but as a hierarchy. At the bottom are biological factors: our DNA and its interactions with the environment in the earliest stages of life. These factors have a crucial role in shaping our personality traits and, therefore, the patterns of decision and motivation on which we fall back constantly throughout our lives. In turn, traits and patterns lead to our characteristic behaviours and actions, which amount to the 'style' of our engagement with the world. The image proposed is not, however, that of a rigid structure, with biology in the basement and behaviours on the upper floor. Rather, it is that of a lift moving constantly between the three main levels and in both directions: behaviours affect traits and traits affect DNA expression just as much as the other way around. This is looking at personality as an "interrelated dynamic system": a chemical solution into which different elements and compounds are dissolved. The 'old-timers' – Freud, Jung, Adler, and Murray, for whom the business of personality psychology was "the nature of human nature" – would certainly agree. Freud would place in this primordial soup Eros and Thanatos, the tensions between life and death instincts; Jung would stress identification with universal archetypes. Modern psychologists talk of "abstract dispositions" with a defining role in shaping aspects of personality higher up in the hierarchy.

Antonio Damasio offers a useful summary of the forces involved in the emergence of personality. He writes:

> What we usually describe as 'personality' depends on multiple contributions. One important contribution comes from 'traits', whose ensemble is often referred to as 'temperament', and which are already detectable around the time of birth. Some of those traits are genetically transmitted and some are shaped by early developmental factors. Another important contribution comes from the unique interactions that a growing, living organism engages in a particular environment, physically, humanely, and culturally speaking. This latter contribution – which is made under the continuous shadow of the former – is recorded in autobiographical memory and is the footing for autobiographical self and personhood.
>
> *(1999, p. 222)*

With this, we are beginning to rummage in the attics and cellars where motivations for actions might lurk. To decide that Tamburlaine is 'reckless and brutal' or 'cunning and logical' is an important step, but leaves unbridged the chasm between actor and character. To cross it, one has to look for the sources of these characteristics in the character's personal history. The child is father to the man: the construction of fictional character biographies is arguably the most complex as well as the most effective means of firing the histrionic imagination. Here, trait personality must give way to an older and, yes, more imaginative psychology.

Notes

1 A different study estimated that people judged personality typically at the mid-way point (75%) between random guessing (50%) and perfect accuracy (100%) (Back and Nestler, 2016).
2 Taken from the NEO Personality Inventory-Revised. Other questionnaires include the Eysenck Personality Questionnaire (EPQ), Exvia-Invia (Cattell and Eber) and the Myers–Briggs Type Indicator.
3 The reader interested in delving deeper into the subtleties of the FFM, including the full list of subsidiary traits for each of the Factors, should look at the NEO-PI-R, the questionnaire most frequently used to assess the Five Factors. An entry point is https://en.wikipedia.org/wiki/Revised_NEO_Personality_Inventory
4 McCrae and John (1992) offer a comprehensive view of the evolution and main features of the model. I follow below their outlines of the five Factors.
5 The remaining 40 per cent of the experimental group of infants displayed different, though less pronounced, behaviours.
6 Kagan's experiments echo a classic study also involving children, called the "strange situation". According to how they reacted to the absence of their mothers, infants were classified as "secure", "ambivalent", or "resistant". The latter sometimes displayed an "avoidant" pattern, whereby they ignored their mothers on their return. In later life,

"avoidants" tended to immerse themselves into their work as an alternative to socialising; they also tended to have poor relationships.

7 Equally, the chemical oxytocin, which is crucial to facilitate birth but is connected to levels of stress, can shape temperament if the mother is stressed during pregnancy or birth.

Bibliography

Trait psychology: Allport, G. W., 1937. *Personality: A Psychological Interpretation*. New York: Holt; Eysenck, H. J., 1967. *The Biological Basis of Personality*. Springfield, IL: Charles C. Thomas; Brody, N., 1994. 'Heritability of traits'. *Psychological Inquiry*, 5, pp. 117–119; Matthews, G., Deary, I. J., and Whiteman, M. C., 2009. *Personality Traits*. 3rd Edition. Cambridge: Cambridge University Press; *as the "psychology of the stranger"*: McAdams, D. P., 1992. 'The Five Factor Model of personality: a critical appraisal'. *Journal of Personality*, 60, pp. 329–261; McAdams, D. P. 1994. 'A psychology of the stranger'. *Psychological Inquiry*, 5, pp. 145–148.

Traits and inference: Allik, J., De Vries, R. E., and Realo, A., 2016. 'Why are moderators of self-other agreement difficult to establish?' *Journal of Research in Personality*, 63, pp. 72–83; Allik, J., 2018. 'The almost unbearable lightness of personality'. *Journal of Personality*, 86, pp. 109–123; Back, M. D., and Nestler, S. (2016). Accuracy of judging personality, in Hall, J. A., Schmid Mast, M. and West, T. W. (eds.), *The Social Psychology of Perceiving Others Accurately*. Cambridge: Cambridge University Press, pp. 98–119; Haselton, M. G., and Funder, D. C., 2006. 'The evolution of accuracy and bias in social judgment', in Schaller, M., Simpson, J. A., and Kenrick, D. T. (eds.), *Evolution and Social Psychology*. New York: Psychology Press, pp. 15–38; Borkenau, P. et al, 2004. 'Thin slices of behavior as cues of personality and intelligence'. *Journal of Personality*, 86, pp. 599–614; Kenny, D. A., 2004. 'PERSON: a general model of interpersonal perception'. *Personality and Social Psychology Review*, 8, pp. 265–280.

Traits and states: Eysenck, 1967; Eysenck, H. J., and Eysenck, M. W., 1994. *Happiness: Facts and Myths*. London: Taylor and Francis; Mischel, W., 1968. *Personality and Assessment*. London: Wiley; Funder, D. C., and Ozer, D. J., 1983. 'Behavior as a function of the situation'. *Journal of Personality and Social Psychology*, 44, pp. 107–112; Caspi, A., Elder, G. H., and Bem, D. J., 1987. 'Moving against the world: life-course patterns of explosive children'. *Developmental Psychology*, 23 (2), pp. 308–313; Pervin, L. A., 1994. 'A critical analysis of current trait theory'. *Psychological Enquiry*, 5, pp. 103–113; *and set-point theory*: Lucas, R. E., 2007. 'Adaptation and the set-point model of subjective well-being: does happiness change after major life events?' *Current Directions in Psychological Science*, 16, pp. 75–79; Headey, B., 2008. 'Life goals matter to happiness: a revision of set-point theory'. *Social Indicators Research*, 86, pp. 213–231; *and temperament*: Fajkowska, M., 2018. 'Personality traits: hierarchically organized systems'. *Journal of Personality*, 86, pp. 36–54; Eysenck, H. J., 1972. 'Human typology, higher nervous activity, and factor analysis', in Nebylitsin, V. D., and Gay, J. A. (eds.), *Biological Bases of Individual Behaviour*. New York: Academic Press.

Classification of traits: Wiggins, J. S., 1979. 'A psychological taxonomy of trait-descriptive terms: the interpersonal domain'. *Journal of Personality and Social Psychology*, 37 (3), pp. 395–412; Wiggins, J. S. (ed.) 1996. *The Five-Factor Model of Personality: Theoretical Perspectives*. New York: Guilford.

Questionnaires: Cattell, R. B., Eber, H. W., and Tatsuoka, M. M., 1970. *Handbook for the 16PF Questionnaire*. Savoy, IL: Institute for Personality and Ability Testing; Costa, P. T., and McCrae, R. R., 1992. *Revised NEO Personality Inventory (NEO PI-R) and NEO*

Five-Factor Inventory (NEO-FFI). Lutz, Florida: Psychological Assessment Resources; McCrae, R. R., and John, O. P., 1992. 'An introduction to the five factor model and its applications'. *Journal of Personality*, 60, pp. 175–215; Eysenck, H. J., 1975. *Manual of the Eysenck Personality Questionnaire*. London: Hodder & Stoughton; Cattell, R. B., Eber, H. W., and Tatsuoka, M. M., 1977. *Handbook for the 16 Personality Factor Questionnaire,* Champaign, IL: IPAT; Briggs Myers, I., and McCaulley, M. H., 1985. *Manual: A Guide to the Development and Use of the Myers–Briggs Type Indicator.* Sunnyvale, CA: Consulting Psychologists Press; *and self-reporting:* Wiggins, 1996.

Value of the lexical approach: Block, J., 1995. 'A contrarian view of the five factor approach to personality disorder'. *Psychological Bulletin,* 117, pp. 187–215; Wiggins, 1996; Goldberg, L. R., 1981. 'Language and individual differences: the search for universals in personality lexicons', in Wheeler, L. (ed.), *Review of Personality and Social Psychology, Volume 2.* Beverly Hills, CA: Sage, pp. 141–165.

Blended traits: Briggs, S. R., 1988. 'Shyness: introversion or neuroticism?' *Journal of Research in Personality,* 22, pp. 290–307.

Traits and context: Kagan, J., 2010. *The Temperamental Thread: How Genes, Culture, Time and Luck Make Us Who We Are.* New York: The Dana Foundation.

Personality as a hierarchy: Fajkowska, 2018.

Childhood traits and personality: Kagan, J., 2007. *What is Emotion? History, Measures, and Meaning.* New Haven, CT: Yale University Press; Kagan, 2010; Hazan, C., and Shaver, P. R., 1990. 'Love and work: an attachment-theoretical perspective'. *Journal of Personality and Social Psychology,* 59, pp. 270–280;

Proactive/reactive animal behaviour: Koolhaas, J. M. et al, 1999. 'Coping styles in animals: current status in behaviour and stress-psychology'. *Neuroscience and Biobehavioural Reviews,* 23, pp. 925–935.

Temperament and biological preparedness: Kagan, 2007; Kagan, 2010; Carter, S. et al, 2008. 'Development of temperament symposium'. The Philoctetes Centre. Available at: https://www.youtube.com/watch?v=kEU-az-NzTc; Roberts, B. W., and Jackson, J. J., 2008. 'Sociogenomic personality psychology'. *Journal of Personality,* 76, pp. 1523–1544; Liu, N., and Pan, T., 2015. 'RNA epigenetics'. *Translational Research,* 165, pp. 28–35.

Personality as an interrelated dynamic system: Murray, H. A., and Kluckhohn, C., 1953. 'Outline of a conception of personality', in Kluckhohn, C., and Murray, H. A. (eds.), *Personality in Nature, Society, and Culture.* 2nd Edition. New York: Knopf, pp. 3–32; McCrae, R. R., 2009. 'The physics and chemistry of personality'. *Theory & Personality,* 18, pp. 670–687; Wiggins, 1996; Damasio, A., 1999. *The Feeling of What Happens: Body and Emotion in the Making of Consciousness.* London: William Heinemann.

8

PSYCHOLOGIES

II – Conflict and energy

A wilful arousal of enthusiasm . . .

Last run before the Dress Rehearsal. The play drags, the lines come out stilted, acting is artless. Lunch. The slough of despond! One hour later, a 'speed run' (what in English is called, reasonably, an 'Italian' run and the French call, for reasons unknown even to them, a 'Spanish'). People run about. The director waves his arms in the air. The tragic characters put on funny accents. The play flies! After that, at the first Dress Rehearsal, the lines flow, people 'give and take', acting is free and easy. Yet, on the timepiece hanging around the neck of the hard-put-upon DSM, the timing is the same – no difference on the clock between the dregs and the heights. Why? What has happened during the speed run that made such a difference? No one could measure it, tell you its colour or its taste, but we felt it in our bones – *energy* was unleashed.

The theatre director and anthropologist Eugenio Barba marks the distinction between our normal or "daily" state of energy and a heightened or "extra-daily" form appropriate for the stage. The latter seems to involve a wanton "wasting of energy". In Japan, Barba recalls, at the end of a particularly good performance, spectators thank the actors with one of the loveliest expressions I have encountered in the theatre: *otsukaresama*. Literally translated, this means, "You have tired yourself for me".

Where does it come from, this special energy under whose influence, Peter Brook says, "invention follows invention in lightning chain reaction"? Psychologists who draw conclusions about the workings of the human mind from animal studies assert that the thing that moves us before anything else has had a chance to leave a trace on a newborn's brain is the instinct to forage for food, and, thus, to *search*. This, they say, is the fundamental emotion that we experience as powerful surges of interest and the arousal of enthusiasm for things and people. It is also worth recalling that the keystone of the complex edifice of characteristics, objectives, and actions

Stanislavski constructed was the actor's will to undertake the role. The wilful arousal of enthusiasm for the role, followed by the purposeful direction of attention to its features, is a necessary precondition for the organic emergence of characteristics. It is this most basic of emotions my friend working on Viola first needed to connect with in *herself*, as a pre-condition for engaging with the emotions of the character: Viola's fears, lust, or naughty sense of play and creativity. The question remains, however, how to entice this energy to rise in the dulled spirit with which most of us come to rehearsals, how to recognise its presence, how to convoke it to the acting feast at will? How to sharpen it and turn it into physical reality?

The, essentially descriptive, psychology of traits, types, and temperaments I surveyed thus far has little to say on this topic. On the other hand, the psychoanalytic approach places the concept of energy at the very heart of its model of the psyche. In one of his earliest published papers, Freud wrote:

> In mental functions something is to be distinguished – a quota of affect or sum of excitation – which possesses all the characteristics of a quantity (though we have no means of measuring it), which is capable of increase, diminution, displacement and discharge, and which is spread over the memory-traces of ideas somewhat as an electric charge is spread over the surface of the body.
>
> *(2010, p. 314)*

His model conceives of the psyche as a dynamic system in perpetual motion, like the mechanism of a clock, pulled by a number of opposing levers and counter-levers, weights and balances. The movements of the psyche produce a form of energy, Freud's "sum of excitation" or libido. Jung later widened the scope of the term libido, giving it a more general sense of desire, longing, and urge. For him, libido denotes an overwhelming "hunger", an *appetitus* derived from different sources – a "will to power", for example, as much as Freud's sexual drives – and represents the intensity of the sum total of the energy generated by the psyche. The libido flows like electric current between negative and positive poles; it ebbs and flows between extremes, which Jung refers to as "the opposites". These opposites exist at various levels of the psyche: consciousness is opposed to unconsciousness, thinking to feeling, extraversion to introversion. The further apart the opposites are, the greater the energy. Moreover, the opposites are the precondition of the existence of energy – no opposites, no noticeable energy. Jung even describes the psyche as a play with characters, in which the characters are clusters of energies interacting with one another.

Throughout the twentieth century, psychoanalysis and the arts have exchanged such key concepts and processes, not least with regard to issues of personality and identity. For decades, the arts were enthralled by the admixture of quasi-medical procedures and mystical 'performance' that psychoanalysis offered. For its part, as the theatre historian Alan Read argues, ever since the young Freud became fascinated during his Paris apprenticeship by public demonstrations of cure by hypnotism, the psychoanalytic method has also had a tinge of theatricality about it, something of the shamanistic practices of the confessor or the exorcist. Psychoanalysis and performance alike are permeated with a sense of play, of a 'game' being conducted according to rules both parties agree to follow. Whether explicitly or by osmosis, psychoanalytic thought has, thus, helped to shape the ways in which plays are constructed and many actors work. And, as philosopher Patrick Campbell notes, the influence was mutual:

> In making the hidden visible, the latent manifest, in laying bare the interior landscape of the mind and its fears and desires through a range of signifying practices, psychoanalytic processes are endemic to the performing arts. Similarly, the logic of performance infuses psychoanalytic thinking, from the 'acting out' of hysteria to the 'family romance' of desire.
>
> *(2001, p. 1)*

A suitable case for treatment

So, to grasp something of the intersection between psychoanalytical views of personality and theatre character, "look here upon this picture . . .":

> The woman is fifty-four, about medium height . . . Her face . . . must once have been extremely pretty, and is still striking . . . Her nose is long and straight, her mouth wide with full, sensitive lips . . . Her high forehead is framed by thick, pure white hair. Accentuated by her pallor and white hair, her dark brown eyes appear black. They are unusually large and beautiful, with black brows and long curling lashes. What strikes one immediately is her extreme nervousness. Her hands are never still . . . In contrast to this, her expression shows more of that strange aloofness which seems to stand apart from her nerves and the anxieties which harry them . . . Her most appealing quality is the simple, unaffected charm of a shy convent-girl youthfulness she has never lost – an innate unworldly innocence. There is at times an uncanny gay, free youthfulness in her manner, as if in spirit she were released to become again, simply and without self-consciousness, the naive, happy, chattering schoolgirl of her convent days. [At other times] she hides deeper within herself and finds refuge and release in a dream where present reality is but an appearance . . .

". . . and on this":

> The man has a pleasing external appearance, has a reserved countenance, is serious and somewhat arrogant. His measured, noble stride catches one's attention – it takes him a good while to walk across the room; it is evident that he avoids – or conceals – any haste or excitement . . . When he discusses his relationship to his dearly loved mother, he quite obviously accentuates his noble pose in an effort to master his excitement: even when tears well up in his eyes and his voice becomes choked, he raises his handkerchief to dry

his eyes with the same dignified composure. This much is clear: his behaviour, whatever its origin might be, protects him against violent emotions. His lordly behaviour is closely related to a secondary character trait, a tendency to deride his fellow men and the malicious joy he derives from seeing them come to grief.

The first of these pen portraits is taken from the stage directions describing Mary Tyrone in Eugene O'Neill's *The Long Day's Journey into Night*. The second, with slight adaptations, is psychoanalyst Wilhelm Reich's description of one of his patients.

O'Neill could not possibly have expected some of the specific physical attributes ("long curling lashes, nose long and straight, mouth wide with full, sensitive lips", etc.) to be replicated by the various actors who were going to play Mary. This is the portrait of the woman as *he* imagines her. The point of including such physical details in the stage directions, however, is that they are rich in intimations of psychological correlatives. Sometimes these are direct ("her hands are never still"), at others more impressionistic: the 'dark-eyed Irish beauty who retains a convent-girl's shy charm' is someone we can picture as both a physical and a psychological type. O'Neill brings together physical traits, gestures, and – crucially for this approach – biographical details. And his description points to tensions between outer appearance and what this conceals, which promise to be rich in meaning.

Reich also turns his gaze towards the tension between outer demeanour and inner drives. He continues: "The lordly quality in his behaviour is a *protection* against the excessive extension of his ridicule into *sadistic* activity. The sadistic fantasies are not repressed; they are gratified in ridiculing others and warded off in the aristocratic pose". Patient and character alike seem ready for the analyst's couch. And, unlike trait psychology, the psychoanalytic approach does not simply describe what it sees but also offers a view – from a particular angle, granted, but a view none the less – on *why* someone might look and behave in certain ways. Not a 'why' rooted in immutable DNA and pre-natal events that feel so distant, but in life experiences, in a 'biography' with parents, siblings, teachers, and role-models, to which we can relate.

As we have seen, the contemplation of the model starts with a record of the basic data about the character offered by the play: age, social status, family background, and relationships – what the characters say about themselves and what other characters in the play say about them. The actor then translates such data into characteristics: Mary Tyrone might be 'introverted', 'skittish', 'diffident', 'romantic', 'depressive', etc. The next step is to compare inferred characteristics with the behaviours explicitly outlined by the text: is Mary's "detachment" a symptom or a deep-seated trait? In the spirit of the psychoanalytic approach, the actor asks 'what is behind' certain ways of behaving, certain decisions or actions.

Thinking of characters in terms of what they might be hiding, especially from themselves, is a useful approach. Freud's revolutionary idea was to postulate the existence of the unconscious as a vast repository of impulses and desires, repressed in early childhood as an unavoidable part of becoming socialised. Within the internal dynamic of the personality, a few unconscious contents occasionally become available to consciousness; most do not. Freud likened the mind to an iceberg, its tip alone visible to consciousness. Jung uses a richer metaphor:

> Consciousness, no matter how extensive it may be, must always remain the smaller circle within the greatest circle of the unconscious, an island surrounded by the sea; and, like the sea itself, the unconscious yields an endless and self-replenishing abundance of living creatures, a wealth beyond our fathoming.
>
> *(1998, p. 14)*

Reich's and O'Neill's character descriptions cited above are, thus, underpinned by a shared assumption: personality and behaviour are determined by forces outside conscious control. These will not be denied (Freud, it has been said, was at war with the illusion of free will). Stanislavskian acting adopts an equally deterministic perspective on personality. In this view, a cause-and-effect relationship exists, first between formative experiences and character traits, then between these and the character's decisions and actions. Those behaviours that are visible to conscious-ness must, therefore, be interrogated, as they are signifiers of hidden, unconscious forces. The motivations of characters can only be accessed by painstakingly peeling away the skins of outer behaviours. Acting in the mainstream Western tradition is rooted in similar cultural assumptions: characters in plays by Miller or Pinter and in subtle, multi-layered films from Bergman to Tarkovsky to Martin McDonagh are built on this. With certain variations, actors trained in this tradition usually construct their characters on this model and, regardless of period and genre, create two-tier personalities *deliberately*. Certain traits (Judge Brack's bonhomie, Lovborg's nonchalance) are displayed, only to mislead. Enough is hinted at by text and actor to stimulate the spectator to infer what is hidden underneath.

This 'assumption of the hidden' powerfully shapes contemporary understand-ings of acting. Most drama is, of course, concerned with the uncovering of a mystery. A continuous dialogue is always established between the spectator's expectations and events as they actually occur on stage, and these are either con-firmed or disproved. But adopting a view of character as the product of conflicting inner forces shifts the focus away from revelations to do with facts – hidden ele-ments of plot – to the mysteries of inner life. What a character says, and often what it does, are now assumed to be informed by a secret motivation, hidden from the character itself. It will be the actor's business to reveal it.

In the theatre of the mind

The notion of the 'hidden' informs the various psychoanalytic models of personal identity. Such constructs of personality continue to hold powerful sway over the histrionic imagination. Well known though these are, it is, therefore, worth outlining the principal assumptions regarding the structure of personality made by Freud and his followers.

The psychoanalytic perspective sees personality as the product of a fundamental imbalance between the different structures of the psyche. These, principally the unconscious id and the conscious and socially orientated ego, are in conflict and competition with one another. The relative balance between them is set in infancy – the Freudian postulate is that the extent to which children manage the tension between pleasure-seeking erotic impulses and the constraints placed on their fulfilment by reality defines their mature personalities. The Freudian view of personality formation is, therefore, essentially negative – it assumes that the personality is formed as a defence in reaction to fear of external influences, in particular of repressive demands made by the parents. Personality is a product of neurosis and neurosis is the unavoidable consequence of becoming socialised. However, personality traits, initially shaped by fear, are later reinforced by the pleasure principle – distorted instincts are gratified and become the traits on which individuals rely to survive and thrive. Our biographies, the ways in which we take decisions and conduct our lives, are said to be subject to forces of assertion and repression that are in dynamic conflict with one another – hence, the theory is labelled 'psychodynamic'.

Freud starts by positing four phases of psychosexual development: the oral, anal, and phallic phases are described as steps in the gradual development of the child towards a fully integrated, mature stage, the genital. Between birth and around the age of five, infants and young children progress through these phases, which often overlap. During each phase, libido or psychic energy is invested on the mouth, anus, and sexual organs, respectively, parts of the body on which the child relies for satisfaction of its elementary nurturing needs: food, warmth, and affection. One of the tenets of Freudian theory is that children do not progress smoothly through these early stages of development and – as a result of interactions with their environment, their parents first and foremost – are likely to develop 'fixations' on one or the other of these early sources of satisfaction. Transition to the mature, balanced genital stage – in which impulses and desires are controlled and directed towards a socially acceptable and mutually reinforcing relationship with a partner – is not automatic and is, in fact, seldom fully realised. As a result, when reaching maturity, people are prone to behaviour patterns, attachments or eruptions of emotions that appear 'out of character'. Such behaviours actually point to the real make-up of the personality: "We thus realise", Freud writes, "that the phenomenon of types arises precisely from the fact that, of the three main ways of employing the libido in the economy of the mind, one or two have been favoured at the expense of the others".

Mature behaviours are, therefore, traced back to one of the organs which defined the earliest stages of development:

Oral personalities place great emphasis on the mouth, both physically and metaphorically. They enjoy eating and drinking to the point of addiction; when under pressure, they tend to bite their nails, or smoke compulsively. They are also eternal optimists, to the point of credulity. In one of the metaphorical associations that suffuse his writing, Freud suggests that a tendency to believe (to 'swallow') anything one is told is connected to an aspect of oral development – some people are, literally, 'suckers'. Equally, the discovery that one can bite and chew as well as suck turns in some people into a tendency towards 'biting' sarcasm.

If toilet training, the defining event of a child's development between eighteen months and three years of age, proceeds successfully, the resulting personality is likely to be highly productive and creative. If it does not, the mature person will be either messy, disorganised, cruel, and vindictive (the 'anal-expulsive' traits) or – if the child reacts to criticism by withholding faeces – the so-called 'anal-retentive triad' emerges: stinginess, exaggerated tidiness, and intransigence, coupled with an unbending, obsessive attitude to others.

In the phallic stage, which occurs between ages three and five, the focus is on the genital organs. This stage is closely associated with Freud's well-known hypothesis of the Oedipus and Electra complexes: sexual desire towards one parent and consequent enmity towards the other, with their associated fear of castration, envy, guilt, and repression. In their attempt to show that they have not been 'castrated', some men will, in maturity, become compulsive philanderers, others will strive obsessively towards professional or financial success. The reverse of this coin is a life defined by failures in both sexual and work relationships, said to be the outcome of fear and guilt felt for challenging the father. Women who become fixated at this stage are described as overly flirtatious, even provocative, but with a tendency to recoil from the actual sexual act.

The fully integrated 'genital' personality is seen more as an ideal towards which one aspires without necessarily being able to reach it fully.

Later, so-called neo-analytical revisions shifted the emphasis away from the unconscious and toward the role of the ego in the formation of personality. In Erich Fromm's radical reassessment, social influences are given greater weight than instinctual drives. Fromm stresses the formative influence of the "common life experience" to which we are all subjected – social, political, and economic conditions that shape us just as much as, if not more than, the incidents of our childhood. The object of the 'social psychology' thus created becomes the investigation of the ways in which experiences shared by a group – poverty or wealth, rural or urban living, positions within the social hierarchy, professions – define certain common psychic attitudes. While acknowledging as a "given" the instinctual apparatus described by Freud, Fromm argues that this is eminently malleable and is modified by social factors brought to bear on our development through our immediate family relationships. Fromm also rejects the patriarchal, even misogynistic, implications of Freud's view of personality, and stresses that human identities are the joint products of the unconscious and of societal reflections. The individual unconscious is, thus, shaped by social forces and psychic energy emanates from socially determined, not instinctual, drives. The cause-and-effect relationship between erogenous zones and personality traits is, therefore, the reverse of that posited by Freud: what comes first is an embedded psychological 'attitude'. If, during analysis, reference is made to one of the erogenous zones, this is simply "the expression of an attitude toward the world in the language of the body". Thus, Fromm argues, there is nothing anal about the 'anal type' save for the lingering use of certain images that may be linked to anal experiences. This personality type is repositioned as the 'authoritarian type' and associated with the 'psychic attitudes' of the capitalist. The emphasis is also on grouping people according to their 'social character' – the typical character structure which people within a given society exhibit, regardless of individual differences.

A third approach, given strong emphasis in clinical practice in Britain, is the so-called object-relations school. This approach replaces the heavy emphasis both Freud and Fromm placed on instinctual drives and the unconscious with a focus on the ways in which infants bond with their mothers. According to the well-known psychoanalyst Melanie Klein, object relations are established "with the first feeding experience" and develop in the first six months of infancy. During this period, the infant separates the sensations of what is good from what is bad. Contents infused with either positive or negative feelings toward the mother form in the infant's unconscious. This is the first time in which the distinction between 'me' and 'not me' occurs. Positive feelings aroused by the mother's love and nurturing are *introjected* (assimilated or internalised) and idealised. Negative feelings, which arise when that nurturing is withdrawn even temporarily, are *projected* (externalised) on to the mother. From then on, the projection mechanism forms the basis of our relationship with "external objects" – essentially, other people. Introjection is the source of our "internal objects", the symbolic characters who populate the theatres of our minds. Internal and external objects operate side by side and are "always interdependent".

Our internal worlds are, thus, populated by imaginary, archetypal figures loaded with emotional contents, the products of our experiences and of our emotional reactions to these experiences. People constantly seek in the external world equivalents or representatives of these "tenants of the internal world", in Klein's phrase. At first, these are the mother and the father, but then this process extends to other important relationships. The object-relations perspective replaces the idea of early life neurotic fixations with that of *patterns* formed in early childhood in the relationship of infant and parents and which are constantly repeated throughout our adult lives. Recent attempts at marrying this view with the findings of neuroscience argue that the interactions between care-giver and infant lead to the formation of synaptic connections, or networks in the brain, and that these form the basis of behavioural patterns on which the adult relies in later life. It is our interactions with others (a function of the ego) rather than repressed unconscious drives that trigger the release of psychic energy as well as shape it into positive or negative forms. The patterns formed in early childhood are the lens through which we view all our relationships; they give us our sense of who we are. Personality is, therefore, defined by the ways in which we habitually relate to others.

The object-relations school has, therefore, devised its own psychological typology, different from that proposed by Freud. Four scales are used to measure the nature of our interactions with others: the 'alienation' scale measures how easily or not we trust others and our ability to get close to them. People who score high on this scale are suspicious, circumspect, and tend to think that others will fail them. The 'attachment' scale measures how concerned we are about being liked or disliked and how sensitive to rejection. The third scale looks at how 'egocentric' or altruistic we are and at the extent to which we view relationships through the prism of our personal needs. The final scale measures our social competence: the extent to which we are ready to engage openly with others or, on the contrary, to become shy and unresponsive, especially in groups.

Two principles underpin all the psychoanalytic perspectives on personality:

First, the overwhelming importance given to early phases of development, which are said to determine patterns of behaviour throughout life. In order to understand the adult, therefore, one has to understand the child – delving into a person's biography is considered essential. Second, an approach toward understanding people not only as individuals, but also in relation to others who share similar experiences and 'neuroses'.

Jerome Kagan lists a number of major influences that reinforce or contradict the inclinations shaped by an infant's temperament. I think these amplify some of the methods of psychoanalysis and are worth summarising here, as they can also provide a useful check-list when constructing a character model and biography:

1. *Identification with a group* – by the age of four, children are aware of the features they share with their parents and with members of their wider group – colour, race, religion, social class – and begin to identify with these groups. For identification to take place, two conditions are needed: first, children have to recognise the distinctive features they share with others. The other is to experience a 'vicarious emotion', usually pride or shame, when they see something, good or bad, happening to a fellow member of the group. Only when both of these conditions are met does identification take place – most people recognise common features, but fewer experience vicarious emotions.

2. *Gender* – conformity with, or rebellion against, the expectations related to gender common to the child's social group.

3. *Class and ethnicity* – status in the hierarchy. Feelings of superiority and/or inferiority towards other groups.

4. *Sibling position* – these differences have been analysed in numerous studies. One, for example, looked at famous scientists who challenged the orthodoxies of their time and found that, overall, first-born children tended to be trustful of authority, while those born later were sceptical. Copernicus and Darwin, among many others, had older siblings.

5. *Size of community in which one grows up* – is the character in a position to compare itself with lots of people, and so most likely see itself as middling, or with relatively few peers, and so acquire an inflated opinion of its own abilities?

6. *Culture and history* – the values of the era with which characters feel they are associated. One might say: "I am a child of the Sixties", implying libertarianism and tolerance; of others it might be said: "These are Thatcher's children" or "this is typical of millennials".

Whether formative influences are those of early childhood, social, or a dynamic interaction between the two, the psychoanalytic view of personality as the terrain of competing forces provides a nuanced, layered view of the structure of character. If the dynamic encounter between instinctual drives, on the one hand, and relationships, on the other, plays a defining role in personality formation, then dramatic character will also need to be considered as twofold in nature. To be clear: I am not making here the traditional distinction between character and action, between *who* the character 'really' is (its psychological 'essence'), on the one hand, and *what* it does and *how* it behaves (the social aspect), on the other. I am considering the proposition that two forces, very different from one another, are in a dynamic relationship – now in conflict, now cooperating – and contribute to establishing the *core traits* of the character.

At one level, we are in the presence of a character with a strong sense of a unitary 'I'. At the same time, there is also an acknowledgment that internal psychic forces are constantly vying with one another to shape the character's traits and motivate its actions. I am not arguing for an exclusive emphasis on the social aspects of the character, otherwise we would get only stock characters or the rigidities of the socialist–realist stage. The social dimension, while crucial, must not be allowed to overwhelm; but neither must an obsession with sexual or emotional drives. The question for the actor is one of relative emphasis: in some interpretations the instinctual drives will be foregrounded, in others, the social. But, since both formative influences are powerfully represented in the character's make-up, one cannot discard either of them without impoverishing the performance. To return to the case study with which this argument began: if the interpretation is not to remain stuck in psychological solipsism, Antonio the merchant prince will have to be visible, albeit in the background, even when the emphasis is on Antonio the neurotic, and *vice versa*.

Attitudes and functions

The view that personality is the product of not one but a number of factors, that these interact dynamically with one another, and that they can be accurately inferred from behaviours, gave rise to the typology developed by C. G. Jung, who dedicated an entire, highly influential, book to the topic.

To understand Jung's analysis, let us return for a brief moment to my friend still trying to puzzle out the meaning of that splendid ring so contemptuously thrown to the ground: "What means this lady?" Her Viola may respond emotionally – fear of the consequences of the caprice of a great aristocrat on the fate of a poor orphan in disguise. She might respond through her intellect – wry amusement at the poser brought about by the success of her disguise. Again, she might respond intuitively – looking for an instant answer to the puzzle, then almost discarding it with a shrug, before coming back to it from another angle. She might even respond through her senses, her entire being concentrating on the sensations of Olivia's ring which she turns over and over again between her fingers. All these responses are possible in theory, though in practice some make more dramatic sense than others. How will our Viola decide?

In his effort to distance himself from what he saw as the reductionist preoccupation with sexuality, hunger, power, etc., which characterised the work of his predecessors, Jung asks similar questions of the generality of human experience. He asks whether individual differences between people can be attributed to their reactions to the objective world. If so, do these common traits fall into any discernible patterns? Could one bracket such individuals, across time, distance and cultures, into groups with a shared way of looking at the world?

In his book *Psychological Types*, Jung undertakes a wide-ranging survey of modes of thought across 3,000 years of Western and Eastern civilisation and his point of departure is the Classical division into temperaments or humours. (Working in Soviet Russia at around the same time, but starting from a different set of assumptions, Pavlov also followed this model in his own attempt at classifying personalities.) On the basis of his analysis, Jung declares that one can discern a fundamental inclination in individuals towards consistently dealing with the world in accordance with two 'attitude-types' and four 'function-types'. The latter are so described because they are determined by one of the four psychological functions that, according to Jung, make up the human psyche: sensation, thinking, intuition, and feeling. A function is defined as a form of psychic activity that remains constant under varying conditions, but Jung writes:

> I can give no *a priori* reason for selecting these four as basic functions, and can only point out that this conception has shaped itself out of many years' experience. I distinguish these functions from one another because they cannot be related or reduced to one another.
>
> *(1971, p. 437)*

His functions are divided into two pairs: thinking and feeling are "rational", while sensation and intuition are "irrational" functions. Sensation and intuition are "irrational" because through them we expose ourselves to continuous experience (we 'absorb' the environment) without stopping to assess what we perceive or to take decisions about these perceptions. Thinking and feeling, on the other hand, are "rational" because through them we make judgements and take decisions. In order to do this, however, we need to suspend temporarily the collection of data from the environment through our "irrational" functions.

In developmental order, sensation comes first. Jung writes:

> By sensation I understand what the French psychologists call *la fonction du réel* which is the sum total of my awareness of external facts given to me through the function of my senses . . . Sensation tells me that something is: it does not tell me what it is and it does not tell me other things about that something; it only tells me that something is.
>
> *(1990, p. 11)*

Having perceived reality through sensation, we engage our thinking to name our perceptions. We then turn these into abstract concepts and make rational judgements about them. Thinking tells us *what* a thing is.

Intuition is a slightly more elusive concept. For Jung, intuition is fundamentally our capacity to have hunches. Like sensation, intuition is a function of perception: the perception of signals from the environment "so feeble that our consciousness simply cannot take them in". Unlike sensation, however, intuition is "perception via the unconscious" – we are not aware of detecting these "feeble" signals.

Finally, feeling is the second rational function. Unlike thinking, which was concerned with naming the object, feeling, says Jung, is the function through which we assign "value" to things. Feeling tells you whether a thing "is acceptable or agreeable or not. It tells you what a thing is worth . . ."

Jung further argues that mature personalities develop in accordance with the "best foot foremost" principle: that people recognise early in life that one or the other of these functions secures approval and success and, therefore, tend to rely on it and underplay the others. As a result, personalities are shaped by the habitual reliance on one of the functions and Jung describes a 'Sensing type', a 'Feeling type' and so on:

> People who have a good mind prefer to think about things and to adapt by thinking. Other people who have a good feeling function are good social mixers, they have a great sense of values; they are real artists in creating feeling situations and living by feeling situations. Or a man with a keen sense of objective observation will use his sensation chiefly, and so on. The dominating function gives each individual his particular kind of psychology.
>
> *(1990, p. 16)*

These preferences form the basis for his classification of personalities into 'psychological types' corresponding to sensation, thinking, intuition, and feeling. These are mainly theoretical constructs, however, as one would be hard put to find 'pure' types, entirely dominated by one of the functions. The 'types' give only a general orientation and they have sometimes been described as providing a good compass, but a poor map. Jung himself spoke of them as "somewhat Galtonesque family portraits", stressing their inevitable tendency to oversimplify human nature. All one can say, therefore, is that a person is *predominantly* sensitive, or a thinker, or has the weighty presence of a sensuous type.

However, such reductions are necessary if one is to accept the two underlying principles behind a model of the personality based on functions:

a. that in any individual one and only one of the functions is fully developed, while the other three are in various states of underdevelopment;
b. that the functions are in a dynamic relationship, either opposing or helping each other.

In consequence, Jung and his disciples establish a hierarchy between the functions. The four functions are designated:

a. The *superior*, dominant or primary function – this is the most developed function, the one that the individual will bring most into play. The superior function is characterised by confidence, stability, and aplomb, and determines the 'type' of the individual.
b. Alongside it comes the *auxiliary* function, a "helper function that is slightly unconscious". While less developed than the superior function, it is "nonetheless accessible and useful to the person in his or her daily life". The auxiliary function is taken from across the rational–irrational divide: thus, for example, if the superior function is sensation, the auxiliary function will have to be either thinking or feeling but can never be intuition.
c. A *tertiary* function. This is not strictly speaking Jung's term, as he tends to refer to the second and third functions in one breath under the generic term "auxiliary". However, contemporary Jungian theorists point out that this third function is rarely developed sufficiently to 'help' the superior function and thus warrant the name of auxiliary. The term "tertiary" is therefore preferred, linking it to . . .
d. The fourth or *inferior* function. This is the function diametrically opposed to the superior function. In a thinking type, feeling is the inferior function, in a sensation type, intuition, and *vice versa*. The inferior function lies deepest in the conscious psyche and is, therefore, laden with unconscious contents, emotion in particular. This function tends to bring into consciousness vitiated perceptions and to play havoc with the order established by the superior function. It is, none the less enormously important as an engine for personality development. According to Jung, its integration with the superior function is one of the chief goals of psychic development.

In any case, a particular personality is a 'cocktail' of the four functions, mixed in various degrees. Thus, one person can be said to be primarily a Sensing type, but to use feeling as the "auxiliary" function, or *vice versa*.

Each function has its own peculiar, characteristic energy. This energy, says Jung, derives from our conscious self, from our ego. The ego is positioned, as it were, at the centre of the four functions and directs its energy, its will to engage with the world, towards its preferred function. Think of Viola's ring as a pebble thrown into a lake: it causes ripples of psychological energy. The substance of the ripples is not determined by the stone, but by the water. The functions are the four 'lakes' open to the actor. She will decide by using her strongest function, by putting her 'best foot foremost'. The transformative actor, however, will be guided not by her own dominant function, but by that chosen for the character: if Viola is a feeling type she will react through fear, if a thinking type through wry amusement, and so on.

Just as they incline towards one or the other of the functions, people also display preferences for one or the other *directions* of energy. Psychic energy moves forward from the 'I' to the object in order to furnish the needs of consciousness; it moves backwards, away from the world and towards the psyche in order to fulfil the needs of the unconscious. These basic inclinations divide mankind into "extravert" and "introvert" categories, the two "attitudes" which, in addition to the functions, define personalities. The categories do not exclude each other and Jung writes, "When you call somebody an introvert, you mean that he prefers an introverted habit, but he has his extraverted side too. We all have both sides . . ." The terms extravert and introvert have become common currency – they describe the two directions of the flow of psychic energy, but they refer primarily to two distinct ways of relating to the world. They are, in other words, categories of personality, broader than the four functions and arching over them. Jungians, therefore, speak of an 'introvert thinking type', 'an extravert sensing type", etc. – eight such types in all. A detailed description of each of the types is beyond the scope of this book, but to get a sense of how this typology works in practice, here are a couple of descriptions. The first deals with the overall 'sensation' type, with little attempt at nuance:

> The sensation type takes everything as it comes, experiences things as they are, no more and no less; no imagination plays around his experiences: no thought attempts to look deeper into them or explore their mysteries – a spade is a spade; neither is any real valuation made; what counts is the strength and pleasure of the sensation.
>
> *(Fordham, 1991, p. 42)*

The typology can be further refined by introducing the 'attitude'. Thus, the 'extraverted sensation type' is

> . . . represented in someone whose gift and specialised function is to sense and relate in a concrete and practical way to outer objects. Such people observe everything, smell everything, and on entering a room know almost at once how many people are present. Afterward, they always know whether Mrs. So-and-So was there and what dress she had on.
>
> *(Hillman and Franz, 1986, p. 27)*

Not a million miles away from descriptions of characters . . .

However, modern clinical analysts tend to use the typology sparingly – when it comes to the complex personalities of individual patients these broad definitions are considered somewhat limiting. When it comes to analysing theatre characters, on the other hand, they combine to offer interesting possibilities: not only does the Jungian model allow for a multi-faceted structure of the character, it also offers a method for grouping characteristics into cognate families. The psychological traits of the character can be assigned to one or other of the functions and attitudes. One of the functions is likely to have listed against it a larger number of traits than the others, indicating that it is the "superior" function, the way in which the character puts its "best foot foremost". Even more interesting, however, are those traits that, while not as numerous, are, none the less, noticeable and coalesce against the auxiliary function. These give the character structure its complexity and depth – the character is 'this', but also 'that'. Finally, and I think most rewarding, is the notion that the character might possess an 'inferior' function – the direct opposite of its dominant characteristics, against which it constantly strives.

It has often been observed that characters – just like people in daily life – have a strange tendency to believe themselves to be the exact opposite of their true natures, at least at the start of their journeys. Lear sees himself as logical, Gloucester as authoritative, Edgar as analytical. According to Marie-Louise von Franz, Jung's close collaborator:

> This comes from the fact that the inferior function subjectively feels itself to be the real one; it feels itself the most important, most genuine attitude. So, a thinking type, because he knows that everything in his life matters from the feeling aspect, will assure you that he is a feeling type. It does no good, therefore, to think what matters most when trying to discover one's type; rather ask: 'What do I habitually do most?'
>
> *(Hillman and Franz, 1986, p. 20)*

In theatre terms, one could therefore consider that a character is formed by going away from its opposite function and then waging a constant struggle to keep it at bay. Pentheus, the tyrannical king in *The Bacchae*, for example, could be played as a Sensing type (solid, stolid, weighty). His inferior function is, thus, intuition – the very mercurial, unpredictable, and therefore dangerous qualities represented by Dionysus, the stranger whose appearance in the city is (at first glance) so furiously resented. But, in the Jungian view, Pentheus actually secretly relishes the arrival of Dionysus to his city, because it fulfils a subconscious need to deal with the Dionysian 'once and for all'. This analysis may go some way toward explaining the psychological roots of the phenomenon of the 'great illusion' to which so many characters (Harpagon, Ekdaal, and Jimmy Porter spring to mind, out of hundreds of possible examples) are prone and which often leads actors astray. From the psychoanalytical perspective, it is this deeply hidden motivation that generates the special form of acting energy of which Brook, Barba, and others were in such awe. Moreover, considering the independent character as a cocktail of functions and attitudes that generate specific energies implies that these, like all forms of energy, can be transmuted one into the other. Psychological transformations are, therefore, made possible by the deliberate activation and manipulation of the four functions. As Jung puts it:

> Psychological functions are usually controlled by the will . . . When the functions are controlled they can be excluded from use, they can be suppressed, they can be selected, they can be increased in intensity, they can be directed by will power, by what we call intention.
>
> *(1990, p. 15)*

Art or anti-art?

Psychoanalytically inspired views of personality, including the postulate of universal neurosis and the typologies based on it, have penetrated popular consciousness to the extent that some key terms are now part of common parlance. Someone who is particularly meticulous, perhaps to the point of pedantry, might be described as 'anally retentive', a slightly oily charmer is 'libidinous', a friendly, outgoing, and sociable person is 'extravert', a self-centred person is 'narcissistic'. Such terms represent vernacular simplifications of their original, complex meanings in psychoanalytical thought. None the less, they have become shortcuts for describing personality, and actors readily use them when examining characters. They are useful because they describe, however superficially, recognisable groupings within which it is possible, as well as tempting, to place individual behaviours. Other approaches rooted in adaptations of psychoanalytical concepts (more or less well understood), including such widely known techniques as sense and emotion memory, have been incorporated into processes designed to explore the actor's inner resources. These are not my concern here, and I note Uta Hagen's sensible caution:

> There are teachers who actually force actors into dealing with something buried (their response to the death of a parent, or the trauma of a bad accident). What results is hysteria or worse, and is, in my opinion, anti-art.
>
> *(1973, p. 49)*

Even when kept within appropriate boundaries, a discussion of character through the lenses of psychoanalytic thought and practice is of a different order than the scientific frameworks deployed elsewhere in this book. The psychoanalytical method has been challenged repeatedly on the grounds that it falls short of the exigencies of scientific scrutiny. As noted in the Introduction, the principal objection is that the claims of psychoanalysis are founded on observational data alone, made by individual practitioners without external, objective corroboration. This so-called 'qualitative' approach is open to the criticism that writers favour those cases that support their perspectives: Freud, for one, based his theory on adult patients, yet wrote extensively about childhood development. Moreover, it is often noted that, from Freud onwards, key writers on psychoanalysis drew far-reaching conclusions from a relatively small number of case studies. These pale in comparison with cross-population studies drawing data from thousands of samples, the stock-in-trade of scientific psychology. As a result, not only are psychoanalytical conclusions open to the challenge that they may not apply outside individual cases, they also often strike one as somewhat literal and naïve, if not downright tendentious. Psychoanalyst Felix Deutsch, to take but one example, describes interpreting a patient's tendency to turn away from him by crossing her legs but never completing the posture as a sign of her thoughts of defiance against her mother and "a wishful turning to her father". Such interpretations are inherently subjective, shaped by the observer's viewpoint and biases rather than by the objects of study. One researcher's findings are, therefore, likely to be different from another's. Paradoxically, for actors this very subjectivity is an asset, not a hindrance: individual actors will bring their own psychological contents to the interpretation of fictional character data. Not only does it not matter that these will differ from another actor's insights, but this can be a positive advantage.

The other main criticism of the psychoanalytical method revolves around the so-called 'defensive reaction formation'. Let us say that a researcher wanted to test the oft-cited supposition that anally retentive personalities exhibit an excess of tidiness, precision, and efficiency. When checked against a group of subjects, the data may well show that this was indeed the case. But it may also show that anally retentive people are, in fact, inefficient, vague, and messy. The psychoanalyst will justify this finding by saying, "Ah, yes, but what the data had recorded was really a defence against the underlying neurosis. These people are obsessively neat, this causes them a great deal of anxiety, and their coping mechanism is to become messy." Psychoanalytic theory always assumes that the ego erects defences against the potential ravages of repressed cravings and that, as a result, these emerge in highly modified forms, whether in dreams or in odd behaviours. There is no way out of this form of circular reasoning: if the data fit, they validate the theory; if they do not fit, they are explained away as distortions caused by defensive mechanisms.

Again, what is clearly a matter of concern to the scientific investigator can be a gift for the actor. Actors playing Angelo will be familiar with the supposition that the character's self-image as a super-efficient civil servant disguises repressed sexuality and sadism. Whether these are then assigned to the inner struggle between 'anally retentive' and 'anally expulsive' tendencies in his personality will matter very little, if at all. What will matter is the window this analysis opens into character formation: the fundamental assumption of conflicting forces shaping the personality and the journey towards insight and revelation traced by the character arc. The outcome of the active contemplation and embodiment of a model is what Jung calls the "transcendent function", the psychological state that "arises from a union of conscious and unconscious contents as well as the real and imaginary".

One should also acknowledge that certain Freudian observations, in particular in relation to his taxonomy of type, have actually been validated by scientific studies. Members of a group assessed as having high levels of anal anxieties were also found to be obstinate and compulsively neat. Correlations have also been found between oral imagery, obesity, and alcoholism.

Scientifically validated or not, psychoanalytical approaches continue to exercise a considerable pull. It has been observed that this is in large part due to their intuitive appeal: key concepts are conveyed through suggestive metaphors and build what even contemporary standard postgraduate texts on psychology still consider to be the most comprehensive and internally coherent picture of the human psyche. Regardless of scientific scepticism, these metaphors capture aspects of reality in ways that we find emotionally attractive and, as a result, psychoanalytically inspired processes are prominent in mainstream Western approaches to acting.

In his rehearsal diary, Antony Sher punctuates his account of working on Richard III with entries about real-life sessions with Monty Berman, his analyst. In a funny–serious passage, he describes seeking the latter's advice:

> We put Richard on the psychiatrist's couch and analysed him in depth.
> 'I suppose I would have to start with that mother.' [Monty] points out that there isn't a single moment in the play when the Duchess of York talks of Richard without contempt and hatred.
> 'What is it like to be hated by your mother?' . . . Monty explains that, as Richard hasn't received love as a child, he won't be able to show any himself; hence his contempt for human life.
> An absence of love. Caused by a hating mother. This is what I will base my performance on. But I will have to be quite secretive about it, because it sounds so corny – his mother didn't love him.
>
> *(2014, locs. 2017–2046)*

Sher's description illustrates both the attraction and the limitations of the psychoanalytical method: it prompts consideration of formative experiences, but ultimately always ends up with the relationship with the parents. One might perhaps take the next step and ask oneself "how would I feel, what would I do, if I had been unloved by my mother to that extent?", but I am not sure most actors could access the sensation of that absence of love with the intensity experienced by a child. Sher eventually transcends "his mother didn't love him" and finds Richard's overriding motivation in his deformity: his biting wit, he decides, is a form of self-defence; his profoundest drive is to revenge himself, to destroy a world that hated him. 'Mother-drives' and social drives are united. By his own admission, Sher has always felt himself an outsider – a feeling with deep roots in his national, ethnic, and sexual identities as a South African-born, Jewish, gay man. The actor's personal drives are brought to coincide with those of the character. When this transition between cerebral analysis and deeply felt identification occurs, actor drive and character motivation meet.

Whether it is then helpful to drill down to their causes in terms of infantile neuroses is doubtful. The emphasis on infantile experiences can easily lead up an artistic *cul de sac*, as in the notorious 'phallic' Brook–Gielgud production of Seneca's *Oedipus*. Deciding how Falstaff may or may not have felt about his mother's breast is certainly a blind alley; yet thinking of him as 'oral' may extend to the way in which he uses language as much as to the way in which he eats, drinks, and kisses. It might be useful to explore, as Stanislavski did, the fact that Desdemona's mother may be long dead and how this affected her relationship with her authoritarian father; but is it useful to ask whether Othello was an only child or had several siblings? I don't think so. To take another example, working on John Ford's *'Tis Pity She's A Whore*, asking when, in their childhood, Giovanni's and Annabella's mother died and how this affected their sibling relationship is relevant; to ask whether Friar Bonaventura is motivated by a homosexual attachment to his brilliant student may be relevant; to ask whether Soranzo is violently jealous because of an unresolved Oedipus complex is certainly not.

Bibliography

Arousal of energy: Barba, E., 1994. *The Paper Canoe: A Guide to Theatre Anthropology*, translated by R. Fowler. London: Routledge; Brook, P., 1968. *The Empty Space*. New York: Avon Books; Benedetti, J., 1988. *Stanislavski: A Biography*. London: Methuen; *in infants*: Izard, C. E., 1978. 'On the ontogenesis of emotions and emotion–cognition relationships in infancy', in Lewis, M., and Rosenblum, L. A. (eds.), *The Development of Affect. Genesis of Behaviour, Volume 1*. Boston, MA: Springer; Panksepp, J., 2005. 'On the embodied neural nature of core emotional affects'. *Journal of Consciousness Studies*, 12 (8–10), pp. 158–184; Panksepp, J., 2014. 'Toward the constitution of emotional feelings: synergistic lessons from Izard's differential emotions theory and affective neuroscience'. *Emotion Review*, 7 (2), pp. 1–6.

Energy and the psyche: Freud, S., 2010. 'The neuro-psychoses of defence'. In *Complete Works (CW)*. Ivan Smith Online Edition: https://openlibrary.org/works/OL16678137W/ Freud_Complete_Works; Jung, C. G., 1960. 'On psychic energy', in *Collected Works, Volume 8: The Structure and Dynamics of the Psyche*, translated by R. F. C. Hull. 2nd Edition. London: Routledge and Kegan Paul.

Psychoanalysis and theatre: Read, A., 2001. 'The placebo of performance: psychoanalysis in its place', in Campbell, P., and Kear, A. (eds.), *Psychoanalysis and Performance*. London: Routledge, pp. 147–166; Campbell, P., 2001. 'Introduction', in Campbell, P., and Kear, A. (eds.), *Psychoanalysis and Performance*. London: Routledge; Walsh, F., 2013. *Theatre and Therapy*. London: Palgrave Macmillan.

Psychoanalytic 'Character Analysis': Reich, W., 2013. *Character Analysis*, translated by V. R. Carfagno. 3rd Edition. Farrar, Straus and Giroux: Kindle Edition; Jung, C. G., 1998. *The Psychology of the Transference*, translated by R. F. C. Hull. London: Routledge; Allport, G. W., 1937. *Personality: A Psychological Interpretation*. New York: Holt; *and determinism*: Brown, N. O., 1985. *Life Against Death, The Psychoanalytical Meaning of History*. 2nd Edition. Wesleyan University Press: Kindle Edition; *and Stanislavski*: Pitches, J., 2006. *Science and the Stanislavsky Tradition of Acting*. Abingdon: Routledge.

Psychosexual development: overall views: Freud, 'An outline', in *CW*, 2010; Fenichel, O., 1945. *The Psychoanalytic Theory of Neurosis*. New York: Norton; Neel, A., 1971. *Theories of Psychology*. London: University of London Press; Carver, C. F., and Scheier, M. F., 2004. *Perspectives on Personality*. 5th Edition. London: Pearson Education; *and libido*: Freud, 'Libidinal types', in *CW*, 2010; *and Fromm's alternative view*: Fromm, E., 1970. 'The method and function of an analytic social psychology', in *The Crisis of Psychoanalysis, Essays on Freud, Marx and Social Psychology*. New York: Henry Holt, pp. 135–162; Funk, R., 1998. 'Erich Fromm's concept of social character'. *Social Thought and Research*, 21 (1&2), pp. 215–230.

Object Relations: Klein, M., 1946. 'Notes on some schizoid mechanisms'. *International Journal of Psychoanalysis*, 27, pp. 99–110; Klein, M., *Envy and Gratitude, and Other Works 1946–1963*. London: Vintage; *and neuroscience*: Wilkinson, M., 2006. *Coming into Mind, The Mind–Brain Relationship: A Jungian Clinical Perspective*. London: Routledge; *and trait measurement*: Bell, M., Billington, R., and Beckler, B., 1986. 'A scale for the assessment of object relations: reliability, validity, and factorial invariance'. *Journal of Clinical Psychology*, 42, pp. 733–741.

Influences on temperament: Kagan, J., 2010. *The Temperamental Thread: How Genes, Culture, Time and Luck Make Us Who We Are*. New York: The Dana Foundation.

Jungian typology: Jung, C. G., 1971. *Collected Works, Volume 6: Psychological Types*, translated by R. F. C. Hull. London: Routledge and Kegan Paul; Jung, C. G., 1990.

Analytical Psychology: Its Theory and Practice (The Tavistock Lectures). London: Routledge; Fordham, F., 1991 (1953). *An Introduction to Jung's Psychology*. London: Penguin; Hillman, J., and Franz, M.-L. v., 1986. *Lectures on Jung's Typology*. New York: Spring; Spoto, A., 1995. *Jung's Typology In Perspective*. Asheville, NC: Chiron.

"Anti-art": Hagen, U. with Frankel, H., 1973. *Respect for Acting*. New York and London: Collier Macmillan.

Psychic energy residing in the id: Freud, 'An outline' and 'New lectures'. In *CW*, 2010.

Qualitative approaches in psychoanalytical observation: examples of: Freud, 2010; Jung, 1998; Deutsch, F., 1947. 'Analysis of postural behaviour'. *Psychoanalytic Quarterly*, 16, pp. 195–213; *scientific validation*: Rosenwald, G. C., 1972. 'Effectiveness of defences against anal impulse arousal'. *Journal of Consulting and Clinical Psychology*, 39, pp. 292–298; Masling, J. M., Rabie, L., and Blondheim, S. H., 1967. 'Obesity, level of aspiration, and Rorschach and TAT measures of oral dependence'. *Journal of Consulting Psychology*, 31, pp. 233–239; Bertrand, S., and Masling, J. M., 1969. 'Oral imagery and alcoholism'. *Journal of Abnormal Psychology*, 74, pp. 50–53; *and "coherent model"*: Carver and Scheier, 2004.

Limits of application to acting: Sher, A., 2014. *The Year of the King: An Actor's Diary and Sketchbook*. Kindle Edition. London: Nick Hern Books.

9

PSYCHOLOGIES

III – Character on the couch

At the end of the previous chapter, I wrote: "To ask whether Soranzo is violently jealous because of an unresolved Oedipus complex is certainly not helpful . . ."

However, two early readers of that passage, both experienced actors, demurred. Neither of them is heavily 'Method' orientated, yet they both felt that my description tended to place unwarranted boundaries on the application of a psychoanalytic perspective to understanding character. Thus, in relation to Othello, one said, "If I had grown up one of four brothers as part of a boisterous, competitive, and aggressive family group, then I might well include this in my autobiography of this character to help me justify his martial make-up. Actually, having grown up a fairly solitary only child, I could still imagine using it. Together perhaps with a demanding father, another soldier, who drove us all tirelessly towards feats of military and masculine prowess". And again, about Soranzo, "Vigorous, healthy, self-assured, sadistic masculinity of a traditional, old-fashioned kind – who is to say it is not the very paradigm of Oedipal rage?" A sentiment which the second actor, who had himself twice played Giovanni, echoed: "Might I not find an interesting explanation in Soranzo's relationship with his parents for his morbid attraction first to Hippolyta, then to Annabella?" I am not citing these reactions principally in order to qualify my own position, which I still think strikes a reasonable balance between those who find the psychoanalytic approach pregnant with possibilities and those who consider it overly speculative and tendentious. In terms of my theme, I think the interest of such comments lies in the way in which they illustrate how – just as was the case with work on objects or animals – it is not the actual 'psychoanalysis' of the character that matters, but the intensely personal reflections to which the application of a psychoanalytic approach gives rise in the mind of the actor. In particular, posing the question "What is my character's problem?" is often a very useful starting point for the actor's engagement with a role. In order to begin the process of character construction, the actor will need at some point to ask whether a neurosis lies at the heart of the character.

A Super-Objective for life

According to Freud, in early infancy all psychic energy resides in the unconscious, the "id". The id invests this energy in objects, activities, or mental images. The more important the object or image, the more energy is invested in it; the power of this investment is as potent decades later as on the day it was formed and, Freud decrees, "is virtually immortal". What makes us who we are is not – as Descartes would have it – our ability to think, but our desires. In an analogous way, a psychodynamic view of theatre character considers that core characteristics are formed by an equally potent generative force, the Super-Objective, the character's overwhelming desire.

The Super-Objective is one of the best known and most debated – some even say "most misinterpreted" – of Stanislavski's concepts. The Russian term *zadacha* has been variously and confusingly translated as 'objective', 'action', 'task', 'target', 'goal', and so on. Since the 1930s, 'objectives' and 'actions' have often been used in idiosyncratic ways, reflecting the outlooks of particular acting schools and causing generations of English-speaking acting teachers and students endless headaches. In my own teaching practice, I have tried – with moderate success – to simplify matters by replacing them with the 'wants' of the character and the 'means' by which these were achieved. In the newest and most accomplished translation of Stanislavski's work, Jean Benedetti sought to cut through the confusion by translating *zadacha* straightforwardly as "task" – hence "Supertask" replaces the older "Super-Objective". The use of this down-to-earth term chimes with contemporary trends towards emphasising the 'actioning' aspects of Stanislavski's thought: the actor's focus is on establishing a chain of concrete physical 'tasks' and overcoming the psychological 'obstacles' posed by other characters, who are executing their own 'tasks'. The older term 'objective' did, however, contain within it a subtler meaning: an objective is something one strives to achieve, certainly, but also implies an "impulse . . . an inner urge, a desire not yet satisfied". For this reason, as well as because it continues to be the more familiar term, I have decided to retain it here. And since, in certain respects, my argument moves away from traditional understandings of this concept, I thought it worthwhile to look afresh at what Stanislavski has to say about it.

In a well-known chapter in *Creating a Role*, Stanislavski describes in detail his preparatory work for playing Chatski, the central character in *Woe from Wit*, a comedy by the classic Russian writer Alexander Griboyedov. Chatski, a nineteenth-century nobleman, is desperately in love with Sophia, a young coquette. After three years spent abroad, he rushes home on an impulse in order to propose to her, only to find her ill disposed towards him and attentive to other suitors.

In his dissection of the play's opening scene, Stanislavski establishes a hierarchy of objectives. These include immediate physical tasks ("ringing the bell, entering the house, greeting the doorman"), simple psychological actions played on other characters ("to appraise the changes that have taken place in Sophia in my absence; to caress her by look and word; to shake her up with reproaches") and "larger objectives" which capture the main thrust of the action ("to hasten the moment of our meeting, to understand the reasons for her coldness"). The sequence of objectives is further coloured by what Stanislavski calls the "inner tone" of the performance, the "submarine current" of the emotions which overtake the character: is Chatski animated simply by a desire to return home to friends and familiar surroundings, or is he driven into a frenzy by the need to see and touch the object of his desire? The "tone" gives the action its "musical key" (minor – the key of a friend; major – the key of a lover) and eventually its essential tempo.

Underpinning what Stanislavski calls this "score" of the role are the play's "Super-Objective" and the main character's "through-line". Stanislavski sees the Super-Objective above all as the overriding idea of the play, its central theme. In the case of the greats – he cites Shakespeare, Tolstoy, Dostoyevsky, Chekhov – this is assumed to reflect the "spirit" of the writers themselves, their overall visions of human nature and of society. Stanislavski declares: "The Super-Objective is the quintessence of the play. The through line of action is the leitmotif which runs through the entire work". Actors are called upon to put themselves in the service of these central themes. To take a better-known example, Oedipus's Super-Objective might be 'to find the culprit so as to assuage the Gods' wrath and save my city'. Such formulations encapsulate the individual motivation of the character as well as the political message of the play. In order to embody them effectively, actors must find *in themselves* analogous impulses. Stanislavski reasons that what would motivate him to engage in Chatski's rash, if sincere, actions, is "the desire to stop an inexperienced girl from taking a wrong step". With uncommon generosity, he goes on to describe the personal memory-image that he associates with Chatski's motivation: a crush on a little girl he once met as a child. Thus, Stanislavski looks in himself for the urge to act as the character does.

But what of *the character's* motivation? The question "what is it in *Chatski* that makes him fall in love with a girl of fourteen, cultivate this dream for three whole years from thousands of miles away, then rush home on a wild impulse expecting to find his passion reciprocated?" is left unanswered. The actor's question: "What is my character's problem?" now comes to the fore. Where, the actor wonders, are the sources of the action in this character's psychological make-up? If one adopts a psychodynamic view of personality, answers to this question are to be found in the deepest sources of psychological gratification, in the search for the ultimate emotional satisfaction. Yes, characters strive to achieve erotic satisfaction, but they are also driven by other sources of "psychic energy": hunger for power or yearning for serenity, the need to possess (people or material goods, or both), fear of annihilation, and the need for safety, etc.

Chatski, our actor might say, is an idealist, a dreamer, and an obsessive – one of Jung's Feeling types. He is fascinating, yet dangerous for his society, whose stability he threatens (in the play, Sophia reacts to his attempt to 'save her from herself' by declaring him insane). Highly-strung dreamers such as Chatski swing perilously between the impulse to withdraw into their shells and the compulsion to emerge in agitated bouts of self-assertion. Chatski had already 'withdrawn' into an exile that lasted three years. As Stanislavski points out, the play starts with his frantic rush to Moscow, to the girl at whose feet he is going to deposit his heart,

> ...beside myself,
> Two days and nights on end, and never closing eye
> I travelled fast over the many hundred miles, through wind and storm,
> In turmoil, many times I fell ...

and ends with Chatski's equally precipitous flight from Moscow, a gesture of rejection and defiance against the pettiness of Muscovite society. The pendulum swings – the idealist, who had emerged from his shell for a characteristic moment of self-assertion, retires back into it, hurt.

The immediate goal that animates Chatski as he comes on stage is indeed 'to see Sophia in order to propose to her'. But, seen from the point of view of the independent character, the Super-Objective is the force that animates the character throughout its entire life. If Chatski's Super-Objective is 'to save Sophia from an unsuitable marriage', or even 'to get Sophia to agree to marry me', as Stanislavski implies, then these must come to an end when Chatski, despondent, departs from Moscow. Seeing Chatski as a character with a past before the play began as well as a future once it is over, suggests that the vital force that animates him in Moscow will persist in Paris, Venice, or Baden-Baden, wherever his life-long grand tour takes him. Considering the character as independent of the actor means constructing for it what Antonio Damasio calls "an autobiographical self", shaped just as much by its dreams of the future as by its lived past. These dreams are reflections of its deepest drives – *its* Super-Objective, not that of the writer or of the actor. Damasio offers a subtle argument:

> The changes which occur in the autobiographical self over an individual lifetime are not due only to the remodelling of the lived past that takes place continuously and unconsciously, but also to the laying down and the remodelling of the anticipated future. I believe that a key aspect of self evolution concerns the balance of two influences: the lived past and the anticipated future. Personal maturity means that memories of the future we anticipate for the time that may lie ahead carry a large weight in the autobiographical self of each moment. The memories of the scenarios that we conceive as desires, wishes, goals, and obligations exert a pull on the self of each moment. No doubt they also play a part in the remodelling of the lived past, consciously and unconsciously, and in the creation of the person we conceive ourselves to be, moment by moment.
>
> *(1999, pp. 224–225)*

Elizabeth Hapgood, Stanislavski's first translator, notes that Stanislavski had also considered examining Chatski's actions in two more 'keys', the free man and the patriot, but did not get to record his thoughts. To justify his current infatuation to himself, Chatski the 'free man and patriot' (presumably in the sense of 'unconventional' and 'radical') might say: "I wish to struggle, not only for Sophia's integrity, but for that of my country, too." But Chatski's deepest, life-long motivation is more likely to be 'to re-make the world in my image' or 'to find a kindred soul in order to change the world in our image' than in his present circumstances. The Super-Objective of the *play* (Sophia!) triggers the deep-seated motivation or Super-Objective of the *character* ('to re-make the world in my image'); it is the latter which generates the energy that propels the character through life. The immediate objective is a concrete, sensuous reality, part of the Given Circumstances. The character's motivation, however, is an inner event, determined by its deepest psychological inclinations. In the psychological terms outlined earlier, Stanislavski's "inner tone" and "through line" are *states*, changing as situations change; the Super-Objective of the character is rooted in *traits*. This distinction becomes clear when one considers that the same outward behaviour assumes radically different meanings according to the personality which carries them out: we saw how Viola could react to the ring in four different ways, according to the nature of the waters in her 'lake'.

A further phenomenon intervenes in the dialectic between actor and character model; one that has intriguing parallels in the psychoanalytic process. People walk into the therapist's consulting room in the expectation of an 'event' which will ease their pain: the return of affection when this has been withdrawn; a child when their marriage is collapsing; their parents not divorcing; getting their jobs back . . . Yet therapy provides nothing of the sort. Instead of satisfying their concrete needs, it brings them to an understanding of *why* they need them and often to the insight that their expectations were really a disguise for a different kind of need altogether. During analysis, Wilhelm Reich explains, analysands are invited to search for something without necessarily knowing what that is – only that their conduct indicated the need to search.

The search for character motivation often travels on a similar path: the actor starts by thinking the character is motivated by a certain Super-Objective, only to realise, often late in the rehearsal process, that another is actually at play. Olga, the eldest of Chekhov's *Three Sisters*, sees herself (and is constantly described by the others) as an embodiment of the spirit of duty: toward her orphaned younger sisters, her pupils at school, toward the maintenance of civilised values in that coarse garrison town. Her Super-Objective is, therefore, usually formulated on the lines of 'to do my duty' or 'to protect my family'. I always wondered about this and a few years ago, in an excellent production by Declan Donnellan with a Russian cast, my doubts were answered: contrary to expectation, the Olga of that production revealed herself to be a pleasure-seeking, self-centred, and resentful woman. This tall, imperious Olga walked across the stage with determined, long strides, smoked defiantly in public, and was altogether assertive in both voice and body. All of a sudden, the festive luncheon which occupies the first act of the play was bathed in a completely different light: not as the celebration of the younger sister's name-day which Olga dutifully organises, but as an opportunity, eagerly seized, for Olga herself to be the centre of attention of the assembled officers. And, in a startling dramatic moment, Olga's reaction in Act II to her sister's distress at having been molested was one of impatient indifference: those famous lines, ostensibly about being exhausted by the drudgery at school ("my head aches, my poor head") as well as the subsequent revelation that, far from going to Moscow, she had accepted the position of headmistress, became the embodiment of a very different Super-Objective: '*I* want to be admired' or perhaps 'I want to hold dominion over others'. The actor had seen through the obvious and had found a deeper, more realistic layer of motivation. The revelation that this intense psychological drive, loaded with emotion, lay hidden under the Super-Objective suggested by the text made for an arresting and thoroughly modern interpretation.

Attitudes

How did the actor playing Olga come to that conclusion? Here an element – for me, all-important – intervenes to shape decisively the relationship between actor and character model. To explain it, I will need to look in more detail at the concept of 'attitude', on which I touched in the previous chapter. First, a theatre report from the Continent:

Anthropologist Jonas Tinius spent a year observing in detail the work of a theatre company in the Ruhr. The company is typical of the myriad regional theatres to be found all over Germany: led by Roberto Ciulli, a respected director, it produces a mixture of classics and modern plays and considers it important to interpret the plays in its repertoire through contemporary references. Above all, it features a stable company of actors, some of whom have been with the theatre for several decades. Rehearsals are – at least by Anglo-Saxon standards – protracted: they can last for up to a year and always start with an in-depth examination and debate around the ideas and possible meanings of the play. Guided by the company dramaturg, whose role is to provide research and analytical perspectives, members of the company formulate a common understanding of what they consider as the play's central theme.

Over the years of working together, members of the company have developed a particular approach, which they call *Haltung*. This German word is variously translated as attitude, stance, bearing, posture, or demeanour. In the usage of this company, however, it has developed ever-richer layers. It describes, for example, the stance each actor adopts towards his or her own development as an artist. It also extends to the way in which the actors conduct themselves toward one another. The company is also conscious of the fact that attitudes to work are shaped by "evaluative beliefs" rooted in pre-formed dispositions towards class, gender, race, etc. This is why, in order to arrive at *Haltung*, members of the company spend extended periods examining their own beliefs, the social contexts from which their plays emerged and, finally, how the two interact. *Haltung* confers meaning on the overall artistic and social endeavour in which the theatre is engaged within its community. And *Haltung* is not a given: it needs to be constantly and consciously pursued, cultivated and transmitted to new members of the company.

Plays selected for the repertoire are viewed through *Haltung* and this *prise de position* helps the company to determine what a play might 'be about'. In other words, *Haltung* guides them toward reaching an interpretative stance and selecting the angle from which they will approach the play, collectively as well as individually. As Tinius explains:

> *Haltung* might therefore better be translated as the 'conduct of conduct', since it describes not the finished decision about how actors and actresses should comport themselves, stand or walk in a particular situation, but rather a process of developing the *capacity* to relate to characters.[1]
>
> *(2017, p. 234, emphasis original)*

The actors rely on *Haltung* to help them determine not who the character is, but what it might represent. Brecht is explicitly cited as a formative influence and, as in the practice of the Berliner Ensemble, "the actors [are] expected to ask where their characters stood and how they (the actors) stood towards their characters". Characters therefore 'stand for' something, they are conceived as instantiations of representative categories, in the service of a guiding interpretation. It is on this basis that actors begin to construct their characters and *Haltung* is a silver thread woven into the fabric of the entire acting process. I believe that the actor playing Olga in that exciting interpretation did so through her own equivalent of *Haltung*.

This practice is, in many respects, very different from Anglo-Saxon approaches and rehearsal patterns. I am not here to argue for the superiority of one over the other, and there will be advocates on both sides. What I find of interest is the link between *Haltung*, interpretation, and the actors' approach to character construction.

As will have become clear, one struggles to find in English a precise equivalent to the German *Haltung* or the French *prise de position*. I would like to suggest, however, that, used in particular ways, the term Attitude (I capitalise it to signal its particular meanings in our context) encapsulates the connection between ideas, psychology, and the body which the German also holds.

Etymologically, 'attitude' is derived from the Latin *apto*, which means aptitude and fitness for purpose. It is also related, however, to *acto*, which refers to postures of the body. The two roots, *apt* and *act*, have been traced to the Sanskrit *ag*, which means to do or to act. The linguistic analysis points to the intrinsic link present in all our actions between, on the one hand, physical shape and movement (the motor function) and, on the other, a purposeful direction of psychological faculties (the mental function).

In classical psychology, the term attitude is used to describe a *predisposition* towards reacting to environmental stimuli in a particular way. The idea and term 'attitude' were already used by both Darwin and Dewey and soon gained wide circulation. Jung considered the concept to include any "readiness of the psyche to act or react in a certain way" due to an "*a priori* orientation to a definite thing, no matter whether this be represented in consciousness or not". Wilhelm Reich describes how strong impulses ("strivings") are "expressed in a specific *attitude* or *mode of existence*" and how these attitudes, in turn, shape individual personalities. Surveying the evolution of the concept, Gordon Allport could chart a shift occurring in the first decades of the twentieth century from an emphasis on mental inclinations alone to studying the intrinsic links between mental and physical elements, as displayed in a person's attitudes. Indeed, by 1935, the experimental psychologist Nina Bull could write: "In nearly all cases today, the term appears without a qualifying adjective, and implicitly retains both its original [etymological] meanings: a mental aptness and a motor set".

Bull went on to build an entire 'Attitude Psychology Theory', founded on the indivisible link between physicality, posture in particular, emotion, and thought. Bull's most striking contribution consisted of a series of experiments using hypnosis. The subjects were placed into deep trances and given the instruction: "I shall say a word which denotes an emotion or state of mind. When you hear the word you will feel this emotion, experience this state of mind strongly. You will show this in your outward behaviour in a natural manner. You may do anything you like". The hypnotised subjects were then asked to react to emotion-laden words suggesting fear, disgust, triumph, etc. As each word was offered, the subjects automatically adopted postures that were both appropriate to, and expressive of, the emotion suggested by the experimenter. In a second set of experiments, Bull reversed the sequence: subjects were this time placed in lighter trances, so that they could communicate with the experimenter. They were then given suggestions of positions associated with emotions such as joy or anger: "There is a feeling of relaxation and lightness in your whole body . . ."; "Your hands are getting tense and your arms are getting tense. You can feel your jaw tightening . . ." When questioned, the subjects very quickly described themselves as experiencing the relevant emotion.[2] Moreover, when asked to remain in that position but experience different emotions, they were mostly unable to do so.

Bull's experiments pointed to deep-seated links between certain musculoskeletal arrangements and certain feelings. It is very likely that such links have developed through evolution: the body adopts those positions which are most effective to fight danger or to fly away from it; these arrangements are accompanied by corresponding physiological changes in the autonomic nervous system, hormonal discharges, etc. However, Bull also noted that her subjects' physical responses were only preparations for action, never the actions themselves. In anger, for example, the "subjects would clutch their hands in readiness to strike, but they never actually struck at anything". This phenomenon had already been described by Darwin and interpreted by early psychologists, who noted that certain movements (say, gripping or clawing), which had originally been useful in the wild, were reduced in evolved humans to mental tendencies only. These, Bull calls "movement in suspense" and she hypothesises that if preparation for movement does not immediately result in a physical "consummation", the energy thus aroused turns into a subjective awareness: a feeling. There are, she writes

> . . . three stages in readiness for action . . . the neural readiness, or latent attitude . . . which precedes the emotional sequence; the activated readiness or

motor attitude . . . which initiates the emotional sequence, and the conscious readiness or mental attitude of orientation and intention, this being
the essential part of feeling in the emotional sequence . . . The processes are
overlapping and neither can be understood without the other.

(1968, p. 14)

'Attitude' captures this integrated sequence well, as the word holds both meanings: a physical posture ("the boy was standing in an attitude of despair" is the
OED example), as well as the mental ('her attitude to politics is one of profound
indifference'). Attitude implies a physical "readiness" for action, associated with a
"neural readiness" to act *in a certain way* and, thus, determine the nature or quality
of the eventual action. *Brewer's Dictionary* quotes a line from an article in the USA
publication, *Police Review*, which I think says it all: "In this job, you gotta have
attitude, hang loose, ready for anything".

Traditionally, most psychologists considered that when we observe the expression
of joy or distress in others, we involuntarily imitate their facial arrangements. This
was meant to lead to us experiencing the same emotions, through a proprioceptive
process of so-called 'emotional contagion'. But, it has been argued of late, there
are times when observing someone else's sadness, say, may arouse in us altogether
different feelings: joy or anger, for example. 'Something else' intervenes at a non-
conscious level, to shape our reaction. This 'something else' that gives the reaction
its colour is, I suggest, the pre-formed *Attitude: an indivisible blend of personality traits,
physical posture, and social views.*

Some Attitudes can also develop over the long term and become ingrained, habitual. They will then determine not only the way one acts in particular instances, but
also shape behaviours across time. Bull writes: "Once [a neural readiness] has been
established in the central nervous system, this organisation becomes a permanent acquisition; it is always there, ready for activation". To illustrate this, Bull likes to use a phrase
from the American South: a person 'fixes' to act. To 'fix' to cry, strike, or caress means
first of all to adopt specific physical positions or postures (again, language captures the
joint nature of the phenomenon in the dual meanings of both posture and position).
In turn, the postural stance causes changes in our internal functions (blood pressure,
hormones, etc.). Nerve impulses from the internal organs ('interoceptive') and from
the posture ('proprioceptive'), combined with some awareness of the original stimulus,
produce the experiences we describe as sadness, fury, or tenderness. The crucial stage
in this sequence is the moment of *suspension*, the "delay" just before the action – in that
moment, the pre-formed attitude "mediates" the action and shapes its nature:

. . . according to the present thesis the sorry feeling is mediated by the attitude of readiness, or fixing to cry, not by actually crying . . . the same holds
true of anger and fear. And so, from the present point of view, we feel angry
as a result of *readiness* to strike, and feel afraid as a result of *readiness* to run
away, and not because of actually hitting out or running.

(1968, p. 5, emphases original)

I cannot stress strongly enough the unified nature of the concept 'Attitude': describing the various stages of its operation in the way Bull does is not to be taken to imply a separation of the mental from the physical. As I have argued all along, changing the shape of one's body goes together with changes in the mental position, and *vice versa*; the effect on the nature of the emotion experienced is a result of this integrated phenomenon. Attitude, with its mixture of personal and social elements, also contributes to the body shape constructed by the actor. Attitude plays a crucial role in shaping *which* actions the character carries out and *how* these are executed. Attitudes of the body are one with the attitudes of the mind, and, as Nina Bull asserts: "attitude leads to action . . . [and] All action predicts attitude". Attitudes, I would submit, are a crucial influencer of the way images rise into awareness and turn into character narratives; these narratives then turn into characteristics and characteristics into posture, gesture, and vocal quality. Attitudes, thus, affect profoundly the way in which the actor engages with the character.

As we have seen, developing a *Haltung/*Attitude also means developing an ethics of acting. Attitude non-consciously informs all the subsequent decisions the actor makes regarding model, characteristics, physical life, etc. Observing the work of the German company, Jonas Tinius was thus able to note: "The form of conduct [*Haltung*] I witnessed developing during rehearsals, conjoins aesthetic deliberation, forms of acted-out improvisation, and the emergence of gestural movements". Attitude eventually shapes the reactions of the actor-in-character to stage events: the actor will react spontaneously in *this* and not in *that* way because of the Attitude that has informed the work on character.

Classical movement discourse also made broad use of the term attitude. As I described in Chapter 3, in the eighteenth and nineteenth centuries, actors would stop the stage action and hold an expressive position for a significant length of time. The practice, as well as the term, survives (in greatly modified forms) in the *attitudes* of classical ballet. The concept of attitude eventually reached the theatre via the work done by Rudolf Laban on the links between personality and movement. Laban first changed some of the original meaning of the word within the vocabulary of dance and applied attitude to patterns of movement rather than to fixed positions. For Laban, as for Bull, an Attitude encapsulated in a single psychophysical concept physical expression, the mental impulses which give rise to it, and their mutual interdependence. He then drew on the psychological uses of the term to develop his concept of the "Inner Attitude". This describes a combination of psychological traits that ordains that the subject either acts physically "in a definite direction" or reacts "in a definite way".

In an innovative extension of this concept, the dancer and teacher Yat Malmgren, a Laban disciple, subsequently developed the Laban–Malmgren System of Movement Psychology and Character Analysis, a training methodology specifically conceived for actors. His approach unites in an original synthesis Rudolf Laban's analysis of the dimensions of movement and his concept of Inner Attitude, Jung's psychological functions, and Stanislavski's concept of the Super-Objective. This methodology is explicitly designed to sensitise the actor to the links between movement and inner life, to analyse the independent character and then facilitate the creation of a bridge between actor and character. Its main purpose is to encourage transformation. As it brings together some of the key elements of transformative acting I have described so far, I shall deal with it in some detail.

Inner attitudes

Character Analysis is based on a deceptively simple idea: that between certain psychological and certain physically based concepts *there is a direct correspondence*. As we saw, Jung had described the psyche in terms of four psychological functions: sensing, thinking, intuiting, and feeling. Moreover, Jung emphasised the physiological foundation of psychological processes, emotion in particular, and the mutually reinforcing relationship between the two. Laban had also hypothesised that a link could be drawn between psychology and movement elements and, toward the end of his career, decided to put his theory to the test. A couple of well-known Jungian analysts had invited him to give movement classes to their patients, as a helpful addition to the latter's therapy. Aided by William Carpenter, one of his collaborators, Laban was thus able to analyse the movement patterns of the patients using the four dimensions or "Motion Factors" of Weight, Time, Space, and Flow and then put them side by side with their psychological profiles. Enlarging from this study, Laban and his collaborator considered that the psychological signals conveyed by expressive Movement (with a capital M, to distinguish it from mere mechanical motion) could be understood by means of associating each Motion Factor with one of Jung's psychological functions, which they called their "Mental Factors". They argued that:

> Sensing is connected to Weight (on a scale of Light to Strong).
>
> Intuiting is connected to Time (on a scale of Sustained/Slow to Quick).
>
> Thinking is connected to Space (on a scale of Flexible to Direct).
>
> Feeling is connected to Flow (on a scale of Free to Bound).

These connections were purely experiential.[3] No proof existed, apart from that offered by their observations, which told them that a person's 'weighty presence' was associated with her sensuous engagement with the world; that a 'thinker' tended to go 'in and out' of his 'inner space' in order to solve a problem. Nevertheless, Laban found in this association of Motion with Mental Factors a way of explaining how, by analysing those features individuals emphasised when they moved, one could detect which of the mental functions was dominant in their personalities.

Yat Malmgren, to whom the development of this incipient work was eventually entrusted, considered that the same reasoning could be used to analyse theatre characters. To apply his approach to a familiar example: at some point in her excavation, my friend will have to ask herself whether Viola's presence is Strong or Light, whether she is Direct or Flexible (convoluted) in her intellectual dealings with the world, Quick or Sustained in her thoughts and decisions, Free or Bound in her emotional reactions. A 'brave and adventurous' Viola will more than likely have a Strong presence, be Flexible in Thought, Quick in her inner tempo, and Free emotionally: her Attitude (in Bull's psychophysical sense) will come across in a 'Slashing' tempo – this Viola will 'whip' all around her. A 'timorous' Viola might be Light and Direct yet closed in her thoughts, cautious and therefore slow (Sustained) in her decisions, and fearsome, withdrawn (Bound) emotionally. This Viola will 'Glide', eyes averted, from Illyrian beach to Court, from Court to Olivia, and from Olivia to Sebastian. Granted, the first interpretation is more appealing (and funnier), but the approach allows for both. A more sophisticated look at the character might combine the elements differently still: a 'shy' Viola might have strong Weight, underplayed at first, then gradually revealed. The Laban–Malmgren System does not prescribe an interpretation – it simply gives the actor an analytical vocabulary with which to reach her own conclusions. In particular, it enables her to infer from concrete data the psychological make-up of the character. If Viola is adventurous and brave, her Sensing function will be put forward in her dealings with the world. Her reaction to Orsino, her attachment to her brother, her empathy with Olivia, all point to a strong emotional capacity as well. She may be a combination of sensation and feeling, with the first being the superior function. If, on the other hand, Viola is 'shy" and 'timorous', then her Bound emotions come to the fore. Her Sensing function is weakened – Feeling is the superior function.

Building on these foundations and incorporating other important concepts from Laban's published work, Malmgren constructed a training methodology designed to sensitise actors to the links between physical activity and mental and emotional states. His is a wide-reaching work, whose complex features extend beyond the scope of this book. Of specific interest for my present topic, however, is the way in which the Laban–Malmgren System adapts for theatre use the psychodynamic view of personality.

I should first note that, in combining them with his dimensions of movement, Laban had simplified Jung's ideas considerably. We saw that Jung used "attitude" to describe the basic orientation of the psyche towards or away from the object (extraversion and introversion respectively). Thus, he distinguished between "attitude-types" and "function-types", where the latter refer to the four functions which can exist in either the extravert or the introvert attitudes. Laban merged these two Jungian concepts – the Inner Attitudes, his principal tool for describing personality, are combinations of two of Jung's functions and also incorporate the notions of extraversion and introversion. Furthermore, Jung had divided the functions along a major fault line, into rational (thinking and feeling) and irrational (sensation and intuition). The two functions within each of these two categories were said to be incompatible with one another: a personality that overemphasised thinking suppressed feeling, and *vice versa*. Laban disregarded this incompatibility and assembled his character typology by combining psychological functions both within and across the rational–irrational divide. By considering that any of the functions could be the superior function and combining it with any of the other three as a possible auxiliary,

Laban arrived at a total of six broad types of personality, or Inner Attitudes. They are usually presented as pairs of opposites – to enable easier access to the reader new to these categories, I am also giving each of them a 'label'. These are very general descriptions but also indicate the archetypal nature of these categories:

- A Sensing–Thinking character type called Stable ('the intelligent ruler').
- An Intuiting–Feeling character type called Mobile ('highly emotional').
- A Sensing–Intuiting character type called Near ('down to earth').
- A Thinking–Feeling character type called Remote ('ascetic, spiritual').
- A Sensing–Feeling character type called Adream ('the lover').
- A Thinking–Intuiting character type called Awake ('the intellectual').

In each character type one of the functions is dominant, while the other is secondary. However, one should also stress that the linking dash indicates that the two functions may be read in either direction: one Stable personality can be Sensing–Thinking, where the Sensing aspect is dominant, while another Stable personality is Thinking–Sensing, where the Thinking aspect prevails, and so on. Which of the two dominates determines to a certain extent the nature of the personality because it reflects the primary psychological function – the Jungian 'type' to which the person belongs.

Coming from a therapeutic perspective, Laban had considered that all six Inner Attitudes could be present in the psyche of the same individual, albeit in different strengths. Movement therapy, therefore, consisted in replacing the Motion Factor on which a person habitually relied with one of the others and could, thus, aid psychological development. Overall, the combined movement and psychotherapy to which Laban's classes contributed was meant to encourage the evolution in the individual of those Inner Attitudes that had remained underdeveloped.

Applying this concept to theatre, Yat Malmgren takes from Laban the idea of an Inner Attitude as a 'cocktail' of Motion and Mental Factors through which actors *conceive* and which they gradually reveal to the spectators as these *perceive* the characters. The Inner Attitude is, therefore, a fundamental psychological orientation, the equivalent of Stanislavski's "innermost centre" of the character. While, as I describe below, it is a complex and dynamic structure, it is, none the less, rooted in a predisposition so pronounced that the character's stance toward the world always follows the same pattern. Unlike those of daily-life personalities, who evolve throughout their lives, the Inner Attitudes of characters are static. There is, therefore, no question of the system being applied to anything other than theatre characters. I stress this because one often senses in actors introduced to it for the first time a natural antipathy toward the idea of human beings being pigeon-holed or (that dreaded word) 'typecast' into one or other of the Inner Attitudes. As I outlined earlier, Jungian analysts are clear that the idea of a 'pure' type is incompatible with the natural complexity and fluidity of the live human psyche. Nevertheless, the idea of the preponderance of one function upon the others, "setting a definite stamp on the character of an individual" is also central to Jung's thought and leads inevitably to the idea of types. Yat Malmgren bases his system on the extension into the realm of theatre characterisation of this idea of a "definite stamp".

A dual character

How, then, does one determine that a character belongs to one Inner Attitude rather than another? Laban's Inner Attitudes simply described people's fundamental inclinations and their expression in movement. I outlined above how our 'Viola' could analyse her characteristics and consequent dimensions of movement in Laban's basic terms. To this analysis, Malmgren adds the Stanislavskian concept of the Super-Objective. Malmgren's reasoning is that in order to grasp a character's Inner Attitude, one starts with the question 'What does my character desire above all else?' The answer to this question determines the Super-Objective *as it is perceived by the character.* If asked, Creon (in Sophocles' Theban plays) would most likely say that what drives his every action is 'to keep the city together'. Analysed with the tools of the system, Creon – an embodiment of authority and penetrating intelligence – is a combination of Sensing and Thinking (Stable Inner Attitude). Natasha in *Three Sisters* wants above all 'to own': she is an embodiment of convention and grasping acquisitiveness, defining qualities of the Near Inner Attitude (Sensing dominates). Desdemona's Super-Objective seems to be intimately linked to her relationship with Othello – feelings and sensuality dominate, a blend characteristic of Adream (a made-up word suggestive of hyper-sensitivity, of a personality defined by the Feeling function). Their *conscious* Super-Objectives indicate which is their superior function and, therefore, what their Attitudes (here in the sense of 'best foot foremost') toward the world are. This aspect of the Inner Attitude is, therefore, essentially extravert, directed towards other people, institutions, or events.

Here, the other meaning of the concept Attitude comes into play. To achieve his prodigious 'Stability', Creon has had to commit to a political idea: the welfare of his city. This commitment is emotional, quasi-religious – Creon has embraced totally the *idea* of the state. At the end of *Three Sisters*, at the very moment when she seems to have achieved her materialistic goals – when she possesses the Prozorov man, house, and heir – Natasha seems as shrill and discontented as ever (she is actually shrieking as she makes her final exit). This points to a deeper motivation than her desire for possessions. Her drive, the thing she wants to attain by means of her acquisitions, lies in the *idea* of power. Desdemona's relationships (to Cassio, Emilia, even to Iago, and ultimately to Othello himself) reflect her fundamental altruism. Desdemona is driven by the *idea* of self-sacrifice, a commitment she does not question until the very moment of her death. These emotional aspects of the concept Attitude are introvert – in psychoanalytic terms, they are linked to deep-seated psychic contents.

Thus, as seen through this psychodynamic perspective, the character has a dual nature. Readily inferred from the data of the play are the *aspirations* the character has to affect the people and social institutions with which it interacts. As I outlined in an earlier discussion, seen as an 'intrapersonal' concept, personality is judged according to the 'impressions' we leave on others. These are shaped by our social roles, our status in relation to others and by the image we wish to project, what Jung calls our "persona". We generally identify with our public image and are, therefore, entirely sincere when we declare that our motivations follow from it: these are the stories we typically tell about ourselves, what psychologist Robert Hogan describes as our "idealised identity". This, the Laban–Malmgren System describes as the 'Outer Character'.

Acting approaches which reject the idea of an independent character tend to rely on the concept of role, described by social psychologists such as Erwing Goffman as a "socially scripted" behaviour, judged to be appropriate for particular identities: teacher and student, soldier and officer, father and daughter, and so on. This position assumes that self-knowledge (we are what we think we are) is the same as character. A psychodynamic view of character, on the other hand, main-tains that we cannot know ourselves to that extent and therefore posits a deeper level of personality. At that deeper level lies a different Super-Objective, consisting of a powerful emotional attachment to an idea, to an abstraction which ultimately *drives* all the character's aspirations and actions. This, the Laban–Malmgren System designates as the 'Inner Character'.

To illustrate the distinction between the two layers of the character, Yat Malmgren offers one of a number of analyses of Iago's character within the terms of his system. At one level, Iago is motivated by resentment at being overlooked for promotion, by sexual jealousy, and class and racial enmity. His conscious Super-Objective lies in his desire for promotion, seduction, monetary gain – all typical materialistic goals. To achieve these goals, Iago relies heavily on his intui-tion. In the Jungian view, intuition is a function of past experiences, forgotten by our conscious mind but stored in the unconscious and ready to be brought to bear when we need to take fast decisions about unexpected events. Iago's intuition is a mixture of prejudice – 'decisions' taken long ago about black people (all wild and gross), women (all fickle), and even rich Florentines like Cassio (all privileged and entitled) – with a perverted 'emotional intelligence' which allows him to sense weaknesses in others. Within the term of the system, Iago's dominant function is, therefore, Intuiting. Iago also has sensuality: his Sensing is developed, albeit not to the same extent as his intuition, and therefore constitutes his auxiliary function. The analysis could stop here and the character could be, and has been, played as a stage villain, a "great, creeping cunning cat" as Macready described a fellow nineteenth-century actor in the role. However, one can consider that Iago also has a hidden Super-Objective: he would like, in this psychodynamic interpretation, to be another Othello, to possess the powerful sensuality that makes the Moor into a successful soldier and lover. Iago would like to be fascinating: instead, he is just plain clever. This is his secret, unfulfilled self-image. At times the character identi-fies with it, at others he resents it as an impossible goal and a source of intolerable pressure. Either way, it constitutes an important layer of motivation, as it drives him – it is the source of his manic energy. Were the character to be asked "Who are you?" he would reply, if honest, in accordance with his self-image, uncon-scious of his true nature. The unconscious contents thus aroused "invade", to use a Jungian term, the conscious part of the character and give it its force as well as its peculiar quality. The actor, of course, is conscious of both.

Stanislavski himself offers a good example of the distinction between overt motivation and inner drive. While rehearsing to play Argan, the main character in *The Imaginary Invalid*, he assumed for a long time that his character's Super-Objective was a desire 'to be cured'. Therefore, he studied carefully the minutiae of his character's 'diseases'. Unfortunately, while this approach matched the character's own thought process, the interpretation turned out to be pathetic rather than comic. Then came the realisation that the character's acknowledged Super-Objective may be different from its unconscious desire. When Stanislavski began playing the Super-Objective 'to be cossetted as if I were ill', the characterisation fell into place and Argan, now a spoiled great pretender, became one of his finest comic creations.

The Inner Attitude as a whole remains the deep, deep background which colours what the character is doing, as the composition of the soil gives the wine its taste. Spectators, however, are subjected to a constant stream of actions, the character's immediate tasks. They get drunk on the wine; how are they to be given access to the soil?

Based on his detailed observations of movement patterns in patients, Laban concluded that the inner workings of their personalities were usually revealed not directly through purposeful gestures, but, rather, through "transitions between essential actions", that is, through non-conscious moves carried out *in between* functional activities. In a brilliant insight, Laban proposed that these incomplete movements were so revealing because they frequently fulfilled a "recovery" function. Between the repeated, purposeful moves needed to punch a nail into wood or to glide across the ice-rink, physical energy has to move inwards so as to regain momentum. In so doing, Laban posits, it comes into contact with deep psychological layers – the engines of expressive movement. The existence of these 'purposeless' movements was, in fact, the initial puzzle which had led Laban to search for the psychological sources underpinning observable movement.

Yat Malmgren linked this observation to the different levels through which the body expresses itself in acting. The Inner Character, the deepest part of the Inner Attitude, he proposes, is primarily revealed to the spectator through posture. This is enhanced by what Laban called "shadow moves", the "tiny muscular movements such as the raising of the brow, the jerking of the hand or the tapping of the foot, which . . . accompany movements of purposeful action like a shadow". In acting, posture and shadow moves may be constructed but eventually become automatic and are also automatically read by spectators: children as young as three have been shown to be able to read the intentions of a person from unintentional moves. This, psychologists Paul Ekman and Wallace Friesen have shown in a groundbreaking study, is due to so-called 'leakage', the betrayal of withheld information by means of automatic movements in those areas of the body which are not the primary means of communication. Most of us focus on the faces of the people with whom we interact; this is why, if they wish to hide from us their thoughts or intentions, their efforts will be concentrated on their faces: the face can betray the most and, thus, must conceal the most. As a result of the focus on the face, areas of the body least likely to come into focus – legs and feet, for example – are most likely to 'leak' involuntarily and are the locus of shadow moves.

That part of the Inner Attitude of which the character is conscious (the Outer Character), on the other hand, is revealed through semi-voluntary yet recurring moves, such as Michael Chekhov's "psychological gestures", as well as through purposefully directed gestures. The actor may manipulate all these elements of movement at will. In so doing, a window opens to transformative work based on a "reflexive feedback loop" of embodiment, in which gesture, verbalisation, and impulse form an inseparable whole.

An articulate account of how this methodology can work in practice is offered by the actor Kate Garthside. A former student of Yat Malmgren's, Garthside played the character of Gervaise Macquart in an adaptation of Émile Zola's *L'assommoir*.[4] Gervaise is a working class washerwoman struggling against poverty and prejudice in nineteenth-century Paris. Responding to her character's tragic emotional life, Garthside's initial impulse was to consider it to be Adream (Sensing–Feeling). Testing her initial reaction by using the system, Garthside reconsidered the character's Inner Attitude by asking what its conscious Super-Objective was. She then took the view that the character was in fact defined by her aspiration to lift herself out of the limitations of her social condition. Gervaise was a tragic character indeed, but unaware of her tragedy, thus lacking one of the characteristic aspects of Adream, awareness of a heightened emotional state. Garthside's conclusion was that the character was in fact Near (Sensing–Intuiting): emotion played a part, but was not intrinsic to the character essence, which was determined by material aspirations.

The difference in Inner Attitude came to the fore when Garthside was rehearsing the high point of the role's trajectory: Gervaise is faced with the loss of her laundry, the source of her livelihood and status. She sits for a long time in silence listening to the men around her discussing her plight until eventually she screams: "I hate the fucking lot of you", and walks out slamming the door. That single line had to express the way in which the character deals with her feelings at a moment of major significance. When she was playing Gervaise as Adream, Garthside felt the emotion was "flying out" and was "acted", "over-indulgent" – a self-conscious display, expressed vocally and gesturally as a whining Slash. However, in Near characters, Garthside remembered, emotion is halted, strangled at birth by the 'spade's a spade' attitude of the character. The tempo of the line, coming from a Near Inner Attitude, now changed to a tough Punch. This sensation rang true and confirmed her analysis; she was then able to build a character defined by the characteristics of Near. Garthside considers that she might have reached the same conclusion even without her analysis, intuitively, but that without the *vocabulary* of the system she would not have arrived at the clarity of thought which gave her intuition a definition necessary to construct characters such as Gervaise consciously and methodically.

From such examples it is clear that in the Laban–Malmgren System the dramatic action – the people, events, circumstances – of the narrative retains through analysis a prescriptive control on the behaviours of the character. However, it has been argued convincingly that, in both its learning methodology and its application, the Laban–Malmgren System is fundamentally experiential. Overall, actors trained in the system cite one feature as its enduring legacy: the way in which as students it *created a systematic way of linking physical activity with mental and emotional states and, thus, enabled them to give words to their sensations*. They retain an enduring perception of a phenomenological level of truth in the propositions put forward by the system. Simon Callow writes:

> Yat Malmgren's work . . . addresses itself directly to the very nature of act-
> ing: not 'What it is for?' or 'What are the conditions which give rise to it?'
> It attempts to say what it *is*. It amounts to a praxis of character in action, an
> account of the physical embodiment of character and impulse.
>
> *(1984, p. 39, emphasis original)*

And Oscar winner Colin Firth:

> [Yat Malmgren put] . . . psychological concepts into space, into action, into
> the physical world. . . . I found that after a couple of years of it, it started to
> make an enormous amount of sense; it came as close as anything anybody
> really can do to teaching acting . . . It made sense to me, and I still use it.[5]

The examples above point to the *raison d'être* of the system: to provide a route towards the deliberate design of character, first and foremost as a physical pro-cess. The Laban–Malmgren approach has helped to shape the thinking and work of some of the most expressive actors of our time: two Academy Award win-ners, Anthony Hopkins and Colin Firth; two 'Bonds', Sean Connery and Pierce Brosnan; and from the younger generation, actors as diverse as Helen McCrory, Michael Fassbender, Tom Hardy, and Emilia Clarke. I am making this particular selection from a much longer list in order to emphasise that, while being designed to encourage transformative acting, Laban–Malmgren principles can be applied across the full spectrum of acting modes. One would, therefore, be wrong to assume a mechanical application of the system in the practice of professionals. In the con-servatoires in which it is taught, the system sits alongside other approaches, as one aspect of a complex curriculum, and actors assemble their personal methodologies from all these influences. Neither do most actors using its tools expect it and its implied aesthetic of transformation to dominate their work. They are aware that the requirements of their roles mean that they will find themselves at any number of points on the transformation scale.

None the less, those trained in the system find it difficult to discard altogether its core teachings. The theoretical apparatus underpinning the system is complex, yet the movement-based, experiential approach through which it is taught goes beyond theory or technique, to a form of embodied learning with lasting effects. By creat-ing a language of acting, and through it bringing sensation to consciousness, the Laban–Malmgren System contributes to the development of what the French call *disponibilité*, having a keyboard of acting possibilities and fingers nimble enough to be able to play it. The system is concerned, as Simon Callow puts it, "with making the word flesh, literally".

How this might work in our mind-brain and how actor and character come together in indivisible unity are the subjects of the chapters to come.

Notes

1 This, Anne Bogart, who was strongly influenced by German theatre, calls "source work", an "invitation to obsession".
2 A different study, carried out by Duclos and colleagues with subjects who were not under hypnosis, came to similar conclusions.
3 Indeed, Laban's journey to this conclusion was fraught with hesitations.
4 West Yorkshire Playhouse, Leeds, 1992.
5 www.firth.com/articles/03backstagewest.html

Bibliography

Psychoanalysis and motivation: Freud, S., 2010. 'New lectures', in *Complete Works (CW)*. Ivan Smith Online Edition: https://openlibrary.org/works/OL16678137W/Freud_Complete_Works; Jung, C. G., 1960. 'On psychic energy'. In: *Collected Works, Volume 8: The Structure and Dynamics of the Psyche*, translated by R. F. C. Hull. 2nd Edition. London: Routledge and Kegan Paul; Reich W., 2013. *Character Analysis,* translated by V. R. Carfagno. 3rd Edition. Farrar, Straus and Giroux: Kindle Edition.
Objectives and Super-Objectives: Merlin, B., 2015. 'The self and the fictive other in creation, rehearsal and performance', in M. Evans (ed.), *The Actor Training Reader*. Abingdon: Routledge, pp. 119–131; Stanislavski, C., 1994. *Creating A Role*, translated by E. Hapgood. London: Methuen.
Autobiographical Self: Damasio, A., 1999. *The Feeling of What Happens: Body and Emotion in the Making of Consciousness*. London: William Heinemann.
Haltung: Tinius, J., 2017. 'Art as ethical practice: anthropological observations on and beyond theatre'. *World Art*, 7 (2), pp. 227–251; *and "evaluative beliefs"*: Dijk, T. A. v., 1987. *Communicating Racism: Ethnic Prejudice in Thought and Talk*. Newbury Park: Sage; *and "source work"*: Bogart, A., and Landau, T., 2005. *The Viewpoints Book: A Practical Guide to Viewpoints and Composition*. New York: Theatre Communications Group; *and Brecht's influence*: Thompson, P., 2010. 'Brecht and actor training: on whose behalf do we act?', in Hodge, A. (ed.), *Actor Training*. 2nd Edition. London: Routledge.
'Attitude' and psychology: Jung, C. G. 1971. *Collected Works, Volume 6: Psychological Types*, translated by R. F. C. Hull. London: Routledge and Kegan Paul; Storr, A., 1973. *Jung*. London: Fontana and Collins; Reich, 2013; Bull, N., 1968 (1951). *The Attitude Theory of Emotion*. New York: Nervous and Mental Diseases Monographs (Coolidge Foundation); Bull, N., 1962. *The Body and its Mind: An Introduction to Attitude Psychology*. New York: Las Americas.
Posture and emotion: Bull, 1968; Duclos, S. E. et al, 1989. 'Emotion-specific effects of facial expressions and postures on emotional experience'. *Journal of Personality and Social Psychology*, 57, pp. 100–108; Hatfield, E. et al, 1994. *Emotional Contagion*. New York: Cambridge University Press.
The Laban–Malmgren System: Mirodan, V., 1997. 'The way of transformation (The Laban–Malmgren system of dramatic character analysis)'. PhD Thesis. Royal Holloway, University of London; Mirodan, V., 2015. 'Acting the metaphor: the Laban–Malmgren

system of movement psychology and character analysis'. *Theatre, Dance and Performance Training*, 6 (1), pp. 30–45; Hayes, J., 2010. *The Knowing Body: Yat Malmgren's Acting Technique*. Saarbrüken: VDM Verlag Dr. Müller; Fettes, C., 2015. *A Peopled Labyrinth: The Histrionic Sense: An Analysis of the Actor's Craft*. London: GFCA; *and Garthside example*: Mirodan 2015; *basis in Jung*: Jung, 1971; Jung, C. G., 1990. *Analytical Psychology: Its Theory and Practice (The Tavistock Lectures)*. London: Routledge; Spoto, A., 1995. *Jung's Typology in Perspective*. Asheville, NC: Chiron; *basis in Laban*: Laban, R., 1947. *Effort*. London: Macdonald and Evans; Laban, R., 1960. 'Light–darkness'. *Laban Art of Movement Guild Magazine*, 25. Laban, R., 1971. *The Mastery of Movement*, edited by L. Ullman. 2nd Edition. London: Macdonald and Evans; *and "idealised identity"*: Hogan, R., 1996. 'A socioanalytic perspective on the Five-Factor Model'. In: Wiggins, J. S. (ed.), *The Five-Factor Model of Personality: Theoretical Perspectives*. New York: Guilford; *parallels with Stanislavski*: Benedetti, J., 1988. *Stanislavski: A Biography*. London: Methuen; *and a "reflexive feedback loop"*: Kemp, R., 2012. *Embodied Acting, What Neuroscience Tells Us about Performance*. London: Routledge; *accounts of using*: Callow, S., 1984. *Being an Actor*. London: Methuen.; *and applications in performance*: Mirodan, 1997.

Shadow moves: Laban, 1971; North, M., 1958 (November). 'Scientific penetration gives basis for guidance and treatment'. *Laban Art of Movement Guild Magazine* 21; McCaw, D. (ed.), 2011. *The Laban Sourcebook*. London: Routledge; *and the revelation of inner states and intention*: Ekman, P., and Friesen, W. V., 1969. 'The repertoire of non-verbal behaviour: categories, origins, usage and coding'. *Semiotica*, 1, pp. 49–98; Shultz, T. R., Wells, D., and Sarda, M., 1980. 'Development of the ability to distinguish intended actions from mistakes, reflexes and passive movements'. *British Journal of Social and Clinical Psychology*, 19, pp. 301–310.

PART III

The melding of actor and character

10

IMAGINING THE CHARACTER

Seeing around corners

I am re-reading the descriptions in the earlier chapters: textual clues, memory images, imaginary bodies, physical transformation, on the one hand; traits, temperaments, and psychodynamic views of personality, on the other. True to both acting practice and psychology as these are, they do not quite capture *what is happening* in the act of transformation: techniques and psychologies may describe how actor and character interact, but not the mysterious creative jump which occurs between rehearsal room and stage, between preparation and real acting.

Observing actors at work often leaves one perplexed: language and points of reference useful in analysing the *effects* of acting are found not to be of much use in understanding the *process*. Here is one observer, describing the great Billie Whitelaw at work on a text by Beckett:

> Then, as she herself reads the words over and over in the rehearsal, they affect her internally, first as music but later also as language. She allows those words to evoke visual images, sometimes from her own life, and in the end arrives at ideas about the play's meaning despite her aversion to analysis and her continuing emphasis on melody in her delivery. Thus her performances benefit from ideas through the avenue of music.
>
> *(Kalb, 2007, p. 215)*

So how do "words evoke visual images"? Let us ask an actor playing Odysseus at the beginning of the *Philoctetes*. At his first entrance, Odysseus has just landed on Lemnos. How did he get here? By rowing boat after a long journey on the trireme from Troy? Is the Greek boat lying at anchor in the bay or has it been drawn on to the shore? Odysseus jumps on to the beach: is it sandy, rocky, friendly, forbidding?

Is it a lonely place where he might die, or a sunny place from where he will at last begin his return home? Decisions must be taken. How?

If pressed, actors often first hint at a feeling of deep immersion in the topic or object of contemplation, to the temporary exclusion of all other awareness. This is followed by a sensation of 'waking up' and of surprise (at times, awe) at the appearance of odd, unexpected, striking images and connections. On reflection, the most productive among these seem to have little, if any, connection with anything of which they were previously aware. Yet, images must come from somewhere! For the more introspective practitioner, the question keeps nagging: "from where?" But, in general, both actors and observers tend to avoid it. Acting, it is said, is 'intuitive' or it is nothing.

Therefore, I return one last time to the psychoanalytical tradition, which has some useful things to say regarding the nature of intuition. Intuition, Jung hypothesises, is the way in which consciousness relates to the unconscious. The latter is the repository of memories of things of which we were once aware yet have forgotten, and even of subliminal perceptions "too feeble to be conscious". Intuition is, therefore, intimately linked to memory and amounts to "perception via the unconscious" of "realities which are not known to consciousness".

The psychoanalytic school also ascribes the emergence of unexpected images to a specific state of mind they label "phantasy" (spelled in this way to distinguish it from aimless daydreaming). This, says Jung,

> . . . is a complex of ideas that is distinguished from other such complexes by the fact that it has no objective referent. Although it may originally be based on memory-images of actual experiences, its content refers to no external reality; it is merely the output of creative psychic activity . . .
>
> *(1971, p. 427)*

Phantasies are the product of intuition but only arise when the subject deliberately enters a state that Jung describes as "an intuitive attitude of expectation". The psychoanalytic concept of "active imagination" captures much of what happens here. In active imagination, consciousness focuses on images or events and yields to their fascination to the point where a phantasy develops in which the disparate images coalesce into imaginary beings. Once established, these acquire lives of their own; they become 'characters' in imaginary stories with their own, particular, logic. Psychoanalyst Barbara Hannah even argues that such models make it possible for "conversations" to develop between conscious and non-conscious psychic contents. Stanislavski also described a state of "active imagining" in which the actor engages in imaginary exchanges with fictional characters. "You can be the dreamer of your dream", Stanislavski writes, "but you can also take an active part in it". Phantasy, therefore, requires a purposeful direction of mental energy.

Recent research has also shown that fantasising about an object of desire (a glass of water when thirsty, for example) increases blood pressure and, therefore, energy levels. Similarly, building in my mind a character model for Tamburlaine becomes a source of acting energy. The images that arise from this "active phantasy" feel concrete, sensuous, and, above all, lead to my doing things: I can engage, on stage, in Tamburlaine's actions. I can test my intuition through imagining and improvising the planning of campaigns, the taming of horses, hand-to-hand combat. To indulge in the delusion of being the ruler of the world, on the other hand, belongs to the realm of wishful thinking and will not compel me to act. Yet, actors who attempt to 'think themselves into the part' or strive to 'believe in the reality' of a scene, before and beside the actions performed on stage, often confuse the two. For good psychological reasons, this kind of gener-alised daydreaming is sterile in acting. To say to myself that I am Tamburlaine, or that the boards on which I tread are a battlefield in Persia, is an imposition on my sense of reality. It will be perceived as a threat to the integrity of my personality as a whole and will, therefore, be rejected as irrational by that part of my consciousness whose function is to test reality. On the other hand, imagining concrete actions, such as those triggered by Stanislavski's 'magic if' – "if I were Tamburlaine, what would I do?" – will arouse my curiosity and be welcomed as a pleasant and creative "game". So, when I engage, purposefully and actively, in the phantasy that I am Tamburlaine planning to conquer the world, I am able to act and react 'in character'.

The scent of plastic roses

Traditionally, 'being in character' is taken to mean that I can 'think character thoughts'. Stanislavski talks about an "inner stream of images" passing through the actor's mind while in character. These images

> must bear a relationship only to the life of the character being played and not to the actor who does the portraying, because unless his own personal life is analogous to that of the part it will not coincide with it.
>
> *(1968, p. 124)*

The consensus, developed in both the Russian and the American traditions, is that before actors reach the stage at which they can roll in their minds the film of character images, they will have had to assimilate these to their own experiences. Rhonda Blair writes eloquently about the "construction of images of the char-acter's memories, based on information in the play's text", noting at the same time that the actor needs to find "personal meaning" in the images provided by the text. A methodology is thereafter proposed whereby reactions to text and Given Circumstances lead to the creation of a stream of images and thence to a "detailed kinaesthetic score that supports the body-mapping of those images".

Uta Hagen labelled the technique by which data from the play are brought to life by association with personal images "personalisation". Endowing stage objects (Viola's ring) with such personal contents is one of Hagen's best known and most effective techniques:

> A rose, which may be wax or plastic on stage, must be not only endowed with the rose texture, aroma, and thorniness of the real rose in order for me to deal with it with conviction, but would be quite differently dealt with if it is from the favourite plant which I myself grew, or if someone I love gave it to me, or if it is from someone I detest who presented it to me to butter me up.
>
> *(1973, p. 116)*

Again, this process involves a dialogue between character data and actor memories. To the literary-minded, however, an actor's images are likely to appear nothing if not trivial. How can my friend, at one and the same time, render the personal associations aroused by the little metal band in her hand and the sexual innuendo which the editor's notes will tell her the word "ring" held for the Elizabethans? What is a memory of her grandmother's ring compared to the subtle ambiguities of Shakespeare's text? This is unavoidable: the very nature of the personalisation process involves bringing rhetoric down to the level of the individual who is speaking the words. After all, it will not matter one jot once the rehearsal process has taken its course – images need only be potent for the actor and their value lies precisely in their intense personal nature. Personalised images remain the secret tools of the actor at work.

Their effectiveness depends on the sensuous and emotional load they carry. Records of objects and events with which we have interacted are stored in memory in association with the motor activities (reaching, looking, tasting, etc.) and emotional reactions that formed part of our encounters with them. And, while motor, affective, and sensory storage occurs in different systems in the brain, retrieval is always holistic and coordinated in time: we recall a landscape in association with the memory of the effort needed to reach it and the feeling of awe or surprise when we first saw it. "As a consequence, when we recall an object . . . we recall not just sensory characteristics of an actual object but the past reactions of the organism to that object," Antonio Damasio notes. Memory is indeed "affective".

It is, however, erroneous to speak simply of 'retrieving the image' of an object. Cognitive approaches to memory distinguish between inactive long-term memory and basic working memory – the ability of the brain to hold on to images for periods from tenths of a second to a number of consecutive seconds. Reactions to emotional stimuli are a dialogue between long-term and working memories, directed by purposeful attention. Associations are not only imbued with the sensations and emotions of the past, but are also shaped by the context in which they arise in the present; they are, neuroscientist Joseph LeDoux explains, "constructions assembled at the time of retrieval". Thus, each "construction" will be slightly different from past remembrances of the same event. An actor seeking to recall a personal image for the highly specialised purpose of transferring it to a fictional character in fictional circumstances does not, therefore, engage in the like-for-like retrieval of a past event, but in its imaginative reconstruction. This is also affected by what psychologists call "mood dependence" – our mood today will influence the way in which we bring out the past.

When our actor reacts to the appearance of the ring, her technique involves an act of emotional *imagination*. Whatever the memories she summons, they are no more 'real' than Michael Chekhov's famous improvisation in which he restaged his father's funeral with impressive emotional investment, only to disclose at the end that his parents were alive and well. This got him expelled for a time from Stanislavski's classes, yet forced the master to reassess his demand for "absolute truth" in the recreation of emotionally laden biographical events. From a cognitive perspective, emotional recall of images can only be a re-creation, affected just as much by traces left in the brain by past events as by the emotional context in which the retrieval takes place and by its current purpose. I do not, therefore, subscribe to the weight given to emotional recall by certain acting schools. Heavy reliance on the recall of emotional personal memories – even if genuinely attempted at every performance – is almost certain to entail significant variations in both accuracy and intensity. I think that the personal images of the actor have to be merged with those of the character for 'emotional memory' to get fixed and work consistently.

A mutual unconsciousness . . .

The psychoanalytic concept of transference may also offer an insight into what happens when I 'actively phantasise' about Tamburlaine's stream of images and actions. Transference describes the process by which the analysand 'transfers' on to the analyst psychic contents with deep sources in infantile experiences. These feelings may be negative or positive: the 'memory' of a loving attachment or of resentment and rejection. In either case, the patient experiences transference as something new and real; in Freud's words, "new editions or facsimiles of impulses and phantasies" from infancy. Much of the process of analysis is then taken up with disentangling the feelings that develop between patient and analyst from their sources in childhood relationships. Freud also outlines the phenomenon of countertransference, whereby the analyst becomes affected by the unconscious contents brought up by the patient. The bond between patient and analyst, Jung writes in a classic text on this topic, "is often of such intensity that we would almost speak of a 'combination'. When two chemical substances combine, both are altered".

I am, however, less interested in this clinical relationship than in another concept Freud associates with this phenomenon: the "transference phantasy" during which past events, forgotten yet still stored in the unconscious, are transferred into a current experience, image, or thought arising in the consciousness or in the dreams of the patient. In therapy settings, the catalyst for their emergence is the analyst, but transference also frequently occurs in daily interactions. Jung writes: "In any human relationship that is at all intimate, certain transference phenomena will almost always operate as helpful or disturbing factors". The process of contemplation of the model, a psychoanalytical perspective on acting would argue, causes similar transferences to occur of unconscious contents into the present experiences, thoughts, and images of the actor.

The ultimate aim is to reach insight. Jung gives perhaps the most telling description of the process:

> The doctor, by voluntarily and consciously taking over the psychic sufferings of the patient, exposes himself to the overpowering contents of the unconscious and hence also to their inductive action. The case begins to 'fascinate' him . . . An unconscious tie is established and . . . the patient, by bringing an activated unconscious content to bear upon the doctor, constellates the corresponding unconscious material in him, owing to the inductive effect which always emanates from projections in greater or lesser degree. Doctor and patient thus find themselves in a relationship founded on mutual unconsciousness,
>
> *(1998, p. 12)*

For "doctor", let us read actor, and for "patient", character. As the actor contemplates the character model, character data are filtered through the actor's unconscious and exercise the "inductive action" of which Jung speaks. However, this is where the parallel ends, as the induction emanates from the actor's own unconscious by means of identification with the character – "fascination" leading to "an activated unconscious content". Thus, the character is *of* the actor, yet of a part of the actor's psyche which is normally hidden to his or her consciousness. Here, the catalyst is the character model: 'Tamburlaine' brings up from the unconscious images with strong emotional content.

This process is often described as difficult, sometimes painful; in any event, it demands a special kind of mental effort, a redirection of psychic energy, of libido. Jung likens the unconscious contents that emerge to a "third party" flitting between analyst and patient, playing a game, "sometimes impish and teasing, sometimes really diabolical". I like the idea of the character as a playful "third party" playing games, albeit dangerous or disturbing ones.

Even though transference always leads to a desire to re-enact, not merely report the events remembered, most analytic schools stress that the emergence of phantasies must remain confined to the mental realm. The endeavour of the actor, on the other hand, is to give physical form to what happens in the mind and turn it into action. In the safety of the actor–character blend, phantasies are articulated and purposefully en-acted.

Soft attention

In the chapter dealing with physical approaches to transformation, I outlined the 'centring' approaches coming from traditions as different as those of Stanislavski, Copeau, and Suzuki. Ultimately, these are designed to weaken or circumvent the control of consciousness in order to enable access to the state of "active phantasy" I described earlier. I also touched on the way in which initial decisions regarding the character Super-Objective are usually proved wrong by the time rehearsals have reached their term. The act of creation seems to involve a process of *reculer pour mieux sauter*. Grotowski writes:

> But in order to get the result – and this is the paradox – you must not look for it. If you look for it you will block the natural creative process. In looking only the brain works; the mind imposes solutions it already knows and you begin juggling known things. That is why we must look without fixing our attention on the result.
>
> *(1968, p. 245)*

How can we understand what happens when we 'relinquish' the control of consciousness while still remaining engaged, alert and active?

In his well-known essay, 'Transitional objects and transitional phenomena', the British paediatrician and psychoanalyst D. W. Winnicott hypothesised that a special phase occurs in child development during which infants do not distinguish between their own psychic reality and objects in their immediate environment. The distinction between the corner of a favourite, much-chewed security blanket and their own mouths (what is 'me' and what is 'not me') is yet to be fully formed. Winnicott describes this developmental phase as an "intermediate area of experience" and the objects as "transitional objects". For the infant, transitional objects and phenomena do not belong exclusively to either subjective or objective reality, but straddle both realms. To the outside observer, these objects will seem entirely 'other' than the infant; "but not so from the point of view of the baby. Neither does it come from within; it is not an hallucination," Winnicott writes. It is a state in which self and object are not one, yet neither are they separate – for the baby, the distinction between 'I' and 'it' is, as it were, in a state of suspension. Furthermore, some analysts argue that what they call a state of "primary confusion" is not confined to infant stages of development, but continues into adult life, albeit in modified forms.[1] Discussing the mechanisms of empathy, psychoanalyst Joseph Sandler writes:

> There will always be a momentary persistence of the primary state of confusion, however fleeting, whenever an object is perceived or its representation recalled. What happens then is that the boundaries between self and object become *imposed* by a definite act of inhibiting and of boundary-setting. It is as if the ego says 'This is I and that is he' . . . This may more readily occur in states of relaxation or intense concentration in which the bringing into play of boundary-setting may temporarily be suspended or delayed.
>
> *(Sandler and Joffe, 1967, p. 268, emphasis original)*

In a most interesting extrapolation, Lisa Baraitser and Simon Bayly suggest that this psychological state has parallels in the rehearsal process. They write:

> In rehearsal, decisions about subjectivity and objectivity are also temporarily suspended. The performance is not yet formed or fixed, identities can remain

free, performers can exploit versions of themselves, versions whose 'truth-value' (that necessary illusion of the sense of 'the real me' as ultimately separate from the sum of what I do and say) is neither asserted nor denied.

(2001, p. 68)

The active contemplation of the model, therefore, feels like a reverie: a state of "suspension", in which the boundaries between my sense of self ('I') and the character ('it') are significantly blurred. I think Jung captures the sensation very accurately when he talks of an *abaissement du niveau mental*, a lowering of conscious awareness. As a sensation, this feels as if my consciousness loses energy, a dream-like state that, Jung says in language strikingly similar to descriptions of actor–character merger, "bring[s] about a dissociation of personality – in other words, a multiplication of its centres of gravity". "Round and round I go, mountains and sharks and bulls and PC Olds and Ronnie Kray. It starts to confuse," is how Antony Sher describes this stage. It takes a deliberate mental effort to restore that boundary and bring the distinction between 'I' and 'the object' back into consciousness. In this special state, which I would call 'soft attention', such efforts are suspended.

Psychoanalyst Wilfred Bion also uses the term "reverie" to describe the way a mother and her baby are totally absorbed in one another. Mothers, Bion says, "contain" their babies' anger and anxiety, in both senses of the word: they limit them by, with infinite tolerance, absorbing them into themselves and, thus, identifying with them. Contemplating the model similarly involves an element of kindness and tolerance and, above all, of identifying with or 'loving' the character, or, if one wishes, of "containing" it. The character is one of Melanie Klein's "tenants of the internal world," an internal object, already present in the unconscious of the actor and permitted to emerge under the pressure of the actor's purposeful gaze. As it emerges, the character acts as a catalyst in weakening the grip of consciousness on the personality of the actor. In the creative process, actors stoop to conquer – their loss of conscious energy is a precursor to creative insights. The state of primary confusion is extended to the point where it feels as if subject and object merge.

I find Freud's metaphor for the psychological process of identification strangely resonant with the acting experience. Freud says that early childhood identifications can be compared to the "cannibalistic" incorporation of another person: one consciousness (the child) imitates another (the parent), behaves like it, and, "in a sense takes it up into itself". While this is primarily an infantile process and Freud is careful to distinguish between it and later-life attachments, he none the less conceives of the possibility of mature identifications too: "it is however possible", he writes, "to identify oneself with someone whom, for instance, one has taken as a sexual object, and to alter one's ego on his model". Actors 'fall in love' with their characters and alter their egos on the character model.

I mentioned earlier how actors absorbed in the contemplation of the model describe feeling insulated, 'in a bubble', their creative energies turned inwards. Jung hypothesises that "in the empty stillness which precedes creative work" psychic energy is redirected inwards, towards the unconscious, and propels the eruption of unconscious contents through the defences of the ego. He adds, "The same phenomenon can be seen on a smaller scale, but no less clearly, in the apprehension and depression which precede any special psychic exertion, such as an examination, a lecture, an important interview, etc.". Melanie Klein also observes that the process of identification with an object is always accompanied by a weakening of the control of the ego, with the effect of "blurring the distinction between the self and objects, and between the internal and external world". This weakening of consciousness often manifests itself as a desertion of practical purpose and an inability to cope with everyday requirements. This is not to subscribe to the myth of the confused actor, incapable of managing complex, practical situations (actor-managers from Burbage, Garrick, and Irving to Olivier give the lie to such generalisations), but to observe that at the point in the creative process when actors open themselves up to unconscious contents, this has a debilitating effect. Young actors in training often go through this phase, to the frustration of their teachers; to those wise to the experience, however, this temporary loss of focus signals that ultimately useful unconscious processes are in train. This is not to deny the reality of psychological distress which accompanies this state: in fact, experienced actors often cite the fact that engaging in transformative work is 'painful' as a reason to avoid it. None the less, as Jung tellingly observes, one is entitled to assume that psychoanalysts do not choose their career by chance, but for good psychological reasons, including a propensity to be affected by "psychic infections". So do actors.

Seen from a psychoanalytic perspective, the non-conscious processes involved in 'reverie' and leading to transformation may be summarised as follows:

The unity of the actor's identity, the voice that declares 'I am', 'I think', 'I do', breaks down under the impact of unconscious contents, released under the pressure of the fictional character. Those contents, which are available to the ego, emerge and mould themselves around the data of the character, leading to the emergence of an alternative personality. Actors become aware of the possibility of 'the other' in themselves. In this process, consciousness weakens its grip on the personality; this is a disturbing stage for the actor, who feels 'off balance'. Three entities are, therefore, in play: the fictional character, the actor's consciousness, and the actor's unconscious contents. Character model and actor are both transformed by the catalyst of the unconscious.

For the transformative actor, the contemplation and assimilation of a character model constitutes a deliberate and systematic technique. At the same time, the 'gods of acting' still need to be well disposed for insight, in our case the emergence of the character, to occur. A mysterious creative leap is still involved. No amount of methodical analysis and 'work' can do away with this stage and its success rests with the actor's talent, which might be said to be precisely the ability to take the leap.

And psychoanalysts would be the first to highlight the fact that the deliberate, methodical process implied by the analytical approach is leavened with a healthy dose of intuition. Understanding of the 'other', whether patient or character, involves an act of faith: it can be nurtured, but not coerced. As Jung writes regarding transference: "Enforced faith is nothing but spiritual cramp". Peter Brook once described how, after weeks and months of preparation on paper, come the day of the first rehearsal with the actors, he tossed away his heavily annotated script, jumped on to the stage and 'entered the stream'. Antony Sher captures a similar moment:

> The anarchy, the disrespect for the final run-through unleashes my performance from the caution of seven weeks' rehearsal and sets loose the character at last. Although I didn't realise it, or plan this to happen, I needed to behave this disrespectfully as an actor to make the final leap . . .
>
> *(2014, loc. 3811)*

When it arrives, insight – the fully-fledged character – appears suddenly, abruptly, like a cartoon 'bulb' lighting up. As Goethe noted, exciting images jump at us unbidden, exclaiming: "Here we are!"

Believing in Larry

The challenges arising from the generation of images, which earlier psychology had sought to explain by means of concepts such as intuition and phantasy, have recently been revisited by cognitive science.

It is undoubtedly the case that our conscious consideration of the world, not least of other people, generates images. Images enable us to review potential responses to an external event, examine the possible outcomes of our actions and choose those most likely to be of benefit. The body–mind does this by comparing the images triggered by the present situation with a range of previous responses, stored in its neural structures. In his influential book, *The Feeling of What Happens* (1999), Antonio Damasio proposes a scheme for consciousness based on the generation of images. Briefly, his scheme is:

- Organisms, humans included, interact constantly with their environment.
- These interactions result in physiological changes, from the least noticeable (minor increases in blood pressure, short-lived hormonal releases) to the most obvious – seeing shapes and colours, the sensations of hot or cold, etc.
- These changes generate neural connections ("patterns") in the brain. We become conscious of these in the form of "images". Damasio explains that by image he means "a mental pattern in any of the sensory modalities", not only in vision.
- From birth, genetically, as well as through learning, certain patterns of importance to the organism's survival and welfare are retained.
- When fresh patterns are created as a result of physiological changes, the brain compares these to the patterns it already contains, which become activated.
- The brain also engenders a sense of itself in the act of knowing. Consciousness, therefore, consists of constructing knowledge about two facts: that the organism is involved in relating to some object, and that the object in the relation causes a change in the organism.

Damasio further explains, "Images also allow us to invent new actions to be applied to novel situations and to construct plans for future actions – the ability to transform and combine images of actions and scenarios is the wellspring of creativity".

Moreover, our minds deal with images by turning them into narratives: in order to assimilate reality into our consciousness we tell ourselves stories. As a result, when faced with the need to recount an experience, our brain rolls the film of images it associates with different aspects of that experience. Storytelling, Damasio hypothesises, has a biological basis:

> Telling stories, in the sense of registering what happens in the form of brain maps, is probably a brain obsession and probably begins relatively early both in terms of evolution and in terms of the complexity of the neural structures required to create narratives . . . The brain inherently represents the structures and state of the organism, and in the course of regulating the organism as it is mandated to do, the brain naturally weaves wordless stories about what happens to an organism immersed in an environment.
>
> *(1999, pp. 188–189)*

Stories, or "inference chains", form the foundation both of our ability to make sense of those things we observe directly, through our senses and – crucially for my argument – of the ability we develop to believe in the reality of fictional narratives and identities. Our capacity to construct such links emerges early in childhood. In a famous experiment, the psychologist Alan Leslie showed several groups of two-year-olds a table full of toy animals, including Larry Lamb, a favourite figurine. He then told the toddlers that a certain section of the table was a 'muddy puddle'. When Larry Lamb rolled in that section, almost all the children declared that Larry had got muddy. The toddlers were able to draw inferences from the various aspects of pretend reality, of play. Their inferences reflected not what they *saw*, but what they *believed*. Indeed, Leslie argues that any and all imagining involves beliefs in which the concept 'pretend' is involved.

Our ability to consider future situations and outcomes by means of images, and then act on the optimum scenarios these entail, confers on us an immeasurable evolutionary advantage. The body-mind develops structures enabling it to respond to images automatically, non-consciously. Damasio calls these brain structures the "somatic markers": "somatic" because they are about the body (*soma* in Greek), "markers" because they "mark", fixing into brain circuitry images arising, however fleetingly, in the mind. Somatic markers are "automated alarm signals", important weapons in our defensive armoury which, by linking present events to the memory of past dangers, enable us to make life-saving choices in milliseconds, without the need for a laborious examination of possible courses of action. Reactions can, therefore, be triggered in the brain not only by an actual object or event, but also by "conjuring up from memory" an image of that object or event. Imagining a violent or an affectionate scenario, for example, provokes emotional reactions closely paralleling the ways in which we would react if we believed the events were real.

Neurological research suggests convincingly that imagined stimuli follow the same pathways in the brain as real-life ones. The eminent neuroscientist Vittorio Gallese writes:

> Imagining and doing use a shared neural substrate. When one imagines seeing something, some of the same part of the brain is used as when one actually sees. When we imagine moving, some of the same part of the brain is used as when we actually move.
>
> *(Gallese and Lakoff, 2005, p. 456)*

Within the framework of play and fiction, constructing a character model means believing in its 'reality' to the point of being changed physiologically. And, as I have stressed before, no tool is more powerful in this endeavour than the use of personality traits or of characteristics: words.

Acting the metaphors

On reflection, what do we have in acting by way of immediate aids to spur the jump between text and embodiment? Only words. We saw in relation to the psychology of traits how words played a crucial role in our common ability to grasp and communicate perceptions of personality. The same applies to the way in which we conceive action. I once knew a singing teacher who had trained a number of highly regarded opera singers. One of her most effective approaches consisted in telling her students, "When you want to hit a high note, imagine you are pulling a string upwards through your nose". This led to some odd facial contortions but almost always succeeded in producing crystalline sounds. How did it work? How, for that matter, does Moni Yakim's injunction to trainee actors to "put themselves wholly" into a caterpillar or a toothbrush actually produce the sensations of psychophysical change? Or Laban's 'punches' and 'glides'? Or, indeed, Stanislavski's and Anne Bogart's exercises which alter the meaning of gestures by changing the speeds with which they are executed?

Anne Bogart even writes:

> Viewpoints is a set of names given to certain principles of movement through time and space; these names constitute a language for talking about what happens onstage . . . Naming the Viewpoints allows us to dissect reality into something identifiable and perhaps repeatable onstage.
>
> *(2005, p. 7, 199)*

Thus, Bogart recognises that the most immediate merit of her methodology is to have created a vocabulary by means of which actors can conceptualise physical experiences, making them conscious and amenable to manipulation and change.

And Simon Callow, speaking about the terminology of the Laban–Malmgren System, says, "I use 'Remote' or 'Mobile' because the words have a suggestive value in themselves, even without the specific images created in training".

It seems that the utility as well as the fascination of movement-based approaches such as these ultimately reside in the fact that they provide a *sui generis language of metaphors*.

George Lakoff and Mark Johnson have argued that, in certain cases, metaphors are not only a function of language, but integral to consciousness. In traditional faculty psychology our ability to reason – to form and use abstract concepts – was considered to be separate and distinct from our ability to perceive and to move. This tradition considered that, as Lakoff and Johnson put it: "perception may inform reason, and movement may be a consequence of reason, but . . . no aspect of perception or movement is *part* of reason" and that consequently "there is assumed to be an absolute dichotomy between *perception* and *conception*". In their influential work on Conceptual Metaphor Theory (CMT), Lakoff and Johnson proposed an alternative perspective on cognition, that of "embodied reason". According to this view, concepts and their properties are an inevitable and necessary consequence of the way in which our bodies and brains are structured, as well as of our interactions with one another and the physical world around us. We conflate abstract concepts (emotions, ideas) with other concepts of which we have a direct, physical experience (spatial orientation, objects, etc.). When we say that we are 'falling behind' schedule or that we 'look forward' to a party, we grasp a highly abstract concept such as time by means of metaphorical associations with the more concrete and easier to perceive domain of space.

Such conflations across domains give rise to what Lakoff and Johnson describe as "metaphoric thinking". We speak, for example, of a *warm* welcome and of people we are *close* to; or of *rising* political tensions and *falling* prices. In such metaphors, a source-domain (the sensorimotor experience through which we perceive temperature, distance, gravity, etc.) is conflated with a target-domain, that of subjective judgement (intimacy, emotions, justice, etc.) According to Johnson's theory of conflation, such associations are formed automatically and unconsciously in early childhood: thus, "for an infant the subjective experience of affection is typically correlated with the sensory experience of warmth, of being held"; equally, repeated observations in early childhood that liquids or piles of objects rise as they increase and drop as they decrease link the subjective judgement of quantity (more/less) with the sensorimotor experience of verticality (up/down). Such conflations give rise to what Lakoff and Johnson call "primary metaphors": AFFECTION IS WARMTH; MORE IS UP; IMPORTANT IS BIG; CHANGE IS MOTION, etc. (I follow their convention and capitalise metaphor descriptors).

In the Laban–Malmgren System, for example, the actor learning to associate Space (Direct–Flexible) with Thinking starts with the sensations of 'towards' and 'away from', as well as of direct and flexible movements. Thoughts are conceptualised as being either fixed in space (*grasped, captured*) or *drifting*. Complex thinking is revealed physically in the concave body of a listener doubting the speaker's assertions ("Let us sit crooked and think straight," as Brecht says). Thought is perceived as a journey: the THOUGHT IS A JOURNEY metaphor tells us that to accept or relate to an idea is to move closer to it; to doubt or examine it is to distance oneself from it; Thought and Space become inextricably linked.

Similarly, linking Flow (Free–Bound) to Feeling is rooted in the sensation of emotions *flowing* or being *blocked* through the body, expressed in metaphors such as *the adrenaline coursed through my veins; love flowed from his eyes; her heart stopped in her mouth; a wave of jealousy.*

Writing about *All's Well That Ends Well*, Michael Bristol draws a nice line between Helena's defining moral quality, her personality, and her tempo. He writes: "Helena's virtue – her character, as we might say – lies in a quality of alacrity, a willingness and a capability of acting to shape her world". Now, imagine turning this "quality of alacrity" into a physical reality by focusing on the Viewpoint of Time, playing with its various tempi, then translating the resulting sensations back into words. Anne Bogart writes:

> What verbs are implied by performing the same action at different speeds? The *medium* [speed] perhaps implies 'to touch' or 'to retrieve', whereas the *fast* action is maybe 'to grab' or 'to protect', and the *slow* maybe 'to seduce' or 'to sneak'.
>
> *(2005, p. 37, emphasis original)*

The transformative techniques I described in earlier chapters are all built on a "foundational" metaphor similar to those described by Lakoff and Johnson: PSYCHOLOGICAL ACTION IS PHYSICAL ACTION. Psychological functions are perceived as movements: feelings *run high* and are *jarring*; thought *goes (straight) to the heart of the issue* or *around the problem*; intuitions are *quick off the mark* or *slow to catch on*; sensations are connected to gravity – *heavy/strong smell; light touch*. Our psychological experiences are structured in terms of physical forces.

In such metaphors, the physical experience dominates. Lakoff and Johnson explain, "we typically conceptualise the nonphysical in terms of the physical – that is, we conceptualise the less clearly delineated in terms of the more clearly delineated". THINKING IS SPACE makes experiential sense; SPACE IS THINKING does not. The relationship between source and target domains is "asymmetrical" – "inferences only flow from the sensorimotor domain to that of subjective judgment".

Conceptual Metaphor Theory is not without its challenges. As Lakoff and Johnson themselves pointed out, neurological research supporting it was far from conclusive at the time they wrote *Philosophy in the Flesh* (1999), their major work on the subject. Earlier studies had shown that when sports people rehearsed their routines repeatedly in their heads in between bouts of exercise, muscle strength increased more than for those who only engaged in the physical aspects of training. Likewise, when people imagined doing physical exercises, their breathing frequency and heartbeat rates increased steadily, just as when they were doing the actual exercise. Such instances led writers to think of imagination as a form of simulation, yet solid evidence derived from brain studies was still lacking. In 2005, working alongside Vittorio Gallese, George Lakoff posed this challenge:

The sentence *he grasped the idea* should activate the sensorimotor grasping-related regions of the brain. Similarly, a metaphorical sentence like *they kicked him out of class* should activate sensorimotor kicking-related regions of the brain.

(2005, p. 472)

In recent years, a series of experiments have sought to offer 'proof of concept' to CMT. By means of fMRI and PET scans, they strived to ascertain whether a common neural substrate was involved when carrying out an action physically as well as when imagining it. Experiments did indeed show that when we imagine grasping or seeing an object some of the same sections of the brain are used as when we actually see or touch it. Most studies of this type focused on metaphors involving a sense of motion: "grasping" an idea, being "moved" by an image, etc. In an interesting recent study, however, researchers also showed that metaphors such as "I had a rough day" or "I met this really slimy guy" activated those areas of the brain where our sense of texture, which does not involve motion, resides.

From the plethora of experiments constantly being carried out in this area, I am selecting a couple which I think are of particular relevance for acting:[2]

In 2013, neuroscientist Rutvik Desai and his colleagues undertook a complex study using a "hierarchy" of metaphoric expressions. Subjects were placed in fMRI machines and exposed to phrases which were linked, yet operated at three different levels: literal descriptions of an action, appropriate but not overly-idiomatic metaphors, and well-worn expressions containing the implication of an action. Brain reactions to the first two phrases investigated the assumptions on which Lakoff and Johnson had based their theory. Reactions to the third checked whether over-familiarity affected the effectiveness of the metaphors and, thus, whether these should in the end be considered simply as linguistic constructs, with no grounding in physical perceptions. Thus:

Literal: The instructor is *grasping* the steering wheel very tightly.

Metaphor: Congress is *grasping* the state of affairs.

Idiom: Congress is *grasping* at straws in the crisis.

or

Literal: The craftsman *lifted* the pebble from the ground.

Metaphor: The discovery *lifted* this nation out of poverty.

Idiom: The country *lifted* the veil on its nuclear programme.

fMRI scans showed that those areas of the brain involved in controlling movement and sensation were indeed activated by both the literal and the metaphorical phrases. This gave support to the hypothesis that the same neural networks are involved in the actual gesture and in its mental simulation. However, the sensorimotor areas of the brain did not light up when the subjects heard the idiomatic cliché. When the metaphors had lost their initial vivid quality, the brain did not appear to make the connection with the physical correlatives of the words on which the phrase had originally been based. The study concluded that a certain level of concrete engagement was necessary if a coupling between words and movement was to occur in metaphoric thinking. For images and characteristics to be effective in acting, they have to retain their freshness; within certain limits, striking metaphors are the more likely to generate the desired psychophysical change.

Another recent study throws additional light on the nature of this engagement. This study set out to ascertain whether being involved in some form of preparatory physical exercise enables greater comprehension of abstract ideas and, in particular, "implicit cognition" – the ability to infer and deduce from a text. In one experiment, participants were asked to ride a stationary bicycle for one minute; in a second trial they were asked to sit still on the bike in a forward-orientated position. Both they and a control group, which did not engage in the physical activities, were then asked to read a political speech containing a number of metaphors and metaphorical phrases indicating 'forward-moving' or progressive policies and ideas. In subsequent tests, both groups were shown to have understood the superficial aspects of the text equally well. However, those who had recently experienced the sensation of moving forward and had then adopted the forward-leaning posture displayed a higher degree of deep comprehension – they were able to judge with significantly higher acuity the meanings and implications of those phrases which implied 'progress'. Moreover, those participants who adopted a forward posture were much quicker at judging whether comments about the content of the speech were accurate or not. The authors concluded that: "These findings support the hypothesis that understanding of language involves constructing [in the mind] a sensorimotor simulation of the described event".

Such studies confirm what actors have always known: that 'doing it', adopting the posture and engaging in the gestures of a character, "makes the words flesh". They also support those acting approaches whose starting points are movement and physical sensation. As Rick Kemp puts it: "consciously chosen gestural activity provokes ideas".

This, I believe, is what happens during the contemplation and exploration of a character model. The association of psychological descriptors with physical dimensions gives the actor a systematic way of describing the type of "experiential gestalt" of which Lakoff and Johnson speak: "a whole that we human beings find more basic than the parts". Having a dual nature (at one and the same time physical and psychological), character traits move us to action as well as change us, especially when they are linked to emotions. It is assumed that certain so-called 'semantic nodes' in our brains – synaptic connections which store words and their meanings – are associated with other networks ('schemata') linked to the perception of physical realities. These schemata are formed through repeated associations between certain life events and certain changes in our bodies. When reading or hearing about an event, we activate these pre-existing perceptual representations in the brain. Words that trigger them cause the recurrence of the bodily arousal we interpret as feelings. Lakoff and Johnson write:

> New metaphors have the power to create a new reality. This can begin to happen when we start to comprehend our experience in terms of a metaphor, and it becomes a deeper reality when we begin to act in terms of it. If a new metaphor enters the conceptual system that we base our actions on, it will alter that conceptual system and the perceptions and actions that the system gives rise to.
>
> *(2003, p. 145)*

Characteristics move us, in both senses of the word.

Notes

1 This state, which precedes the awareness of separation between 'I' and 'other', is called "primary identification" by Freud, "adualism" by Piaget, and "primary identity" by others.
2 I am grateful to Vittorio Gallese for pointing me in the direction of these recent studies.

Bibliography

Observing actors: Kalb, J., 2007. 'Rockaby and the art of inadvertent interpretation, and considerations of acting in the early plays', in Keefe, J., and Murray, S. (eds.), *Physical Theatres: A Critical Reader*. London: Routledge.

Intuition and the psychoanalytic tradition: Jung, C. G., 1971. *Collected Works, Volume 6: Psychological Types*, translated by R. F. C. Hull. London: Routledge and Kegan Paul; Jung, C. G., 1990. *Analytical Psychology: Its Theory and Practice (The Tavistock Lectures)*. London: Routledge.

Phantasy and active imagination: Jung, 1971; Hannah, B., 1981. *Encounters with the Soul – Active Imagination as Developed by C. G. Jung*. Boston: Sigo Press; Stanislavski, C., 1994. *Creating A Role*, translated by E. Hapgood. London: Methuen; *as a "game"*: Stanislavski, C., 1986. *An Actor Prepares*, translated by E. Hapgood. London: Methuen; Freed, D., 1964. *Freud and Stanislavsky*. New York: Vantage Press; *and inner images*: Stanislavski, C., 1968. *Building a Character*, translated by E. Hapgood. London: Methuen; Blair, R., 2008. *The Actor, Image, and Action (Acting and Cognitive Neuroscience)*. London: Routledge.

Personalisation: Hagen, U., with Frankel, H., 1973. *Respect for Acting*. New York: Collier Macmillan; Blair, R., 2006. 'Image and action: cognitive neuroscience and actor-training', in McConachie, B., and Hart, F. E. (eds.), *Performance and Cognition: Theatre Studies and the Cognitive Turn*. London: Routledge, pp. 167–186; Bristol, M., 2006. '. . . And I'm the King of France', in Grady, H., and Hawkes, T. (eds.), *Presentist Shakespeares*. New York: Routledge.

Retrieving images: Damasio, A., 1994. *Descartes' Error: Emotion, Reason, and the Human Brain.* New York: Putnam; Damasio, A., 1999. *The Feeling of What Happens: Body and Emotion in the Making of Consciousness.* London: William Heinemann; LeDoux, J., 2003. *The Emotional Brain: The Mysterious Underpinnings of Emotional Life.* New York: Touchstone; *mood dependence*: Connolly, R., and Ralley, R., 2007. 'The laws of normal organic life or Stanislavski explained: towards a scientific account of the subconscious in Stanislavski's system'. *Studies in Theatre and Performance*, 27 (3), pp. 237–259.

Transference: Freud, S., 2010. 'Fragments of an analysis of a case of hysteria' and 'An outline', in *Complete Works (CW)*. Ivan Smith Online Edition: https://openlibrary.org/works/ OL16678137W/Freud_Complete_Works; Jung, C. G., 1998. *The Psychology of the Transference*, translated by R.F.C. Hull. London: Routledge.

Soft attention: Grotowski, J., 1968. *Towards a Poor Theatre.* New York: Touchstone Books.

Transitional objects: Winnicott, D. W., 1953. 'Transitional objects and transitional phenom- ena – a study of the first not-me possession'. *International Journal of Psychoanalysis*, 34, pp. 89–97; Sandler, J., and Joffe, W. W., 1967. 'The tendency to persistence in psychological function and development, with special reference to fixation and regression'. *Bulletin of the Menninger Clinic*, 31 (5), pp. 257–271.

Reverie and acting: Baraitser, L., and Bayley, S., 2001. 'Now and then: psychotherapy and the rehearsal process', in Campbell P., and Kear, A. (eds.), *Psychoanalysis and Performance.* London: Routledge; Sher, A., 2014. *The Year of the King: An Actor's Diary and Sketchbook.* Kindle Edition. London: Nick Hern Books; *"here we are"*: Goethe, cited in Pitches, J., 2006. *Science and the Stanislavsky Tradition of Acting.* Abingdon: Routledge.

Reverie, identification and psychoanalysis: Jung, 1998; Bion, W. R., 1962. *Learning From Experience.* London: Karnac; Klein, M., 1997. *Envy and Gratitude, and Other Works 1946–1963.* London: Vintage; Freud, 2010.

Inference chains, pretending and belief: Damasio, 1999; Leslie, A., 1987. 'Pretence and repre- sentation: the origins of theory of mind'. *Psychological Review*, 94, pp. 412–426; Leslie, A., 1994. 'Pretending and believing: issues in the TOMM'. *Cognition*, 50, pp. 211–238; *somatic markers*: Damasio, 1994; *emotional responses to imagined events reviewed in*: Lang, P., 1984. 'Cognition and emotion, concept and action', in Izard, C., Kagan, G., and Zaponas, R. (eds.), *Emotion, Cognition and Behaviour.* Cambridge: Cambridge University Press, pp. 192–226; Harris, P., 2000. *The Work of the Imagination.* Oxford: Blackwell; Gallese, V., and Lakoff, G., 2005. 'The brain's concepts: the role of the sensory–motor system in conceptual knowledge'. *Cognitive Neuropsychology*, 22 (3–4), pp. 455–479.

Acting, language and conceptualisation: Yakim, M. with Broadman, M., 1990. *Creating a Character: A Physical Approach to Acting.* New York: Back Stage Books; Bogart, A., and Landau, T., 2005. *The Viewpoints Book: A Practical Guide to Viewpoints and Composition.* New York: Theatre Communications Group; Bristol, M., 2012. 'How dark was it in that room? Performing a scene Shakespeare never wrote', in Yu, J. K., and Shurgot, M. (eds.), *Shakespeare's Sense of Character, On the Page and From the Stage.* Farnham: Ashgate, pp. 19–34.

Conceptual Metaphor Theory: Lakoff, G., and Johnson, M., 1999. *Philosophy in the Flesh: The Embodied Mind and its Challenge to Western Thought.* New York: Basic Books; Lakoff, G., and Johnson, M. 2003. *Metaphors We Live By.* Revised Edition. Chicago: University of Chicago Press; *challenges to*: Gainotti, G., 2004. 'A metanalysis of impaired and spared nam- ing of different categories of knowledge in patients with a visuo-verbal disconnection'. *Neuropsychologia*, 42, pp. 299–319; *and imagination as simulation*: Yue, G., and Cole, K., 1992. 'Strength increases from the motor program: comparison of training with maximal and imagined muscle contractions'. *Journal of Neurophysiology*, 67, pp. 1114–1123; Decety,

J., Jeannerod, M., et al, 1991. 'Vegetative response during imagined movement is proportional to mental effort'. *Behavioural Brain Research*, 34, pp. 35–42; Gallese, V., 2003. 'The roots of empathy: the shared manifold hypothesis and the neural basis of intersubjectivity'. *Psychopathology*, 36 (4), pp. 171–180.

Neuroscience and metaphors: Gallese and Lakoff, 2005; Lacey, S., Stilla, R., and Sathian, K., 2012. 'Metaphorically feeling: comprehending textural metaphors activates somatosensory cortex.' *Brain and Language*, 120, pp. 416–421; Desai, R. H., Conant, L. L., et al, 2013. 'A piece of the action: modulation of sensory–motor regions by action idioms and metaphors'. *NeuroImage*, 83, pp. 862–869; *bicycle study*: Horchak, O. V., Giger, J.-C., and Pochwatko, G., 2014. 'Simulation of metaphorical actions and discourse comprehension'. *Metaphor and Symbol*, 29, pp. 1–22; *words trigger body arousal*: Kemp, R., 2012. *Embodied Acting, What Neuroscience Tells Us about Performance*. London: Routledge; Kagan, J., 2007. *What Is Emotion? History, Measures, and Meaning*. New Haven, CT: Yale University Press.

11

EXPERIENCING THE CHARACTER

Fusions

"The end of playing," the American scholar Bert O. States says, is the ability of actor and spectator to hold in their minds at one and the same time two categories, self and character, "fused into a single phenomenon". How is such a fusion even possible?

To the scientific psychologist, all the talk about mergers taking place in the unconscious, which has been the focus of the previous chapters, will sound like a peculiar form of mysticism. From the scientific perspective, transformation ought to be considered as a cognitive experience – we *perceive* being 'other', although, in the strict physical sense, we are not. And there is nothing mystical about this – acting transformation is a specialised extension of a natural process of our body-mind.

But before attempting to offer some possible explanations from this perspective, let me first say that I think we are still far from being able to capture with anything like scientific accuracy the transformative experience, however familiar this may feel to actors. The experimental technology available to us is not sufficiently advanced to explain the higher levels of neural integration involved in the creation and reception of complex artistic creations. At the level of the brain, the process remains opaque. What follows is, therefore, based on well-argued, yet still tentative, theoretical models.

Older attempts at an answer skirted around this enigma by citing 'talent' and 'intuition', both concepts we recognise empirically, yet are hard put to define. I have had cause to refer already to Francis Fergusson's notion of the "histrionic spirit", which, "like the ear for music, is a natural virtue". Fergusson continues:

> The great continental repertory theatres of the last generation – the *Vieux Colombier*, Reinhardt's theatres, the Moscow Art Theatre – required of the

actor a discipline of the feelings and the imagination as conscious and severe as the physical disciplines of ballet. The purpose of this discipline was to free the actor's emotions and cultivate his perceptions, so that he could make-believe the situation as invented by the playwright and then respond mimetically with his whole being. An actor or director trained in this way reads the play as a composition to be performed, just as a trained musician reads a score as a composition of sounds and rhythms.

(1949, p. 24)

Historically, such inspirational, if somewhat nebulous, descriptions have defined much of the discourse on creativity in acting. But how does this happen?

A book widely read in the 1960s and 1970s, Arthur Koestler's *Act of Creation* (1964), proposed one way of approaching these mysteries. An innovative thinker with a gift for making complex concepts accessible, Koestler landed on the notion of comparing the paths by which humour, scientific discoveries, and artistic achievements are reached. Koestler suggested that in these three spheres, unique to human endeavour, the mind follows an identical pattern: presented with two domains ("matrices") of thought, unrelated and often contradictory, the mind finds points at which these can intersect. Out of such intersections a new, original, third "matrix" emerges: the punchline of a joke, a scientific Eureka moment, or an arresting turn of phrase.

Koestler gives numerous examples of how this so-called "bisociation" works, from Jewish jokes from the Bronx to Newton's apple and Proust's time travels. I have my own, multi-layered favourite: in 1987, the singer Lou Reed recorded an album entitled *Songs for Drella*, dedicated to his mentor, Andy Warhol, who had recently died. 'Drella' is an amalgam of 'Dracula' and 'Cinderella' and was the nick-name given to Warhol by his close friends, reflecting two aspects of his personality.

Overtaken for a time by other concerns, Koestler's "bisociation theory" has been revisited in recent years by those seeking to dissect creative processes with the tools of cognitive science. In their influential book, *The Way We Think* (2002), Gilles Fauconnier and Mark Turner propose *cognitive blend theory* as a scheme to explain the complex computations taking place within the human brain. In order to grasp this non-conscious mechanism, they use a spatial metaphor: thought, they assert, takes place within "mental spaces". These "small conceptual packets constructed as we think and talk" are needed for speedy problem solving and action. Let us say that I have lost my keys and I need to retrace my steps – when I do this, I "inhabit" a mental space – 'earlier me' walking on the same path. Under certain conditions, two such spaces "blend" in the body-mind to create a third, new space. This draws certain characteristics from its initial sources but has its own – distinctive – identity. This organic, everyday process describes the way in which we understand the world around us at the most basic level. Let me try to follow this thread:

Earlier today, on my way to the British Library where I am now sitting typing this paragraph, I passed a small pop-up shop selling tea and cakes. The sign above it read *Tea Rex*. As I read it, I smiled. Why? Following the cognitive blend scheme, in order to understand and react to the pun, I had to:

1. Hold the image of the name above the teacart in my short-term memory so that it registered in consciousness.
2. Summon from long-term memory the image and name of a species of dinosaur called *Tyrannosaurus Rex*.
3. Recall that when written down, the name *Tyrannosaurus Rex* is abbreviated as 'T-Rex'
4. Translate the graphic symbol into its corresponding sound in English (T – [*ti:*]).
5. Realise that the sound elicits at least two homophones – tee/tea.
6. Blend the two mental spaces – tea and dinosaur – into a third: a witty pun.
7. Further recall that *Rex* is Latin for King, that T-Rex was the 'king of dinosaurs', and, therefore, arrive at the intended message – that the stall was run by the 'King of Teas'.
8. Interpret the metaphor 'King of Teas' to stand for 'best teas'.
9. Separate ("disintegrate") the blend back to its original terms in order to work out in consciousness what the pun meant.
10. Finally, react physically to this mental sequence and smile at the conceit.
    Ten separate steps, taken in the blink of an eye.

In this model, the two initial mental spaces are called *inputs;* these merge into the *blend*. Fauconnier and Turner point out that inputs may consist not only of material realities (objects, events, etc.), but also of mental representations of such realities. Thus, a crucial step in this process is the abstraction of material realities into symbols. People who visit the National Portrait Gallery or Madame Tussauds do so in no small measure because they feel 'in the presence' of famous figures. We look at the portraits and say, "Queen Elizabeth looks magnificent in that dress", or "That's James Joyce". The sign comes to stand for the person: we create cognitive networks that permit us to identify a person by their most salient features. Sonia in *Uncle Vanya* is the plain girl with "beautiful hair"; Falstaff's gut makes him instantly recognisable. "We parse an ocean of diversity quickly and reliably into a few elements coherently arrayed," writes Mark Turner. Had we not developed this ability to turn diversity into unity, little brain capacity would be left to deal with attention, memory, and so on. Remember how Lecoq relied on only three key physical changes and Barbara Berkery on a small number of vowel shifts to signal character? The mind needs only a limited number of elements in order to place its perceptions into correct categories – 'going from many to one' is a key principle of cognition.

This miraculous ability is one of the greatest gains of evolution: we are constantly assailed by myriad events and our minds have developed the rare ability to package them. It is a distinct evolutionary advantage that these functions are discharged away from consciousness and at the speed of light: they are probably carried out by means of distributed networks across the nervous system, which would be inhibited if consciousness were involved. The fact that they are hidden from consciousness, however, makes them feel like 'magical' Eureka moments.

Having abstracted diverse aspects of material reality, our minds then compress these abstractions into a single, unitary experience. If this sounds overly theoretical, think of two puppies fiercely engaged in 'the great game of Who's Boss'. They will chase each other in imitation of stalking their prey, they will nibble at each other's ears and noses in mock fighting, they will hold their tails erect in pretend aggression. Even children playing with pet dogs will simulate conduct associated with hunting and domination. During such behaviour, they *simultaneously* exercise motivations, direct their attention, and execute movements that belong to two very different worlds: hunting and playing. Normally, bringing two different domains into the mind at the same time is a recipe for madness and would have been discarded by evolution as being against the fundamental interests of the organism. Yet, in what Mark Turner calls "forbidden-fruit blending", the brain permits this simultaneous holding together of two domains. The hypothesis is that this very special form of adaptation contributes to introducing variation into the cognitive process and, thus, leads to innovation, unusual associations, and, ultimately, to those creative leaps we hail as major discoveries.

Conversely, the pedantic unpacking of an innocent pun I undertook above left me with an odd aftertaste. It felt perverse to break down a humorous, and therefore pleasurable, occurrence. Blends and compressions feel natural, organic, but their disintegration goes against the grain. The same applies when actors perform. For most of the time, the actor-in-character 'feels like' a single, indivisible, and stable entity. Occasionally, this perception is broken and the actor becomes aware of the distance between the 'I' and the 'it'. When this happens, the actor perceives this as an unpleasant jolt. At the same time, disintegration remains an essential feature of character creation: the character blend has sufficient disintegration capacity for the actor to be able to connect back to the original inputs – the actor holds in consciousness *in a sufficient degree* the awareness that the character is an amalgam of elements of 'I' and 'it'.

As we have seen, actor identity (the sense of 'I') and character identity ('it') are held in working memory as abstractions. This ability to turn them into symbols permits the blend to take place. I also think that actors engaged in transformation specifically translate their 'sense of I' *as actors* (not their daily life identities), into the symbols which, to borrow a concept from chemistry, are the precursors of this reaction. The will of the actor to engage with the role focuses the daily personality into a professional identity, in preparation for the blend. This is part of the actor's Attitude/*Haltung* and constitutes a neurological bias, a learned reflex, developed through training and experience. It supports attention, arousal, and memory functions specific to the acting process. Training and experience also facilitate the special mental effort needed to disaggregate actor from character – the dissociation of the blend back into its inputs.

So, to the earlier list of underlying principles involved in transformation (design, intensity, and rhythm) we must now add the all-important mechanism of abstraction and compression of two disparate realities into a third cognitive synthesis.

Creativity in general, defined as the discovery of unexpected connections and solutions, is, therefore, dependent on the blending capacity of the mind. As cognitive linguist Merlin Donald explains:

> Art is *constructivist* in nature, aimed at the deliberate refinement and elabora-
> tion of mental models and worldviews. These are the natural products of
> cognition itself, the outcome of the brain's tendency to strive for the inte-
> gration of perceptual and conceptual material over time. The term *large-scale*
> *neural integration* refers to the nervous system's cross-modal unification of
> many sources of experience into a single abstract model or percept.
>
> *(2006, p. 4, emphasis original)*

Blends are connected in the mind to long-term schematic knowledge as well as to long-term specific knowledge. In the example above, the mental space I created to register and understand the *Tea Rex* sign connected to my long-term awareness of commercial advertising as well as to the specific understanding of 'street cart sell-ing tea'. Once this basic level of understanding was established, the creative jump consisted in making the connection between tea drinking and a long-lost dinosaur. This is what mental spaces are for: to play with representations of reality that would be impossible in the material world. The brain science behind such schemas is still indeterminate, but the working assumption is – as we saw in the earlier description of Damasio's scheme – that mental spaces are underpinned by networks of neurons which are fired by certain inputs, and then connect (bind) to the already established neural networks in which we store knowledge.

It is well known that memory is distributed throughout our brains. Because we use different organs to register the shape, weight, sound, and colour of, say, a violin, the records of these features are registered in those parts of our brain which variously correspond to sight, touch, hearing, etc. Moreover, the word we use to describe the object is stored in a different part of the brain altogether. Yet, when we need the image of the violin, our brains have no trouble coordinating the speedy retrieval of these records so as to form an integrated image. Antonio Damasio hypothesises that this pattern also applies to the way in which we construct our biographies, and, thus, our sense of identity. He writes:

> I would like to suggest that the memories for the entities and events that
> constitute our present autobiography are likely to use the same sort of
> framework used for the memories we form about any entity or event. What
> distinguishes those memories is that they refer to established, invariant facts
> of our personal histories. I propose we store records of our personal expe-
> riences in the same distributed manner, in as varied higher-order cortices
> as needed to match the variety of our live interactions. Those records are
> closely coordinated by neural connections so that the content of the records
> can be recalled and made explicit, as ensembles, rapidly and efficiently.
>
> *(1999, p. 221)*

I think this perspective can also be applied to the process of character formation. We read 'Elsinore' in *Hamlet* – the word evokes associations with "a number of explicit mental patterns". The "records" vary: views of medieval fortifications, touch of stone, smell of gunpowder, concept of castle, concepts of power or oppression or defence. These are then coordinated and turned into explicit, albeit sketchy, images. However, we know that a non-conscious selection process is also in play: one actor will select 'power', another 'defence' – hence the possibility and inevitability of interpretation, of particularisation. In its current state of knowledge, cognitive blend theory has not been able to determine what causes some images to penetrate into consciousness and others not. Fauconnier and Turner maintain that they only need to be sufficient to satisfy the requirements of the blend sought by the mind-brain. They write:

> The mind can be thought of as a bubble chamber of mental spaces: New mental spaces are formed all the time out of the old ones . . . Yet despite the teeming activity of the brain's bubble chamber and the vastly larger bubble chamber of culture, only some blends will come up, only some inputs will be activated, only some conceptual mutations will happen. Many could have happened in principle, but did not . . . In blending, as in evolution, good enough is good enough.
>
> *(2002, p. 321)*

I like their parallel with the unpredictability of selection in evolution: it would go some way toward explaining why different actors arrive at such different interpretations of the same character, or even of the same lines, and, by extension, the cognitive mechanism behind what we perceive as intuition. But I am also attracted by the causality implied by the psychological perspective. As I discussed earlier, in that view it is the actor's unconscious inclinations (Attitude/*Haltung*) and consequent interpretative choices that determine which images come up. They certainly determine which images are retained: working on Richard, Sher goes through a whole series of animal images, yet ends up by discarding lions and bulls in favour of the spider. True, his final choice is suggested by the text, but is 'intuitively' recognised as the 'right one' by his *Haltung*.

Blends, including the specialised actor–character one instanced here, do not happen of their own accord. Ninety-nine per cent of the public passing by the tea stall would have simply read the sign. Many would, like me, have smiled at the pun. Some would have stopped to buy a cup of tea. But only I dwelt on the sign long enough to parse the cognitive process behind it. And this only because, as I was passing by the stall, my attention was already turning to writing this section. My *purpose* made me look at this piece of reality with specialised eyes and find new meanings in the blends on offer.

This is also what happens when an actor 'reads for character'. As they mature, our brains form numerous connections between neurons, reflecting the various experiences of our lives. But the fact that they are there does not necessarily mean they will become active. It is now widely accepted that the activation of pre-existing neural patterns depends on what is happening in the brain *at a particular moment*. Our present purpose plays a crucial role in determining whether a particular set of connections in the brain will fire up, will be "co-activated", in neurological terminology. The purpose "drives" the blend. Similarly, a pre-condition for character creation is that the attention be purposefully directed towards the possibility of a blend. The actor wills the character blend into existence. Once this begins to emerge, an iterative process is established between the blend and the matches within the inputs, mutually reinforcing one another and growing together: the matches in number, the blend in shape and potency. By potency, I mean the power of the blend to energise the actor and eventually to act autonomously.

For specific neural networks to become activated, two or more inputs must share a cognitive framework that supports their association, a so-called "organising frame". *The Long View*, for example, a programme on BBC Radio, illuminates contemporary issues by setting them alongside similar occurrences in history. These could include England's relationship to continental Europe, the abuse of 'fake news', or the trials and tribulations of growing a beard. In these random examples, the organising frames that permit the connections to be made by the producers and understood by the listeners are, respectively, international relations, news/information, and fashion. We saw that one framework shaping my understanding of the *Tea Rex* sign was commercial advertising. But I could have selected others, too: 'temptation on my way to work', 'English humour', and so on.

Similarly, an actor engaged in the contemplation of the fictional character model uses organising frames such as mimesis, imitation, or transformative acting to activate so-called 'mirror integration networks' in the brain. The cognitive principle, Mark Turner explains, is that "in a mirror network, separate conceptual spaces share an organising frame, which is also projected to organise a blended space".

Directly relevant to my argument is Fauconnier's and Turner's additional observation that, alongside shared frames, character and identity also play crucial roles in the way we think. To arrive at answers to questions such as, "What would I do if I were Baron Tuzenbach challenged to a duel?", to 'put myself in his shoes', I am using my understanding of the Baron's *character*. This understanding is based on the assumption that personal identity is stable across any number of frames. As I have outlined in relation to traits and types, we say about someone, "He is always so proud, or sensitive, or nervous", precisely because we recognise that people may be described by the way in which they display similar behaviours in different circumstances. We also recognise similarities of behaviour among groups of people in order to build a generic category for a *type* of behaviour. And we then create a mental space for 'the kind of person who always does this kind of thing'. Types – from Theophrastus to the masks – are, thus, extensions of these common cognitive processes.

Devising a character biography follows a similar route. Generally speaking, we are inclined to look to formative experiences to explain adult behaviours. Cognitively, a 'shared space' is thus created, conflating adult and child. These links are postulated, not demonstrated. The narrative establishes cause–effect relations between disparate time-frames and, in so doing, creates a sense of shared identity: grown-up 'I' is connected with child 'I' and this connection is compressed into personality traits which are considered to be continuous. Similarly, constructing a character biography involves a blend of actor, mature character, and imagined 'character-as-child'. And in almost all theatre characters worth playing, at the heart of this blend is a profound neurosis, a psychological imbalance that the biography seeks to trace to formative experiences.

The group and mask improvisations I described earlier can also be understood in these terms: identity is exposed to a variety of frames in order to test its resilience and stability. Unlike in actor-in-action mode, in this type of work it is identity (character), not frame (situation), which determines the nature of the imaginative blend.

In this view, character is firmly rooted in the two 'inputs': actor's body, biographical memories, and interpretative choices on the one hand; the fictional data physicalised into a model on the other. The blend begins when the actor starts imitating the model's imaginary body. The fact that these two inputs are so different is an advantage, not a handicap. The integration network created between them is described as a "double-scope network" and, it is asserted, is the cognitive foundation of all artistic endeavour.

A double-scope network has inputs with different (and often clashing) organising frames as well as an organising frame for the blend that includes parts of each of those frames and has an emergent structure of its own. In such networks, both organising frames make central contributions to the blend, and their sharp differences offer the possibility of rich clashes. Far from blocking the construction of the network, such clashes offer challenges to the imagination; indeed, the resulting blends can be highly creative.

As Rick Kemp points out while looking from this perspective at Michael Chekhov's approach to characterisation, "concentrating on the differences between actor and character is more aligned to the principles of conceptual blending than the idea that an actor can completely identify with the character, often associated with Method acting".

This scheme often gives rise to a further question. Who 'leads'? Accounts of acting often describe the process as if the actor were 'shaping' the character or, as I outlined at the start of this book, in the case of the independent character, in terms of the character 'taking over', 'penetrating', or 'filling the vessel' of the actor. Which one is accurate? One way of looking at this within the cognitive blend scheme is to consider that in some blends one of the inputs may be dominant, what Fauconnier and Turner call "double-scope networks with high asymmetry". In such networks, the "organising frame of the blend is . . . an extension of the organising frame of only one input". This seems to be the case in the actor-in-action mode: the dominant framework is the actor. In transformative acting, a better way would be to conceptualise the process as a "dynamical pattern". These are the ways in which living organisms organise themselves in nature and are often described with the aid of dynamical systems theory (DST). DST maps mathematically the mutual interdependence of variables within

a system or 'state'. When organisms react, their reactions are not directed or determined by a primary cause, but are shaped by the mutual interaction between all the
factors involved. A simple example of such mutual interdependence is what occurs
when two grandfather clocks are placed next to one another on the same wall. After
a while, their pendulums synchronise through vibrations, with the wall acting as a
conduit. Neither clock can be said to lead the other – they are both engaged in continuous, mutual adaptations.

The blend constantly seeks to achieve equilibrium. Actors speak of 'being on'.
A hoary anecdote about Laurence Olivier is worth re-telling here: at the end of a
particularly good performance of his much-lauded *Othello*, Olivier locked himself
in his dressing room and was heard pacing about, mumbling and cursing. Frank
Finlay, who was playing Iago, knocked gingerly and whispered through the locked
door, "Larry, what's wrong? You were brilliant." "I know", came the enraged
reply, "but I don't know WHY!" Without for one moment pretending that what
preceded constitutes some kind of 'recipe for brilliance', I would only argue that
the feeling of 'being fully on' that actors experience in such rare moments might be
explained cognitively by the achievement, however brief, of a state of equilibrium
in the actor–character–action blend.

And, as we have seen, while inputs are available to consciousness, the blending
process is invisible to it. This accounts for the sense of mystery that surrounds our
perceptions of the process. As Mark Turner observes, "The creativity is greater than
we usually see, but also more profoundly anchored than we usually see". What
does become visible to consciousness again, is the resulting artefact: in our case, the
embodied character, with its peculiar shape and characteristics. I use the term 'peculiar' advisedly: the result of the blend is recognisably extra-daily – quirky, uneven,
lopsided, and . . . arresting.

The cognitive pattern underpinning character formation therefore entails three
elements ("spaces") merging to form a fourth (the "blend"):

a.   The input spaces are the actor's sense of 'I' and the fictional model. Both are
     held in short-term memory. When the actor contemplates the model, atten-
     tion moves purposefully between these two identities. 'Taking the model for a
     walk' can occur in both physical and mental spaces.
b.   When the two input spaces are brought together, the body-mind begins to
     scan for similarities and to find "matches": shapes of the body that can belong
     to both actor and model, selected personal traits exported into the character.
     This cross-space matching process creates a . . .
c.   Third mental space, perceived in consciousness as images (physical shapes –
     silhouette, gait, and gestures) or linguistic structures (adjectives – characteristics).
     The appearance of this third space in turn triggers the ability of the body-mind
     to "map" these contents against pre-existing information ("frames") held in
     long-term memory: the defining psychological and social characteristics of the
     type to which the character belongs. These are further linked to the mental
     frames created by the Given Circumstances, the world suggested by the play.

d.   Thus, a fourth mental space emerges: the blend, or actor-in-character. This
blend is dynamic and "emergent", that is, it evolves and changes over time.
Elements from the inputs establish relationships with it that did not exist be-
forehand. In a telling phrase, Fauconnier and Turner, capturing the same iterative process I described earlier as a conversation between actor and model, call
this the "running of the blend". As this is an act of imagination, there are
few limits to where "running the blend" may take us: the actor-in-character
becomes a self-standing conceptual network. A new life form is born.

Experiencing

In the end, the cognitive function that underpins these experiences is our simple,
innate ability to imitate one another physically and vocally. George Lakoff and
Mark Johnson place great store on our natural, inborn capacity for mimesis. In a
passage with significant implications for acting, they write:

> Imitating makes use of an ability to project, to conceptualise oneself as
> inhabiting the body of another. Empathy is the extension of this ability to
> the realm of emotions – not just to move as someone else moves, but to feel
> as someone else feels.
>
> *(1999, p. 281)*

Projections may take one of two forms: "advisory projection" and "empathic
projection".

> In . . . Advisory Projection, I am projecting my values onto you so
> that I experience your life with my values. In the other type, Empathic
> Projection, I am experiencing your life, but with your values projected
> onto my subjective experience.
>
> *(1999, p. 281)*

In the context of acting, these two modalities underpin the distinction between the
actor-in-action and actor-in-character. From the moment we are born, we have
this ability to imitate others and, thus, to imagine ourselves being them. Through
"empathic projection" we can experience the world as another person would
experience it. It is also an embodied experience: even reverie, the dream-like state
I described earlier, involves the activation of motor functions.

Thus, Lakoff and Johnson explain,

> . . . in dreaming, the high-level motor programs of our brains can be active
> and connected to our visual systems while the input to our muscles is
> inhibited. In preparing to imitate, we empathically imagine ourselves in
> the body of another, cognitively simulating the movement of the other.
> That cognitive stimulation, when 'vivid', is the actual activation of motor

programs with input into the muscles inhibited, which result in the 'feel' of movement without moving.

(1999, p. 565)

I might imagine Tamburlaine's actions in great detail, but unless and until it is translated into 'acting out', reverie remains fruitless. The point of a body-based approach to transformation is not to imagine the model, but to live it. Stanislavski insisted that the process of "experiencing" (*perezhivanie* – the actor constructing "in his dreams" the image of the character) must always be followed by a physical process. 'Acting out' requires a body as well as a mind: enacting formative experiences in the lives of the characters in improvisations aids the transformative process more than mere associations based on memory.

Imitating a character model thus entails complex mind-brain processes. A couple of decades ago, a group of Italian scientists discovered a class of neurons which became active when a macaque monkey reached out to grasp an object, but also when the monkey observed someone else attempting to grasp the object[1]. These so-called 'mirror' neurons have since been extensively studied in animals, although they are yet to be detected convincingly in humans. Mirror neurons are important elements within brain circuits which reflect motor actions such as grasping or holding on to an object. These circuits become active not only when they control the actual movement, but also when perceiving it while it is being performed by someone else, when imitating it, or when imagining performing it while holding perfectly still. The detection of these brain structures has led to an understanding of imitation not as a process of conceptual reasoning, but as direct simulation, the actual experience of others' emotions and actions. Strong evidence is also emerging of emotion and sensation mirroring through bodily functions other than those of the brain. This has led Vittorio Gallese to introduce the concepts of "embodied simulation" and "intercorporeality" to account for interactions between subjects that cannot be assigned to the classical 'mind-reading' cognitive model. "By this", Gallese writes, "it is implied that mindreading is preceded, both from a phylogenetic and ontogenetic point of view, by non-propositional forms of social understanding". We contemplate characters and 'understand' them not in a cerebral, propositional way, but through our bodies. Just like the two pendulums on the wall I described earlier, a process of "mutual resonance" is established through which we acquire "the basic knowledge we entertain of others."

Intuited through the experience of acting, this type of direct experience through imitation is, to return one last time to Francis Fergusson, the marker of the histrionic sensibility: "a sympathetic response of the whole psyche . . . expressed more or less completely and immediately in bodily changes, postures, and movements".

Moreover, actors who explore the model through improvisations engage in the repeated re-examination and evolution of the form imitated. Mimesis operates in a powerful working-memory space in which the brain uses its body as a "reduplicative device" in order to observe and alter its own functions. In rehearsals, the physical realisation of the model never looks exactly like its mental image. Whereas the processes involved in contemplating the model are largely unconscious, the mimetic process in rehearsals is subject to conscious control. The higher cognition functions of the body-mind actively reflect on the process. "Mimesis is always an attempt to reduplicate some aspect of reality in action, and in the case of skilled rehearsal, the rehearsal itself is a mimetic act", writes Merlin Donald. As a result, the actor constantly creates variations on the character's psychophysical identity and the emerging shape of the character changes with each recurrence.

Spontaneity

None of the techniques and approaches described thus far would mean very much if they didn't somehow lead to stage conduct which is sufficiently spontaneous, free, and fluid to be perceived as believable behaviour. How does one arrive at such a level of automatism when constructing and inhabiting an imaginary body?

Anthropologist Greg Downey spent a considerable amount of time studying the way in which capoeira dancers acquire their intricate, improvisatory skills. On the basis of these observations, he then put forward a view of knowledge acquisition based on the 'plasticity' of the brain:

Cognitive science has come to the conclusion that information is stored in the brain by altering the relative strengths of synaptic connections between neurons – the so-called 'connectionist' view of the way in which the brain operates. With repeated and frequent activation, certain synaptic connections become stronger and better at what they do. Fundamental knowledge is implicit, stored in the connections between units, rather than in the units themselves. This process is strongest during infancy, but the adult brain remains "plastic". A well-known study demonstrated that London taxi drivers showed significant changes in certain areas of the brain after mastering 'the Knowledge' (essentially, after they had learned by heart the map of the city). It is also agreed that acquiring new physical skills involves the re-assignment of neural patterns. The assumption is that sustained alterations in posture and gesture patterns, such as those which occur in rehearsals, result in behaviours which are just as automatic and spontaneous (in that they by-pass the retardation mechanism of consciousness) as other acquired physical skills, whether driving a car, or the intricate fingering involved in knitting or violin playing.

The body "knows", Downey therefore asserts, through the physical, neuro-logical, perceptual and behavioural changes that occur while learning a skill.[2] This is not explicit ('propositional') knowledge, which can be put into words – what Downey calls the "filing cabinet model" of learning – but embodied knowledge. Embodied knowledge is not something one "has", but something one "is". Downey writes: "Embodied knowledge shapes the subject".

Moreover, such knowledge alters the way in which one looks at all sorts of realities, not only at those directly related to the skill being learnt. Attention becomes filtered by the knowledge, so that we mainly register those things that are of interest – we develop a perceptual bias, reflecting the acquired knowledge. As I have outlined earlier, actors begin by re-centring their bodies. They then re-shape them to reflect the model and, through repetition, achieve the type of body 'knowledge' of the character that Downey describes. Through sustained changes to body patterns, the relative strengths of the existing brain patterns of the actor are repositioned, as well as fresh synaptic connections formed. My hypothesis is that this is what happens when actors behave 'in character' – changing one's body through repetition changes what is taken from the environment: one perceives and reacts differently because *one has to*.

This is how actors-in-character manage to achieve spontaneity even while adopting a different body shape. The contemplation and imitation of a model, aided by specific training and rehearsal techniques such as those described earlier, leads actors to perceive their imaginary bodies as if they were, for the duration of the performance, their habitual shapes and tempi. To understand this better, one has to distinguish between the scientific concepts of body schema and body image.

Neuroscientists distinguish between the conscious awareness of the body – the "body image" – and the "body schema". This, philosopher Shaun Gallagher explains, is

> A non-conscious system of processes that constantly regulate posture and movement – a system of motor–sensory capacities that function below the threshold of awareness, and without the necessity of perceptual monitoring.
>
> *(2005, p. 234)*

We move without paying attention to the fact that we move. The body schema is a system of neuromotor functions that operate below the level of consciousness so that we might maintain a constant posture and rearrange our bodies in order to pick an apple from the tree or grasp a glass of water. In so far as it produces a set of recurring movement patterns, it can be said to underpin the individual's Posture–Gesture Merger I described earlier. The actor, however, consciously and deliberately creates what the theatre scholar Gabriele Sofia calls an "artificial body schema". This, Sofia argues, first involves a process of "fragmentation" of the actor's own body schema and then its replacement or "reconstruction" with a new set of neural structures. The key is the time-consuming and repeated experiencing of the physical gestures and posture derived from the character model. In daily life, the body schema is a non-conscious system. On stage, the same level of automatism is achieved through repetition. And, just as in daily life the body schema governs the way the body rearranges itself in order to attain its goals, the artificial body schema is shaped by the need to attain a series of stage goals: in Stanislavskian terms, to achieve one's tasks or objectives. The impression, indeed the reality, of spontaneity is based on this inextricable connection between the chain of tasks (Stanislavski's "score") and the non-conscious body schema it engenders. "In a stage condition when the actor already knows the concatenation of actions", Sofia writes, "his body schema may naturally anticipate the following actions even if they are supposed to be a natural reaction to an incidental event."

This hypothesis is supported by a model of emotion and cognition put forward by cognitive psychologists Mick Power and Tim Dalgleish, in which they describe how a so-called "associative system" develops in the mind. Essentially, they argue that the mind-brain registers associations of external events with internal reactions, such as a loud noise triggering the physiological changes connected with fear. When such combinations repeat themselves, the mind produces an internal model or schema. Then, Dalgleish posits: "If the same event is repeatedly processed in the same way at the schematic level then an associative representation would be formed such that, on future encounters of the same event, the relevant emotion will be *automatically* elicited."

Antonio Damasio's scheme of "dispositional representations" in the brain also helps to explain how this process operates. Research[3] has shown, for example, that when our senses detect certain natural phenomena (loud sounds, large shapes coming into view, physical pain), specialised structures in the brain's limbic system (often the amygdala) trigger the physical characteristics of fear. We do not have to identify the objects attracting fear (thunder, a swooping eagle, or an aching tooth) for a stimulus or combination of stimuli to provoke a reaction in the brain and for the brain to trigger the body state: the "dispositional representation" is a pre-existing pattern of neurons, "dormant and implicit", that enables the brain to place the stimulus in the correct category – danger! Dispositional representations consist of previously acquired knowledge, literally em-bodied in the circuitry of the brain. The process, Damasio summarises, "presupposes the presence of a trigger, the existence of acquired dispositions on the basis of which evaluation will take place, and the existence of innate dispositions which activate body-bound responses". Stage stimuli – Malvolio's sneer, Olivia's ring – are evaluated emotionally by dispositions acquired 'in character' through repetition in rehearsals; these, in turn, activate already existing brain structures or "rules" and, thus, lead to spontaneous physical (re)actions.

This is all the more evident when one considers how the body schema relates to the space around the body and, in particular, to material objects found within or in proximity to what Laban called the "kinesphere" and scientists "peripersonal space" – essentially, the space into which we can reach by extending our arms. In fact, the notion of the body schema first arose when, at the beginning of the past century, neurologists observed that women wearing hats with feathers would naturally duck when going through a door and did so to the precise degree needed to avoid damaging the headgear. The mechanism of the body schema allows the body constantly to adjust to its material environment – wearing a different pair of shoes, putting on a bicorn, or squeezing into a corset fundamentally alter one's sense of self. Actors who rehearse for a long time with key character props – the sword, walking stick, or fan of the classical stage, for example – find that these inanimate objects become 'natural extensions' of their bodies. With the extensions come alterations of the body schema. As Shaun Gallagher observes: "these processes are more than physiological; they . . . shape consciousness in important ways". There may be few better examples in modern theatre than Antony Sher's use of crutches to alter both body and personality as Richard III.

Can a leopard change its spots?

An all-consuming question remains: does constructing an imaginary body by physical means, inhabiting it mentally through conceptual blends, and experiencing such changes for extended periods *actually lead to the actors themselves being changed*?

In earlier chapters, I described classical models of personality which account for our strong sense of a stable and continuous 'I' by emphasising that those traits which describe who we are remain stable across our life span. These models also appear to be reinforced by the theory of temperaments. In this view, people who are strong, naïve, or impulsive tend to be so consistently, in all situations. The leopard cannot change its spots.

Coherent as such classical models might be, they do not account for the significant evidence which has been accumulating in recent years and which shows that, in response to repeated and cumulative life experiences, traits *do* evolve. Research into the genetics of twins, as well as into family connections and adopted children, is gradually leading towards the conclusion that inheritance only amounts to between one third and one half of a person's personality traits. Environmental factors thus account for at least half, and probably more, of our traits. We are not carved in stone. DNA certainly plays an important role, but is more likely to determine not the personality traits themselves, but the ranges within which certain traits manifest themselves inside each of us. Inherited temperament acts as a restricting mechanism, but within certain ranges traits are malleable enough. Remembering the distinction psychology draws between traits and states, the questions are: To what extent? How long does a state need to persist to make a lasting difference? Are changes brought about by altered states reversible? Overall, can a hard border really be set between permanent traits and transient states?

These debates have significant implications for the hypothesis of character transformation: if personalities, those of actors included, are 'set', then so-called transformation can only be considered as a metaphor and is ultimately an external, relatively superficial artifice. If, on the other hand, under certain circumstances traits can change, then the concept of transformation as a fundamental alteration in the psychophysical make-up of the actor can actually be contemplated. Recent models of personality may offer some answers to these questions.

One recent approach sees permanent traits and transient states as parts of the same interdependent system, and seeks to establish a model of personality based on the dynamic relationship between them. The "sociogenomic model" proposed by psychologist Brent Roberts and others starts from the observation that, seen from the point of view of the ways in which they *manifest* themselves, traits and states look identical: thoughts, feelings, and behaviours. The only conceptual difference between them is the length of time over which they persist.

Roberts and his colleagues agree with the traditional observation that traits cause states. At the same time, they argue that certain states that, once they take hold, persist for long periods and become "internalised, automatized, and generalised", may also crystallise as traits. In other words, personality traits can be not only the product of genes and early life, but also of later experiences. In certain circumstances, traits can change. Roberts clarifies: "These changes . . . reflect something more enduring than fluctuating systems because they change a person either permanently or for an extended period of time".[4]

Certain changes, caused by major life events and typically lasting from one to three years, can lead to permanent alterations to personality traits. Roberts labels such changes "pliable" or "plastic": his image is that of a wire bent into shape – it will remain in its new position unless another force intervenes to bend it once more. Just as genetic and early-life epigenetic factors shaped the DNA in the first place, strong and sustained environmental events that take place during a person's life can modify the ways in which the DNA is used in shaping personality traits. Research into humans in this area is, as yet, neither extensive nor conclusive, so, in making this assertion, Roberts relies extensively on research in non-human animals, where such "pliable" mechanisms are found quite often. None the less, it is not unreasonable – using animal models as parallels – to assume that, once acquired through learning and application, a trait such as 'Conscientiousness' could become a permanent feature of the personality.

So-called professional deformations fall into this category. Using the terms of the Five Factor Model, the well-drilled soldier, trained to be obedient in both mind and body, will score low on Openness to Experience, the bookish academic obsessing over minutiae will score high on Conscientiousness, and the skilled diplomat displaying boundless positive energy will be marked high on Agreeableness. In theatre character terms, these are our Woyzecks, Tesmans, and Panglosses.

Of even greater interest from an acting perspective is Roberts's second type of possible personality changes: his "elastic system" describes a mechanism by which personality traits can be temporarily "re-programmed" under the influence of an environmental input, but only for as long as that input lasts. In Roberts's model, elastic transformations sit between short-lived states and permanent "pliable" changes. What might have initially appeared as an immutable point on the scale of a particular trait can, in fact, change strength for a time, then revert to its original position.

I had a close friend who one day left her gas oven unattended and returned home to find her kitchen full of acrid smoke. As a result, this hitherto temperamentally calm and collected young woman developed a bothersome anxiety about leaving domestic appliances unattended. On one occasion, while travelling to rehearse in another town, she even got off the train half-way and returned home to check that she had not left the gas on again (she hadn't, of course). To pre-empt such extreme anxieties, she got into the habit of checking the gas, closing the door, reopening it, checking again that all was in order and then saying aloud "The gas is off". Funny as all this seemed to her friends, she suffered from this anxiety for a couple of months and I should imagine that, had she been administered a standard FFM-based questionnaire at that time, her ratings for Neuroticism would have been pretty high. But simply getting into a vortex of this sort does not necessarily result in a permanent change. My friend moved house, acquired an electric oven with an automatic cut-off device and her anxiety vanished, as did the need for the reassurance ritual. The changes in the intensity of her Neuroticism trait had not been permanent and she reverted to her usual, poised self. As Roberts explains:

> The inclusion of fluctuating processes invites the possibility of *pseudo-change* in personality traits – change occurring only at the state level that mimics change in personality traits and may even show up in personality

trait change. For example, people can think, feel, and act in ways inconsistent with their traits because of demands made upon them by their environment. However, this type of inconsistency may have little or no impact on long-term personality trait change, depending on the frequency and ubiquity of the environment.

(2018, p. 30, emphasis original)

This is not to say that such changes are not 'real', in the sense of being deeply embodied in our physiology. Research has shown that temporary changes in conduct are, none the less, enabled by fundamental, if time-limited and reversible, changes at the molecular, genetic level. Studies on the lasting effects of depression, for example, appear to support the theory of temporary genetic alteration: researchers collected several types of body tissue from patients who had suffered relatively long depressive episodes and compared them with those taken from a healthy control group. Tissues taken from the depressed group showed different gene methylation patterns. As outlined earlier, methylation determines the way in which genes express themselves. Under the effect of the sustained neurochemical changes associated with depression, some traits had undergone what Roberts calls "temporary but semi-enduring amplitude changes". Roberts's dynamic model of personality thus allows for mechanisms through which experiential changes can cause the emergence or modification of traits, understood as fundamental, genetically based components of personality.

Additional evidence is also growing which shows that repeating a physical activity over a prolonged period, especially when that activity holds strong emotional associations, actually creates new structures in the brain. Experiments appear to indicate that both repeatedly executing a movement and focusing on that movement in active imagination over days and weeks – in the way that actors and dancers do – triggers the activation ("expression") of corresponding genes. In turn, these generate the protein syntheses that facilitate the generation of new synapses and neurons, thus creating "new functional units whose connectivity is shaped by experience". Brains are thus 're-tuned'. Just as in daily life, the artificial body schema enables the brain to exercise automated, non-conscious control of the body and its actions. A commonly held misconception on the part of those who observe acting from the outside is that actors are permanently and consciously 'in control' of their emotions and of their bodies, and that they only imitate spontaneity. Nothing could be further from the truth: actors *do* act and react spontaneously, through the mechanism of pre-reflective control described above. What is true is that in order to achieve this level of integration between the mind and the constructed body requires significant investment in repetition.

As will readily be seen, arguments for temporary, reversible, yet embodied trait changes have significant implications for the theory of character transformation. There are numerous, well-documented examples of actors 'staying in character' in an imaginary body both inside and outside rehearsals. Neither are these limited to so-called 'Method' actors, as is commonly assumed – Brando getting ready to shoot *The Mutiny on the Bounty* was indeed 'Method'-trained, but Olivier working on Othello for three years or Zellweger preparing for months on end for Bridget Jones and working in a London publishing house 'in character' (and not being recognised) were most certainly not. To what extent can one say that these actors had actually 'transformed'? Roberts's hypothesis of "pseudo-change" in personality traits gives scientific support to the notion that when an actor adopts the psycho-physical identity of a character model, something occurs which goes far beyond imitation or pretence. This needs to be qualified, however: on the one hand, as I outlined earlier, our temperaments define fundamentals of our personalities such as levels of energy, adaptability, affective sensitivity, etc. In the terms I defined when discussing physical approaches to transformation, actors – like all human beings – possess their own, innate 'tempi', which reflect their basic temperaments. On the other hand, by consciously changing their Posture–Gesture–Merger, adopting altered psychophysical identities and sustaining these changes for extended periods, actors from all traditions can temporarily suppress other temperamental features and open the possibility of changing certain personality traits through an "elastic" process. But I do not believe that such suppression can be absolute – the actor's own temperament will continue to shine through the shell of the character. The temperament remains the 'steady-state' from which actors depart and to which they return. And, attractive as this hypothesis might be, I put it forward only with the weighty *caveat* that the models of personality on which it is based remain tentative and provisional and that a lot of research still needs to be undertaken to confirm or refute them. Nevertheless, on the basis of evidence from psychological research, one can state with a modicum of confidence that during rehearsals, by undergoing repeated and sustained psychophysical changes, actors *may* be able to effect temporary and reversible transformations of their psychophysical identities.

Notes

1 Enthusiasm among theatre scholars for the implications of the discovery of mirror neurons as a possible physiological mechanism for empathy through mimesis must be tempered by the fact that their existence in humans is still to be convincingly proven and by an acknowledgment that their implications for performance continue to be a matter of lively debate.
2 The underlying assumption is that one can 'know' oneself and the world by means of the body.
3 Work done by Panksepp and LeDoux on certain, very powerful, emotions – for example, panic as opposed to fear – appears to indicate that these are generated directly by the stimulus, without the intermediary of representations.
4 Fajkowska supports this assertion overall but is careful to signal that it remains "speculation".

Bibliography

Fusions of self and character. States, B. O., 2002. 'The actor's presence: three phenomenal modes', in Zarrilli, P. (ed.), *Acting (Re)Considered: A Theoretical and Practical Guide.* 2nd Edition. London: Routledge, pp. 23–39; Donald, M., 2006. 'Art and cognitive evolution', in Turner, M. (ed.), *The Artful Mind: Cognitive Science and the Riddle of Human Creativity.* Oxford: Oxford University Press, pp. 3–20; *and the "histrionic spirit":*

Fergusson, F., 1949. *The Idea of a Theatre: A Study of Ten Plays, The Art of Drama in a Changing Perspective*. Garden City, NY: Doubleday.

Bisociation Theory: Koestler, A., 1964. *The Act of Creation*. Harmondsworth: Hutchinson; *and cognitive science*: Mithen S. J., 1996. *The Prehistory of the Mind: A Search for the Origins of Art, Science and Religion*. London: Thames & Hudson; Fauconnier, G., and Turner, M., 2002. *The Way We Think: Conceptual Blending and the Mind's Hidden Complexities*. New York: Basic Books; Deacon, T., 2006. 'The aesthetic faculty', in Turner, M. (ed.), *The Artful Mind: Cognitive Science and the Riddle of Human Creativity*. Oxford: Oxford University Press, pp. 21–55.

Cognitive blends: Fauconnier and Turner, 2002; Turner, M., 2006. 'The art of compression', in Turner, M. (ed.), *The Artful Mind: Cognitive Science and the Riddle of Human Creativity*. Oxford: Oxford University Press, pp. 93–114; Donald, 2006; *and "distributed" memory*: Damasio, A., 1999. *The Feeling of What Happens: Body and Emotion in the Making of Consciousness*. London: William Heinemann; Kemp, R., 2012. *Embodied Acting, What Neuroscience Tells Us about Performance*. London: Routledge.

Mimesis and empathy: Lakoff, G., and Johnson, M., 1999. *Philosophy in the Flesh: The Embodied Mind and its Challenge to Western Thought*. New York: Basic Books; *and physicalisation*: Benedetti, J., 1988. *Stanislavski: A Biography*. London: Methuen.

Mirror neurons: Gallese, V., and Goodman, A., 1998. 'Mirror neurons and the simulation theory of mind-reading'. *Trends in Cognitive Sciences*, 2 (12), pp. 493–501; Ramachandran, V. S., 2000. 'Mirror neurons and imitation learning as the driving force behind "the great leap forward" in human evolution'. *Edge*, 60; Mukamel, R. et al, 2010. 'Single-neuron responses in humans during execution and observation of actions'. *Current Biology*, 20 (8), pp. 750–756; Ulthol, S., and Gallese, V., 2015. 'The role of the body in social cognition'. *WIREs Cognitive Science*, 6 (5), pp. 453–460; Gallese, V., Keysers, C., and Rizzolatti, G., 2004. 'A unifying view of the basis of social cognition'. *Trends in Cognitive Sciences*, 8 (9), pp. 396–403; Gallese, V., 2007. 'Before and below "theory of mind": embodied simulation and the neural correlates of social cognition'. *Philosophical Transactions of the Royal Society B–Biological Sciences*, 362 (1480), pp. 659–669; Gallese, V., and Sinigaglia, C., 2011. 'What's so special about embodied simulation?' *Trends in Cognitive Sciences*, 15 (11), pp. 512–519; Gallese, V., 2017. 'Visions of the body: embodied simulation and aesthetic experience'. *Aisthesis. Pratiche, linguaggi e saperi dell'estetico*, 10 (1), pp. 41–50; *enthusiasm amongst theatre scholars*: Carnicke, S. M., 2009. *Stanislavsky in Focus: An Acting Master for the Twenty-First Century*. 2nd Edition. Abingdon: Routledge; McConachie, B., 2011. *Engaging Audiences: A Cognitive Approach to Spectating in the Theatre*. New York: Palgrave Macmillan; *debates concerning implications for performance*: Shaughnessy, N. (ed.), 2013. *Affective Performance and Cognitive Science: Body, Brain and Science*. London: Bloomsbury Methuen; *and theatrical mimesis*: Fergusson, 1949; Donald, 2006.

Brain plasticity: Downey, G., 2007. 'Seeing with a sideways glance: visuomotor 'knowing' and the plasticity of perception'. In: Harris, M. (ed.), *Ways of Knowing, New Approaches to the Anthropology of Experience and Learning*. New York: Berghahn Books, pp. 222–241; Downey, G., 2010. 'Practice without theory: a neuroanthropological perspective on embodied learning'. *Journal of the Royal Anthropological Institute*, 16, pp. S22–S40; McConachie, 2011; Huttenlocher, P. R., 2002. *Neural Plasticity: The Effect of the Environment on the Development of the Cerebral Cortex*. Cambridge, MA: Harvard University Press; *in taxi drivers*: Maguire, E. A. et al, 2000. 'Navigation-related structural change in the hippocampi of taxi drivers'. *Proceedings of the National Academy of Sciences of the USA*, 97, pp. 4398–4403.

Body image and body schema: Gallagher, S., 2005. *How the Body Shapes the Mind*. Oxford: Clarendon; Gallagher, S., and Meltzoff, A., 1996. 'The earliest sense of self and others: Merleau-Ponty and recent developmental studies'. *Philosophical Psychology*, 9 (2), pp. 211–233; Sofia, G., 2013.

'Achieved spontaneity and spectator's performative experience – the motor dimension of the actor–spectator relationship', in De Preester, H. (ed.), *Moving Imagination. Explorations of Gesture and Inner Movement.* Amsterdam: John Benjamins, pp. 69–85; *and repetition*: Dalgleish, T., 1998. 'Emotion', in Eysenck, M. W. (ed.), *Psychology: An Integrated Approach.* Harlow, UK: Addison Wesley Longman.

Perception and imagery: Damasio, 1999; Kosslyn, S. et al, 1994. 'Visual mental imagery activates topographically organised visual cortex: PET investigations'. *Journal of Cognitive Neuroscience,* 5, pp. 263–287; Cabeza, R., and Nyberg, L., 2000. 'Imaging cognition II: an empirical review of 275 PET and MRI studies'. *Journal of Cognitive Neuroscience,* 12, pp. 1–47; Damasio, A., 1994. *Descartes' Error: Emotion, Reason, and the Human Brain.* New York: Putnam; *and research on fear*: Panksepp, J., 2005, 'On the embodied neural nature of core emotional affects'. *Journal of Consciousness Studies,* 12 (8–10), pp. 158–184; Panksepp, J., and Biven, L., 2012. *The Archaeology of the Mind, Neuroevolutionary Origins of Human Emotion.* New York: W. W. Norton, Kindle edition; LeDoux, J., 2007. 'The amygdala'. *Current Biology,* 17, R868–R874; LeDoux, J., 2012. 'Rethinking the emotional brain'. *Neuron,* 2012, Feb 23; 73 (4): 653–676.

Peripersonal space: Connolly, R., and Ralley, R., 2007. 'The laws of normal organic life or Stanislavski explained: towards a scientific account of the subconscious in Stanislavski's system'. *Studies in Theatre and Performance,* 27 (3), pp. 237–259.

Sociogenomic model: Roberts, B. W., and Jackson, J. J., 2008. 'Sociogenomic personality psychology'. *Journal of Personality,* 76, pp. 1523–1544; Roberts, B. W., 2018. 'A revised sociogenomic model of personality traits', *Journal of Personality,* 86 (1), pp. 23–35; Fajkowska, M., 2018. 'Personality traits: hierarchically organized systems'. *Journal of Personality,* 86, pp. 36–54; *and methylation patterns*: Oh, G. et al, 2015. 'DNA modification study of major depressive disorder: beyond locus-by-locus comparisons'. *Biological Psychiatry,* 77, pp. 246–255.

'Re-tuning' the brain: Van Pragg, H. et al, 2002. 'Functional neurogenesis in the adult hippocampus'. *Nature,* 415, pp. 1030–1034; Rossi, E. L., 2004. 'Sacred spaces and places in healing dreams', *Psychological Perspectives,* 47 (1), pp. 48–63.

12

DECEPTION, SELF-DECEPTION AND THE TRANSFORMATIVE ACTOR

In the early 2000s, in search of a Russian partner for the London drama school whose Principal I then was, I visited the Vakhtangov Institute in Moscow. The school, one of Russia's best-known conservatoires, was at that time still headed by a famous comedian, old enough to have been taught directly by some of the original members of Evgenyi Vakhtangov's companies. I walked into his office having come straight from another meeting with his counterpart at the Moscow Art Theatre School (MAT), who had proudly pointed out that his school sat in a direct line with Stanislavski's company. I asked the old actor if he could explain what the difference was between the teaching at his school and the better-known approaches of the MAT. "Well, you know", he said, "it's like this: Stanislavski had a well-known exercise for developing the imagination of his students. He would take them to the Tretyakov Gallery, point to a landscape painting and ask them to describe in detail what they saw. First-year students at most of the drama schools in Moscow still undertake this exercise. At the MAT school, the student-actor would start by saying: 'I can see a river. On the other side of the river there is a small cottage and just behind the cottage, a copse of birch trees . . .' At our school, the student says: 'I see a wall. On the wall is a canvas, surrounded by a frame. On the canvas, I can see a river . . .'"

His little parable more or less encapsulates the core argument of this book: the to-and-fro between the real and the illusory and the ways by which we arrive at the state of grace in which we can bring ourselves and others to *believe* in the illusion.

A story is told about a lady who, having been moved to tears by a performance of *Othello* at a theatre in New York at the turn of the past century, arrives back at the box office the following morning, still in thrall to the previous night's excitement. With trembling hands, she pushes through the hatch the price of another ticket. Only to pull it back a second later with a shout: "Oh, Lord, there will not be another performance tonight, will there? Desdemona is already dead!" One might indeed expect a 'truly' enraged Othello to have to strangle a fresh Desdemona night after night. Yet, self-evidently, this won't do. What the mechanisms might be that allow passions to appear to be fully experienced, yet at the same time controlled, has been the subject of much speculation. I find of particular interest the view that, in fictional contexts, *belief* plays a role far greater than in daily life in modifying emotion-contingent actions. We saw how, in the 'Larry Lamb' experiment, children as young as two could believe fully in an imaginary scenario, yet, at the same time, were aware of the limits of the fiction. Indeed, I recall that my three-year-old son used to delight in 'talking on the phone' through a plastic banana; I also recall that not once did he try to eat it. It appears that we act differently towards a thing we imagine than towards something in which we actually believe. Belief is a second-level mental phenomenon, which moderates and modifies the imagination.

Imagine, say philosophers Timothy Schroeder and Carl Matheson, going up in one of those high-speed lifts with glass walls and a glass floor that run on the exteriors of skyscrapers. Few of us will fail to experience a tightening of the stomach in fear. Yet, our belief in the safety of the floor modifies the emotion and controls any precipitate actions to which it might otherwise lead. Our belief in the reality of the situation (the lift) moderates the visceral reaction (the fear). Similarly, when responding to *fictional* stimuli the brain receives two complementary sets of messages: one (probably sub-cortical) from the 'reality' experienced, the other (cortical) from our pre-formed understanding of its fictional nature. As a consequence, they argue, even though "one's belief that certain events are only being played by actors has a very modest impact upon one's feelings . . . this belief is quite enough to keep one seated during a convincingly depicted murder". And we take great pleasure in experiencing the consequent neural and chemical surges vicariously, in the safety of our comfortable seats.

It is often asserted that actors who attempt to give 'truthful' performances strive to attain, in Coleridge's over-used formula, 'a willing suspension of disbelief', so that they can engender what Stanislavski called "an unwavering belief in what is happening". Contrary to such received wisdom, I think that the actor-in-action actually strives towards the suspension of *belief* – belief in the reality of the acting artifice and of the 'frame' this places around the 'landscape'. Some interesting experiments in this area have shown that as soon as our mind-brain understands the signals it receives from the environment via our senses, it tends to believe in their reality. Our New York lady was, in fact, acting on what is the general default position. It actually takes a sustained mental effort to adjust this immediate perception and 'disbelieve' what the senses tell you. Contemplation, reverie, and the imitation of a model also create visceral reactions of this type, but in character acting, the awareness of the artifice, the *belief that this is acting*, is sustained and transforms the imagined realities. Anne Bogart captures this dynamic well when she writes that to compose a story requires, at one and the same time, "passionate intimacy" and "enforced distance".

I have, therefore, become convinced that in transformative acting the maintenance of belief plays just as important a role as its suspension. In the kind of acting with which I am concerned, we willingly acknowledge that *we trick our-selves* in order to trick others. Charles Marowitz even considered that the actor's utter absorption when repeating words, moves, and gestures during rehearsals led to "a mild form of self-hypnosis", reducing interference from conscious thoughts and opening up the ability to react spontaneously. Such statements may be thought simply the stuff of acting folklore. Yet, an interesting scientific study recently sought to ascertain whether acting students might be more susceptible to hypnosis than control groups of musicians and non-artists. The conclusion was that they were, as a result of their greater openness to imaginative suggestibility, proneness to fantasy, and acquired skill in focusing their attention in order to become absorbed.

Erving Goffman famously described the world as a theatre in which relation-ships between people were constantly being "staged". Social interaction, he asserted, of necessity involved an element of deception, in the sense that we as well as our interlocutors engage in dramatic performances in which we control the impressions we present to others. Acting is a particular form of deception and its effectiveness is rooted in mechanisms of self-deception.

Deception is a universal biological phenomenon, an essential part of the way in which all organisms, not least primates, interact with their environments and with one another. A subadult male ape under threat of attack by the dominant male in the group will often pretend maternal behaviour, embracing and carrying someone else's infant. Why? Because "adult males attack animals simulating a mother–infant pair only half as often as they attack single animals". In human children, the earliest signs of deception (fake crying and pretend laughing) appear as early as six months and deceptive behaviour is well established by the age of three. We, the parents, are not only complicit in this but encourage it: we tease and trick our children with imagi-nary 'safe threats', we play 'pretend' as soon as our children are able to cooperate. Later in life this evolves into hide-and-seek, magic tricks, practical jokes, *Would I Lie to You* on television, reading fantasy novels and . . . going to the theatre or the mov-ies. As the evolutionary anthropologist Robert Trivers puts it, deception is our ability to fool others in order to gain an advantage or avoid punishment. The practice of deception, he asserts, "stimulates imagination and learning and also prepares the child for living in a world where practising and spotting deception are important". Does this mean that we are not sincere in our actions and utterances? Not in the slightest.

Outlining his 'deception theory', Trivers makes use of arguments drawn from a wide range of animal and human activities to support his main contention: that the better to deceive others, we have become masters at deceiving ourselves. In the process of social interaction, whether in birds, chimpanzees, in the human kindergarten, or at the office, organisms are, of course, not only actors – deceivers – but also victims, recipients of others' deception. In order to protect ourselves we (and they) develop mechanisms for detecting deception. Deception – lying well – is difficult. We give the game away relatively easily through myriad involuntary signals. Among these, three aspects of behaviour are particularly noticeable – two are relatively easy to spot, the third one less so.

The first is nervousness: we are apprehensive of our lie being spotted, with possible repercussions, so we tend to be more nervous (sweaty and clammy palms, blushing, increased heartbeat).

The second is control: to cope with the nervousness, we try to suppress these give-away signals. To do so, we over-control and appear rigid, tense, and artificial, and our voices become strangled and shrill. Denials are too strong, affirmations over-emphatic. This is why children (and inexperienced actors), when asked to replicate natural reactions (to a surprise, say, or to encountering a physical shock such as cold or heat) tend to overact.

The third – and most interesting from my point of view – is what neuroscientists describe as cognitive load. Lying makes intense demands on our brains. First, the brain needs to hide the real state of affairs, the truth of which we are, of course, aware. It then has to create a fiction that fits any data already known by our interlocutor ("Yes, officer, it was the middle of the night, but there was a full moon"). It then has to remember the details of this fiction ("I already mentioned the full moon, didn't I? That is how I spotted the knife in the alleyway"). All this effort takes increased concentration, which, in turn, reduces the brain's ability to carry out secondary, unrelated tasks. People who are lying have to think too hard and, thus, appear unnaturally calm and in control. When we are nervous, for example, we blink a lot, fidget, speak fast: not so when we lie deliberately. Studies, partly related to police interview procedures, have shown that people who lie blink and fidget less and that they either take longer pauses between sentences or reply much too quickly – they are either over-rehearsed or cognitive load takes over and inhibits ordinary behaviour. Trivers writes:

> In short, cognitive load does more than slow down your responses – in a whole host of ways, *it tends to reveal unconscious processes*. These predominate when conscious degree of control is minimised because of cognitive load.
>
> *(2011, p. 12, my emphasis)*

The transformative approaches described in this book may, therefore, be said to increase unconscious control over those factors that, unless controlled, would result in physical activities that would betray the deception. I would suggest that the notion of cognitive load is directly linked to what we generally perceive as 'bad acting'. We react negatively to exaggeration, for example, not primarily because of a cultural bias, but because movement (blinking, high-pitched voices, size and frequency of gestures) which is outside the range of plausibility (not necessarily more, indeed often less, than the ordinary) is perceived as giving strong signals of deception. How many beginner actors have reacted in confusion to those perennial acting teachers' injunctions: 'leave yourself alone' and 'focus', so irritatingly contradictory? Yet, these are designed to address the two major behavioural factors which betray lying: the former – over-control; the latter – the effort needed to cope with cognitive load.

In contrast, movement which falls into a range which is plausible for the circumstances of the action – the physical markers of natural(istic) behaviour, 'grounded' bodies, and 'centred' voices, for example – have become signifiers of good acting because they are, in fact, markers of a well-executed deception, one which we accept and like. It is not that 'natural' behaviour actually deceives us into believing that the stage illusion is real; on the contrary, it reminds us that what we see *is* deception, well executed. The actor sets out to deceive, and my contention is that the more 'natural' the acting, the more we know we are being deceived. Merlin Donald writes:

> Art should be regarded as a specific kind of *cognitive engineering*. As a first princi-
> ple, art is an activity intended to *influence the minds of an audience* . . . This reflects
> a very deep human tendency for the reciprocal control of attention, which
> carries with it a propensity to deliberately engineer the experiences of others.
>
> *(2006, p. 4, emphasis original)*

How does this square with the emphasis I placed throughout this book on the constructed character? I would contend that the interplay between a declaredly constructed Posture–Gesture–Merger and naturalistic behaviour is most satisfying because the former signals the deception, while the latter delivers it effectively across the audience's counter-deception mechanisms. We are, therefore, in a very satisfying 'play' in which we know from the outset that a game is being played, yet we are allowed to involve ourselves fully in it.

As we have seen, identifying the nature of a character through its PGM depends on identifying the pattern or group to which this points. In the great game of deception and defence, the recognition of patterns of behaviour is a key means of detection. As a result, deceivers will do everything in their power to create ran-domness, the absence of pattern – the better to deceive. Two great, biologically determined impulses are at play here: to improvise, to engage in random activities so as to appear truthful, counteracting our other great instinct, which is to create and discern patterns in random activity and rely on them for judgement.

A question then imposes itself: does watching a constructed character give rise to a different order of experience than watching actor-in-action performances?

The evolutionary spiral of deception and detection leads to continuous adap-tations in both deceiver and deceived. It has been argued, convincingly, on the basis of sustained ethological and other evidence, that one such adaptation is the evolution of intelligence, and, more specifically, of what the ethologist Nicholas Humphrey called "Machiavellian" or social intelligence. Briefly, there are three main theories regarding the sources of the evolution of intelligence. Intelligence, it is posited, may have evolved as an adaptation to the need to use tools (the 'mechanical' version of intelligence); it might have evolved as a consequence of the need of wandering primates to recall the precise positions of the better feed-ing grounds, in turn developing an ability to recognise similarities and differences and classify objects accordingly (the 'spatial' or 'natural history' hypothesis) and finally – and most convincingly, I think – intelligence as an adaptation to inter-action within highly social primate groups, and particularly as an adaptation to deception and the detection of deception.

Acting as a form of artistic expression is defined by the fact that it modifies forms of social behaviour. In so doing, says anthropologist Terence Deacon, it involves "special conventional re-framings of 'mundane' speech and social life . . . supported by cognitive capacities that probably evolved for other reasons". I am proposing that at least part of the satisfaction to be gained from watching an actor at work may usefully be understood as a sophisticated form of practising deception and counter-deception, below the threshold of awareness. I suggest that, other factors – style, design, location, etc. – being equal, when the actor-in-action approach dominates, our sense of the fictional is weakened; conversely, when a constructed character is presented, our sense of fiction is intensified.

I would like to return one last time to the argument with which this book opened, this time from the perspective of deception and self-deception. In the introductory chapter, I outlined three types of reaction to the Stanislavski legacy:

- One sought to engender spontaneous psychological responses to the circum-stances of the play by pursuing a chain of objectives or tasks (the Physical Action principle).
- A second rejected this emphasis on analysis and cerebral dissection and relied on moment-by-moment, emotion-driven reactions to create the effect of spontaneity ('processional' acting).
- A third approach expected certain decisions to be made *a priori*, through inferences from the data of the play regarding the character's psychophysi-cal make-up and consequent expressions of these decisions in a constructed physicality and personality. Both of these were 'other' than those of the actor and, thus, invited, indeed required, acting to involve a process of transformation.

The first two, actor-centred, approaches reflect the well-documented bifurcation in the Stanislavskian legacy: the Russian emphasis on action and the American fore-grounding of emotional content. The third invites the reconsideration of an older attitude: the imaginary body extolled by Michael Chekhov drew on a Continental tradition with which Stanislavski had become familiar through Salvini, Isadora Duncan, and Coquelin and which was subsequently reinvigorated by the French revival led by Jacques Copeau and Michel Saint-Denis.

The first two approaches make only partial use of the Stanislavskian legacy. The third was said, with some justification, to have "turned much of the technical apparatus of the Stanislavski System upside down . . . [as it was] concerned with the physical nature of the actor's movement in the creation of new and startling characters". This approach acknowledges that the Stanislavskian methodology is predicated on two – interdependent – processes:

- An analytic phase, during which the actor collects biographical, sociological and historical data from the dramatic text and its contexts, draws inferences from these regarding the psychological traits of the character, then gives these characteristics physical expression.
- A synthetic phase, which is reached at the point where the analysis has been integrated into an overall psychophysical entity.

Anyone looking at photographs of Stanislavski in his most famous roles – Vershinin, Othello, Argan, Krutitsky – cannot but be struck by how different he looks in each of them. As he was to write: ". . . characterisation is a mask which hides the actor-individual. Protected by it he can lay bare his soul down to the last intimate detail".

An insight that Michael Chekhov famously amplified:

> Everything changes for [the actor] at this happy moment. As the creator of his character, he becomes inwardly free of his own creation and becomes the observer of his own work. The actor acquires a Divided Consciousness. He has given to his image his flesh and blood, his ability to move and speak, to feel, to wish, and now the image disappears from his mind's eye and exists within him and acts upon his means of expression from inside. This is the aim of the whole creative process, the true desire of the Higher Ego of the actor. The consciousness now stands divided.
>
> *(1991, p. 155)*

Divided or dual consciousness is an experience whereby actors report a sensation of being 'in the moment', yet simultaneously observing themselves in the act of acting, as it were 'from above'. Psychologists sometimes explain such reports by arguing that what the actors actually experience is moving very rapidly in and out of 'flow', the sensation of total immersion in an activity. I think this widely reported acting phenomenon (Diderot and Henry Irving also describe it) captures the interplay between deception and self-deception in the process of transformative acting. As we have seen, imitation of a model is key to transformation. But imitation is not identification. Actors-in-action attempt to 'identify': one approach seeks to identify with the character by means of its actions, the other identifies the character with the actor. Awareness of character as an artificial construct, on the other hand, opens a necessary distance. Neither is imitation to be equated with 'indication', that dreaded word which implies a disconnect between impulse and expression. Imitation is play – pretending to be someone else, but so well that you *believe* you are 'other', while always retaining the knowledge that this is a pretence designed to deceive.

What I have described above as three distinct approaches to action and character are, therefore, best considered, in light of that part of the Stanislavskian tradition I am foregrounding, as three stages of the same process. Approaching the character as an imaginary 'other' does not invalidate the need for spontaneity of reactions (what Stanislavski calls "a constant state of inner improvisation"). Neither does it negate the need for directed, purposeful action. In the end, however, both of these approaches rely on the *similarities* between the actor and a somewhat hazy idea of the character and are always in danger of stopping at the former. Focusing on the imaginary character's traits, biography, back story, etc., is, I think, more fruitful, because it foregrounds the *differences* between character and actor. But, in a fully constructed and embodied performance, all three are parts of a continuum, achieving that "creative individuality" which Michael Chekhov described as precisely the position in which an actor was best placed to "assert his ego, through the medium of his parts".

At heart, this is an Expressionist view of the relationship between impulse and the body. Expressionism was primarily concerned, however, with the unfettered expression of inner contents. In transformative acting, to the Expressionist forward thrust of energy is added the idea of an outer 'shell', of the patterned form. To fix in the mind the balance I am trying to strike, take a look at a picture of Auguste Rodin's gigantic statue of Balzac: it is recognisably human, yet is rendered otherworldly through the titanic body one can discern under the monumental cloak. Henry James, for whom Ibsen was closer to Expressionism than naturalism, spoke of the latter's characters as having "the extraordinary, the brilliant property of becoming when represented at once more abstract and more living". This kind of portrayal belongs to those extra-daily techniques which, in Eugenio Barba's phrase, "put the body into form, rendering it artificial/artistic but believable". It also has something of the added vividness of the dream: indeed, Freud talks about the "lines engraved more deeply" of those beings who come to visit us in our dreams. In both art and on the stage, this approach involves an enhanced vigour, and a streamlined, *somewhat* distorted silhouette. Thus, it can be said to be Expressionist in intent and realistic in realisation. I would call it 'attenuated Expressionism'. It aligns itself with the tradition of the great Modernist performers and directors of the first half of the twentieth century: Pitoëff, Jouvet, Michael Chekhov, Evreinov, Tairov, Reinhardt, and Copeau, all intensely exercised by questions of form. Yet, for us, their tradition is firmly realistic. Because, as Barba argues, their form was that of a "living but re-invented body . . . of a naturalness which is the fruit of artificiality". This is what Sharon Carnicke calls "Stanislavski's oxymoron – real theatricality". The perception of acting 'truth' as replication of behaviour is rooted in a fundamental misunderstanding of what Stanislavski meant by the word. Acting is not (daily) behaviour.

Strong as this position may sound, I would not wish this praise of transformation to sound doctrinaire. There is, in fact, a school of thought, to which many film stars subscribe, according to which acquiring character 'technique' would poison the spring of their success: their ability to allow the camera unfettered access to their emotions. 'Technique', in this sense, is equated with self-awareness. And self-awareness is often an impediment to the self-assurance and, to use Kleist's words, to the "innocence, bliss and spontaneity" which is the essence of the able, talented personality actor. Above all, the personality side of the equation is summed up in one winning asset: charm. Stanislavski, ever the realist, knew that actors with charm – that "indefinable, intangible quality" – could permit themselves anything, "even bad acting". Ultimately, when it comes to confronting the concept of constructed character with the miracle of charm, the ideal is a combination of personality and transformation. The great reference points – Olivier, Hopkins, Brando, Streep – all, in their own ways, have idiosyncratic, 'charming' personalities as well as a developed sense of constructed character. Speaking of the great Brechtian actor Ekkehard Schall, Joseph Chaikin once wrote: "I never believe he is the character by name. Nor do I believe that he is playing himself. He performs like a double agent who has infiltrated the two worlds".

I am, therefore, not arguing for the obliteration of the actor's personal qualities in the service of transformative characterisation. Indeed, in many cases actor-in-action and character-in-action acting are part of a continuum of professional practice: the same actors can find themselves in the TV studio in the morning, playing roles close to their daily physical shapes and accents, and, that very evening, appear unrecognisable on stage. (Neither is this governed by the medium: while commercial imperatives often favour personality acting for the screen, spectacular transformations occur in all media.) Many actors regularly move along this continuum and, thus, find themselves at various points on the transformation scale.

My conclusion is this: transformative acting exists on a spectrum and transformation is not always appropriate to the professional context in which acting takes place. But when it occurs in an appropriate context, it appears to offer a superior experience because it involves higher levels of deception and attracts higher levels of counter-deception in the spectator. Watching transformation prompts a higher-order mental process: the 'puzzle' presented to the spectator is simply more challenging. It also positions the actor in a different place within the cultural framework: the actor-in-action is essentially an executant, a means of transmission for someone else's artistry. The transformation actor, purposefully shaping his or her materials, is – as Stanislavski never tired of stressing – an artist.

Bibliography

Belief in imaginary scenarios: Shakespeare, W., 1987. *Othello*, edited by J. Hankey. *"Plays in Performance"*. Bristol: Bristol Classical Press; Schroeder, T., and Matheson, C., 2006. 'Imagination and emotion', in Nichols, S. (ed.), *The Architecture of the Imagination: New Essays on Pretense, Possibility and Fiction*. New York: Oxford University Press; *and the suspension of belief*: Gilbert, D. T., Krull, D. S., and Malone, P. S., 1990. 'Unbelieving the unbelievable: some problems in the rejection of false information'. *Journal of Personality and Social Psychology*, 59, pp. 601–613; *and "enforced distance"*: Bogart, A., 2014. *What's the Story: Essays about Art, Theatre and Storytelling*. Abingdon: Routledge.

Actors and self-hypnosis: Marowitz, C., 1978. *The Act of Being*. Charlottesville, VA: Secker and Warburg; Panero, M. E. et al, 2016. 'Do actors possess traits associated with high hypnotizability?' *Psychology of Aesthetics, Creativity, and the Arts*, 10 (2), pp. 233–239.

Deception: Goffman, E., 1959. *The Presentation of Self in Everyday Life*. New York: Doubleday Dell; Kummer, H. 1988. 'Tripartite relations in hamadryas baboons', in Byrne, R., and Whiten, A. (eds.), 1988. *Machiavellian Intelligence: Social Expertise and the Evolution of Intellect in Monkeys, Apes and Humans*. Oxford: Clarendon Press, pp. 113–121; Trivers, R., 2011. *Deceit and Self-Deception: Fooling Yourself the Better to Fool Others*. London: Allen Lane;

Leslie, A., 1987. 'Pretence and representation: the origins of theory of mind'. *Psychological Review*, 94, pp. 412–426; Premack, D., 1988. 'Does the chimpanzee have a theory of mind?' in Byrne, R., and Whiten, A. (eds.), pp. 160–159; De Paulo, B. M. et al, 2003. 'Cues to deception'. *Psychological Bulletin*, 129 (1), pp. 74–118; Vrij, A., 2004. 'Why professionals fail to catch liars and how they can improve'. *Legal and Criminological Psychology*, 9, pp. 159–181; Vrij, A. et al, 2006. 'Police officers', social workers', teachers' and the general public's beliefs about deception in children, adolescents and adults'. *Legal and Criminological Psychology*, 11, pp. 297–312; Vrij, A. et al, 2006. 'Detecting deception by manipulating cognitive load'. *Trends in Cognitive Science*, 10, pp. 141–142; Morgan, P. et al, 2009. 'Replication of functional MRI detection of deception'. *Open Forensic Science Journal*, 2, pp. 6–11; Humphrey, N., 1988. 'The social function of intellect', in Byrne, R., and Whiten, A. (eds.), pp. 13–26; *and 'naturalistic' acting*: Donald, M., 2006. 'Art and cognitive evolution', in Turner, M. (ed.), *The Artful Mind: Cognitive Science and the Riddle of Human Creativity*. Oxford: Oxford University Press, pp. 3–20; *and modifying social behaviour*: Deacon, T., 2006. 'The aesthetic faculty', in Turner, M. (ed.), *The Artful Mind: Cognitive Science and the Riddle of Human Creativity*. Oxford: Oxford University Press, pp. 21–55.

The Stanislavskian legacy: Gordon, M., 1987. *The Stanislavsky Technique: A Workbook for Actors*. New York: Applause Theatre Books; Benedetti, J., 1988. *Stanislavski: A Biography*. London: Methuen; Stanislavski, C., 1968. *Building a Character,* translated by E. Hapgood. London: Methuen; Stanislavski, C., 1986. *An Actor Prepares*, translated by E. Hapgood. London: Methuen; Chekhov, M., 1953. *To the Actor: On the Technique of Acting*. New York: Harper and Brothers.

Divided consciousness: Chekhov, M., 1991. *On the Technique of Acting*. New York: Harper Collins; Diderot, D., 1883. *The Paradox of Acting*, translated with annotations by Walter Harries Pollock, with a Preface by Henry Irving. London: Chatto & Windus; *in Irving*: Dromgoole, N., 2007. *Performance Style and Gesture in Western Theatre*. London: Oberon Books.

Expressionism and artificiality: Barba, E., 1994. *The Paper Canoe: A Guide to Theatre Anthropology,* translated by R. Fowler. London: Routledge; Freud, S., 2010. 'An outline', in *Complete Works (CW)*. Ivan Smith Online Edition: https://openlibrary.org/works/OL16678137W/Freud_Complete_Works; *and "real theatricality"*: Carnicke, S. M., 2009. *Stanislavsky in Focus: An Acting Master for the Twenty-First Century*. 2nd Edition. Abingdon: Routledge.

Personality and the actor: Kleist, H. v., 1989. *On the Theatre of Marionettes,* translated by G. Wilford. London: Acorn Press; Stanislavski, 1968; Chaikin, J., 1972. *The Presence of the Actor*. New York: Atheneum.

INDEX

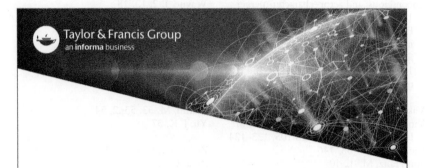